International Investment for Sustainable Development

Balancing Rights and Rewards

Edited by
Lyuba Zarsky

London • Sterling, VA

First published by Earthscan in the UK and USA in 2005

ISBN: 1-84407-039-5 paperback
1-84407-038-7 hardback

Typesetting by JS Typesetting Ltd, Wellingborough, Northants
Printed and bound in the UK by Cromwell Press Ltd, Trowbridge
Cover design by Danny Gillespie

For a full list of publications please contact:

Earthscan
8–12 Camden High Street, London, NW1 0JH, UK
Tel: +44 (0)20 7387 8558
Fax: +44 (0)20 7387 8998
Email: earthinfo@earthscan.co.uk
Web: **www.earthscan.co.uk**

22883 Quicksilver Drive, Sterling, VA 20166-2012, USA

Earthscan is an imprint of James and James (Science Publishers) Ltd and publishes in association with WWF-UK and the International Institute for Environment and Development

A catalogue record for this book is available from the British Library

Library of Congress Cataloging-in-Publication Data
International investment for sustainable development : balancing rights and rewards / edited by Lyuba Zarsky.
p.cm.
Includes bibliographical references and index.
ISBN 1-84407-039-5 (pbk.) – ISBN 1-84407-038-7 (hardback)
1. Investments, Foreign–Government policy–Developing countries. 2. Sustainable development–Government policy–Developing countries. I. Zarsky, Lyuba.
HG5993.I574 2005
338.9′27′091724–dc22

2004013715

Printed on elemental chlorine-free paper

International Investment for Sustainable Development

Contents

List of Tables, Figures and Boxes *vii*
About the Authors *viii*
Preface *xi*
Acknowledgements *xii*
List of Acronyms and Abbreviations *xiii*

Introduction: Balancing Rights and Rewards in Investment Rules **1**
Lyuba Zarsky

Part 1: Links Between Foreign Direct Investment, Development and Sustainability

1 **No Miracle Drug: Foreign Direct Investment and Sustainable Development** **13**
Kevin P. Gallagher and Lyuba Zarsky

2 **FDI and the Environment: What Empirical Evidence Does and Does Not Tell Us?** **46**
Monica Araya

3 **Governing Foreign Direct Investment in Sub-Saharan Africa: Policies and Practices Reconsidered** **74**
John Mugabe

4 **Sustainable Development and Foreign Direct Investment: The Emerging Paradigm in Asia** **97**
Simon S. C. Tay and Iris Tan

Part 2: The Governance of International Investment

5 **All Roads Lead Out of Rome: Divergent Paths of Dispute Settlement in Bilateral Investment Treaties** **123**
Luke Eric Peterson

6 **The Road to Hell? Investor Protections in NAFTA's Chapter 11** **150**
Aaron Cosbey

7 **The Environment and the Principle of Non-discrimination in Investment Regimes: International and Domestic Institutions** **172**
Konrad von Moltke

8 **Corporate Governance and Global Disclosure: Let the Sun Shine In** **197**
Sandy Buffett

Index *219*

List of Tables, Figures and Boxes

Tables

1.1 Ten Largest Developing-country Recipients of FDI Inflows 19
1.2 Does FDI Generate Efficiency Spillovers in Developing Countries? 23
1.3 Does FDI Promote Economic Growth in Developing Countries? 25
1.4 OECD's Environmental Guidelines for MNEs 28
1.5 Locally Sourced Inputs in Maquila Manufacturing Plants 32
1.6 Lacklustre Domestic Performance: Investment and GDP Growth in Mexico 34
1.7 Share of 'Dirty Industry' in U.S. and Mexican Manufacturing 36
1.8 Marginalization in Mexico 39
3.1 Net FDI Inflows in Sub-Saharan Africa, Average 1996–1997 81
7.1 Selected EU Legal Instruments and Institutions for the Environment 184
8.1 International Trends in Social and Environmental Disclosure 210
8.2 Recent Disclosure Regulations for Institutional Investors 212

Figures

1.1 FDI Flows in the World Economy 1990–2002 18
1.2 FDI as a Percentage of GDP in the World Economy 20
1.3 Real Spending on Environmental Protection in Mexico 37
1.4 Maquila Inspections 1992–2001 38

Boxes

2.1 Portfolio Equity Investment and the Environment: Some Key Issues 48
2.2 Debt Finance and Environmental Performance 50
4.1 Sufficiency Economics 107
8.1 OECD Principles of Corporate Governance 201
8.2 Disclosure Principles of the OECD Guidelines for Multinational Enterprises 204

About the Authors

Monica Araya is the director of the Sustainable Americas Project at the Yale Center for Environmental Law and Policy and the Global Environment and Trade Study (GETS). She has worked at the Ministry of Foreign Trade in Costa Rica and as a consultant to a variety of international organizations. She is currently a PhD candidate at Yale University, where she is completing a dissertation on corporate environmental disclosure and multinational enterprises.

Sandy Buffett is a consultant on corporate social responsibility and has consulted to the OECD, US EPA, World Resources Institute and UN Environment Program. She was programme manager at the Nautilus Institute where she managed the International Investment Rules Project and the California Global Corporate Accountability Project. She is the editor of *Whose Business? An Activist Guide to Corporate Responsibility for Human Rights and the Environment* (Nautilus Institute, 2001]) and co-author of *Leverage for the Environment: A Guide to the Private Financial Services Industry* (World Resources Institute, 1998).

Aaron Cosbey is an environmental economist specializing in the areas of trade, investment and sustainable development; international environmental governance; and the greening of business/regulatory reform. He is an associate and senior advisor for trade and investment at the International Institute for Sustainable Development in Winnipeg, and senior associate at Resource Futures International in Ottawa. He is a member of the Canadian Government's Academic Advisory Council on Canadian Trade Policy and the Environmental Sectoral Advisory Group on International Trade, where he chairs the working group on the Free Trade Area of the Americas (FTAA). He has published widely in the area of trade, investment and sustainable development.

Kevin P. Gallagher is an economist and research associate at the Global Development and Environment Institute at the Fletcher School of Law and Diplomacy at Tufts University. His latest book is *Free Trade and the Environment: Mexico, NAFTA, and Beyond* (Stanford University Press, 2004). He is also the editor (with Jacob Werksman) of *The Earthscan Reader on International Trade and Sustainable Development* (Earthscan, 2002). Dr Gallagher has served as an advisor to international institutions and non-governmental organizations, including the Organisation for Economic Co-operation and Development (OECD), the Economic Commission on Latin America and the Caribbean (ECLAC) and the International Union for the Conservation of Nature (IUCN).

Luke Eric Peterson is a writer and consultant on international investment policy to, among other organizations, the Royal Institute for International Affairs and the Swiss Department of Foreign Affairs. His articles have appeared in *The Guardian* and the *New Statesman* in the UK and the *Toronto Star* and the *Ottawa Citizen* in Canada. He is an associate of the International Institute for Sustainable Development's (IISD) Trade and Investment programme and produces a weekly newsletter for IISD on investment law and policy (www.iisd.org/investment/invest-sd).

John Mugabe is chair of the African Forum on Science and Technology for Development of the New Economic Partnerships for Africa's Development (NEPAD) programme in Pretoria, South Africa, and executive director of the African Centre for Technology Studies (ACTS) in Nairobi, Kenya. He is the founder of the ACTS Bio-Policy Institute in Maastricht and is a member of the board of directors of the Biofocus Foundation of the World Academy of Arts and Sciences; the African Conservation Centre (ACC), Kenya; and Biotechnology and Development Monitor of the University of Amsterdam.

Iris Tan is a research fellow at the Singapore Institute of International Affairs (SIIA), where she focuses on environmental issues and East Asian affairs. She is a graduate in Japanese studies and represented the SIIA on national committees to implement the Singapore Green Plan, the country's ten-year programme for sustainable development and environmental protection.

Simon S. C. Tay teaches international law at the National University of Singapore and is chairman of the Singapore Institute of International Affairs (SIIA). In July 2002, he was appointed chairman of Singapore's National Environment Agency. His latest publications are *Sketching Regional Futures: Pacific Asia in 2022* (forthcoming) and *The Enemy Within: Combating Corruption in Asia* (2003).

Konrad von Moltke is senior fellow at the International Institute for Sustainable Development in Winnipeg, Canada, and the World Wild Wide Fund for Nature (WWF) in Washington, D.C. His work is focused on environmental policy and international economic relations, including debt, trade, investment and development. He has contributed to developing the agenda on trade, investment and sustainable development at global and regional levels. He is also adjunct professor of environmental studies and senior fellow at the Institut pour le Développement Durable et les Relations Internationales in Paris.

Lyuba Zarsky is senior research fellow at the Global Development and Environment Institute at the Fletcher School of Law and Diplomacy at Tufts University, Boston, and Senior Associate at the Nautilus Institute for Security and Sustainability. She is co-founder of the Nautilus Institute and directed its Globalization and Governance Program. Her work focuses on globalization and sustainability, including the governance of international investment and global corporate responsibility. She has published and consulted widely to organizations including the OECD, WWF, the Earth Council and the Asian Development Bank. Her latest publications are *Human Rights and the Environment: Conflicts and Norms in a Globalizing World* (contributing editor) (Earthscan, 2002), and *Beyond Good Deeds: Case Studies and a New Policy Agenda for Corporate Accountability* (co-authored with Michelle Leighton and Naomi Roht-Arriaza) (Natural Heritage Institute, 2002).

Preface

This book is the culmination of the International Sustainable and Ethical Investment Rules Project, a collaboration of researchers from the following five non-governmental organization (NGO) think-tanks:

- African Centre for Technology Studies, Nairobi, Kenya;
- Fundacion ECOS, Punta del Este, Uruguay;
- International Institute for Sustainable Development, Winnipeg, Canada;
- Nautilus Institute for Security and Sustainability, Berkeley, California, US;
- Singapore Institute for International Affairs, Singapore.

Conceived and directed by Lyuba Zarsky and Sandy Buffett of the Nautilus Institute, the project aimed to articulate a framework for the governance of international investment that promotes economic development, environmental sustainability, human rights and global security. At the centre of such an investment regime is the fundamental principle that private investor rights must be balanced by investor responsibilities and public goods.

Project collaborators worked together in two meetings in 2001. An initial working group meeting, held in Berkeley in April, defined the objectives and sketched broad terms of reference for research papers. The second meeting brought project researchers together with a wider group of policy experts, activists and business representatives for a strategic consultation on ethics, security and international investment. Held at the Rockefeller Brother Fund's Pocantico Conference Center in New York shortly after the September 11, 2001, bombings of the World Trade Center, the consultation generated ten-year scenarios about the governance of investment that helped to deepen the thinking behind the papers in this volume (the scenarios are available on www.nautilus.org/enviro/).

Researchers from two additional academic institutes – the Yale Center for Environmental Law and Policy and the Global Development and Environment Institute at Tufts University – joined the project at a later stage to fill in key gaps.

All the contributors are not only researchers, but are also passionate and engaged advocates. Their collective efforts to implement trade and investment rules that promote global sustainability and socially just development have targeted the World Trade Organization (WTO), OECD, the European Union and the Common Market of the Southern Cone (MERCOSUR), as well as the North America Free Trade Agreement (NAFTA) and the Free Trade Area of the Americas Agreement. This book is dedicated to the spirit and energy that animates those efforts, and millions like them around the world.

Acknowledgements

We are grateful to the many people who provided the ideas, encouragement and support needed to bring this volume to production. Many thanks to Sandy Buffett for competent management of the International Sustainable and Ethical Investment Rules Project. Thanks to Miguel Reynal and Marie Leichner for encouragement, insight and inspiration.

The staff of the Nautilus Institute, including Christine Ahn, Leif Brottem, Jin Chen, Peter Hayes and John Williams assisted with project administration, communication and research. Special thanks to Joan Diamond for her constancy and gentle prodding in keeping the institute on track.

Many thanks for insightful review of specific chapters provided by Monica Araya, Michelle Chan-Fishel, Aaron Cosbey, Gerald Epstein, Mark Halle, Howard Mann, Luke Peterson, Richard Perkins, Kenneth Van de Velde, Konrad von Moltke and Halina Ward. Thanks to Aljendro Escobar and Antonio Parra at ICSID for responding to author queries for Chapter 5.

For financial support, thanks to the Ford Foundation, the Wallace Global Fund and the Rockefeller Foundation. Special thanks to Melissa Dann for being the first to throw her support behind the International Sustainable and Ethical Investment Rules Project. The Joint Public Advisory Council of the North American Commission for Environmental Cooperation funded work on a previous version of Chapter 6. Funding for Chapter 6 was also provided by the Charles Stewart Mott Foundation.

Thanks to the Rockefeller Brothers Fund for support of a strategic consultation held at the Pocantico Conference Center in New York in 2001. Special thanks to Peter Riggs for participating in the consultation and for his early embrace of scenario methodology as a strategic tool. Thanks also to all the participants of the strategic consultation and to Alain Wouters of the Global Business Network-Europe for excellent and creative facilitation.

requirements have been effective in stimulating domestic industries in both developed and developing countries (Kumar, 2003; Moran, 1998).

Finally, the tilt is perhaps most evident in the new rights it gives to investors in disputes with host governments. NAFTA's Chapter 11, as well as most BITs, grant investors the right to directly sue host governments in a variety of international tribunals. In earlier times, such disputes were handled state-by-state by host and home country governments.

Coupled with poorly defined justifications for a suit, investor–state arbitration mechanisms open the door to an attack by TNCs on the host government's right to regulate. In a rash of high-profile cases in the last five years, TNCs have sued host governments for enacting domestic environmental and health policies which could adversely impinge on company revenues.

In Chapter 5, Luke Peterson examines the procedural problems of the dispute settlement mechanisms found in BITs. In the main, these mechanisms were simply grafted onto BITs from the secretive world of international commercial arbitration. Meant for disputes involving two private parties, they are not required to make public even the fact that a suit has been filed, let alone substantive arguments – notwithstanding the fact that the suit targets public policy measures. Moreover, the multiplicity of BITs and arbitration mechanisms means that an aggrieved TNC can go 'jurisdiction shopping', filing a suit in the arbitration venue most likely to rule in its favour.

Peterson also looks for evidence that the BITs have actually helped developing countries to attract FDI, and finds none. While there may be marginal disadvantage in not having a BIT, there seems to be no net advantage in having one. In short, the BIT imposes a social cost – a dispute settlement mechanism which does not meet the standards for transparency, legitimacy and accountability required when public policy objectives are weighed against private interests – while delivering no net economic benefit.

In Chapter 6, Aaron Cosbey examines problems with the procedural and substantive provisions of NAFTA's Chapter 11. He argues that the intent of Chapter 11 – to protect North American investors from mistreatment at the hands of government – has been construed by TNCs to attack domestic environmental, health and safety measures that might incidentally harm their interests. The attack is made possible by Chapter 11's shortcomings, including the lack of transparency, accountability and legitimacy in the investor–state dispute settlement process; the broad definition of 'investors'; and the overly broad interpretations of host state obligations in areas such as expropriation, non-discrimination and minimum standards of treatment.

Towards a Sustainable and Ethical International Investment Regime

The emerging international investment regime is fundamentally off kilter. In terms of domestic policy, it over-weights the role of FDI as an elixir of development at the expense of homegrown firms and markets. In international agreements, it tilts towards the interests of foreign investors at the expense of domestic firms and host governments' ability to regulate in the public interest.

Balance should be the central principle of an investment regime which aims to promote sustainable development – balance between private rights and public goods; balance between investor rights and investor responsibilities; and balance in development strategies between promoting domestic producers and encouraging foreign investment.

In international investment agreements, there is also a need for balance between universality and specificity, that is, between global norms and local jurisdiction. The global economy is far too differentiated for it to be governed fairly, efficiently and sustainably by an overly prescriptive set of top-down rules.

From one angle of approach, the global–local problem is revealed in the gap between developed and developing countries. Investment rules that ban performance requirements strip developing-country governments of policy tools that have historically stimulated industrial development. As one account put it: 'When equal rules apply in unequal situations, the result is inequity'.

From another angle of approach, the problem is the gap between universal rules and global adjudication mechanisms versus on-the-ground realities and local adjudicating institutions. The European Union has adopted the principle of subsidiarity – the idea that action should be taken at the lowest level of governance consistent with effectiveness. Subsidiarity is especially relevant to environmental management, because ecosystem and natural resource conditions depend on place. Unlike economic regimes, the principle of subsidiarity is found in many international environmental regimes.

The chapters in this book address aspects of the imbalances that currently characterize investment rules and offer pointers towards a better pivot. Focusing on the over-emphasis of FDI in development strategies, Zarsky and Gallagher (Chapter 1) suggest that, rather than attracting FDI *per se*, macroeconomic policies should aim to enhance the overall climate for investment, both domestic and foreign They argue that the central objective of development strategies should be to nurture endogenous local capacities for sustainable production, and that they should be aimed more at local than global markets. With the proper policies and institutions, FDI could potentially be of service in that objective.

John Mugabe (Chapter 3) calls for the integration of social and environmental regulation into the governance of FDI at national and supra-national levels. Pointing towards bitter clashes over the integration of trade and environment, Tay and Tan (Chapter 4) argue that any international investment regime that seeks to promote sustainable development must be based on engaging, rather than bullying, developing countries.

Peterson (Chapter 5) and Cosbey (Chapter 6) address the imbalance between investor rights and public goods. Peterson suggests that a multilateral investment agreement should address the procedural shortcomings and jurisdictional confusion found in the multiplicity of arbitration mechanisms found in BITS. A set of common, transparent rules governing investor–state arbitration would be a good start. Cosbey examines four potential solutions to the problems of NAFTA's Chapter 11, including amendment of the substantive provisions and reform of two key arbitration mechanisms.

In Chapter 7, Konrad von Moltke grapples with defining a balance between global norms and local jurisdiction as found in the interpretation of the principle of non-discrimination. Focusing on standards of post-establishment treatment of foreign investors, von Moltke argues that, at its most fundamental, non-discrimination simply means equality before the law – a worthy objective. When applied to changing and place-specific environmental management requirements, however, the interpretation of non-discrimination can be murky and complex, and can generate perverse outcomes.

Investments are made at different times, in different places, by different companies. Achieving environmental objectives may oblige local and national governments to set standards which are different as those between domestic, as well as foreign, companies. Newer investments, for example, often must meet higher standards than older ones, not least because newer technology makes higher standards feasible. An overly universal interpretation of non-discrimination, set at the regional or global level, could constrain and undermine national and local environmental policy. On the other hand, an overly local interpretation could undermine the principle of non-discrimination.

To find the right balance, von Moltke suggests that investment regimes be modelled on multilateral environmental agreements (MEAs). Based on the principle of subsidiarity, MEAs typically identify a broad global norm and objective, while leaving the specifics of implementation to participating nations. Von Moltke suggests that the parallel in investment regimes would be a global embrace of the broad principle of non-discrimination, while assigning the interpretation of unfair discrimination to local and national institutions.

In Chapter 8, Sandy Buffett addresses the imbalance between investor rights and investor responsibilities by proposing changes in corporate governance. Rules, relationships and expected standards for accountability and disclosure are at the heart of corporate governance. Traditional shareholder-led models of corporate governance have not clearly defined a company's accountability for environmental impacts. However, recent corporate accounting and governance scandals and growing calls by civil society for minimum corporate environmental and social standards provide traction for elevating an enhanced corporate governance and disclosure framework into the international policy arena.

Buffett argues that a good place to start is to define mandatory disclosure requirements for TNCs in their global operations. The OECD's Corporate Governance Principles and Guidelines for Multinational Enterprises both offer a useful framework. However, both are voluntary principles. The inclusion of disclosure obligations in multilateral, regional and bilateral investment agreements would help to move towards the creation of a binding and international multi-stakeholder corporate governance framework.

As a whole, the chapters in this volume point to the conclusion that steering foreign investment towards sustainability and equity will require advocacy and policy action on several fronts. Much water has already passed under the bridge. Even if activists and developing countries continue to fend off a global investment agreement in the WTO, there is still the multiplicity of BITS to deal with, as well as NAFTA. Most important, despite evidence to the contrary, there is the reigning orthodoxy that FDI is an elixir for development, and that investment agreements that favour foreign investors over public goods are needed to attract it.

This book aims to marshal economic and legal arguments that contribute to the rethinking of both assumptions, and to offer pointers to greater balance in the governance of investment. If we have taken even small steps, our purpose will be more than fulfilled.

References

Kumar, N. (2003) 'Performance Requirements as Tools of Development Policy: Lessons from Experiences of Developed and Developing Countries for the WTO Agenda on Trade and Investment', Research and Information System for the Non-Aligned and Other Developing Countries (RIS) Discussion Paper no 52, available on www.ris.org.in/

Moran, T. (1998) *Foreign Direct Investment and Development: The New Policy Agenda for Developing Countries and Economies in Transition*, Washington, D.C.: Institute for International Economics

Zarsky, L. (ed) (2002) *Human Rights and the Environment: Conflicts and Norms in a Globalizing World*, London: Earthscan

Part 1

Links Between Foreign Direct Investment, Development and Sustainability

Chapter 1

No Miracle Drug: Foreign Direct Investment and Sustainable Development

Kevin P. Gallagher and Lyuba Zarsky

Abstract

In the 1990s, foreign direct investment (FDI) came to be seen as a 'miracle drug' – a jumpstart to economic growth and sustainable industrial development, especially in developing countries. Policies to attract FDI became the centrepiece of both national development strategies and supra-national investment agreements.

This chapter examines statistical and case study evidence about the impacts of FDI in developing countries on economic growth, efficiency spillovers and environmental performance. Mirroring the heterogeneity of developing countries, we find that there is no consistent relationship: the impact of FDI on each count has been found to be positive, neutral or even negative. Key determining variables are domestic policies, capacities and institutions.

The chapter also presents and evaluates evidence about the economic, environmental and social performance of Mexico's FDI-led global integration strategy in the 1990s. We find that technology spillovers were minimal or non-existent, that FDI 'crowded out' domestic investment, and that environmental benefits of clean technology transfer were minimal.

We conclude that the purported benefits of FDI are exaggerated and that its centrality in development strategies is misplaced. Rather than attract FDI *per se*, development policies should aim to promote endogenous local capacities for sustainable production. With the right national and global policy framework, FDI could potentially help in that process.

Introduction

In the 1990s, foreign direct investment (FDI) came to be seen in much the same light as export-led growth in the 1970s – a jumpstart to sustained economic growth in developing countries. Optimism was fuelled by a surge in FDI inflows, outstripping other forms of public and private finance. Led by transnational corporations (TNCs), the hope was that FDI would transfer superior technology and management skills, stimulate domestic investment and growth, generate efficiency spillovers and integrate developing-country firms into global markets.

An added twist was that, directly and indirectly, FDI would also boost environmental performance. The direct benefits would be gained from the transfer of cleaner technology and the better environmental management practices of TNCs. The expectation was that TNCs would implement and diffuse in their developing-country operations the high standards required in Europe, Japan and the US. The indirect benefits would be gleaned largely from the impacts of FDI on economic growth. By increasing per capita income, growth would promote cleaner consumer goods and greater citizen demand for environmental protection.

Two standard prescriptions followed. First, since 'more is better', policies to attract FDI should be at the heart of national development strategies. An understanding of what these policies should be has changed over the decades. In the 1980s, the emphasis was on 'getting the prices right', – that is, the elimination of domestic policies, such as energy and food subsidies, which create a cleavage between domestic and global prices. In the 1990s, the trend was towards 'getting the macro-policies right', especially the deregulation of financial markets.

Currently, the focus is on fashioning the right 'enabling environment' for FDI – that is, creating or strengthening legal, regulatory and political institutions that provide transparency, property protection and financial stability to foreign investors. Even if desirable, the creation of such institutions is neither an overnight nor costless affair. If success in attracting FDI awaits their creation, many developing countries, especially the poorest, will be waiting a long time.

The second prescription is that investment agreements – global, regional or bilateral – should aim to 'make the world safe' for FDI, including expansion of the protections for, and the rights of, foreign investors. Greater rights for investors have come at the expense of flexibility and diversity of national development policies. Moreover, TNCs have used new rights to challenge national environmental and health regulations (see Cosbey, Chapter 6).

This chapter examines recent statistical and case study evidence about the impacts of FDI in generating efficiency spillovers, promoting growth and improving environmental performance in developing countries. The studies paint an ambiguous picture: FDI has been found to have positive, neutral or even negative impacts on all three counts. The poorer the country, the more likely that the FDI impact will be negative. While further studies are needed, especially case studies of particular TNCs and sectors, the key variables appear to be the domestic institutional and policy context on one hand, and TNC practices on the other hand.

The central argument of the chapter is that FDI is no 'miracle drug' for economic development, environmentally sustainable or otherwise. Structuring development strategies and investment regimes around the assumption that it *is* a miracle drug may act, ironically, to undermine the positive contributions that FDI could potentially make to nurturing local capacities for sustained economic growth.

Section 2 defines and examines trends in global FDI flows to developing countries, including the concentration of FDI in a handful of countries and the privatization wave of the late 1990s. Section 3 outlines the 'promise of FDI' in terms of economic growth in general and efficiency spillovers in particular, and reviews the evidence about whether and when the promise is fulfilled.

Section 4 examines the linkage between FDI and environmental performance, considering in turn, whether TNCs disseminate global best practice; whether increases in per capita income generate environmental improvements; and whether global competition for FDI 'chills' environmental standards.

In Section 5 we examine evidence about the economic, environmental and social impacts of FDI in Mexico in the 1990s, which adopted a highly 'integrationist' model of development. Despite large increases of FDI inflows into the manufacturing sector, Mexican imports grew faster than exports, economic growth was sluggish and domestic investment contracted. In addition, the scale of environmental degradation swamped benefits from industrial restructuring, and a slow rate of job creation led to a widening of income inequality.

The final section of the chapter concludes that the purported benefits of FDI are exaggerated and that its centrality in development strategies is misplaced. Development policies should aim not to attract FDI *per se* but to promote growth in environmentally and economically sustainable local productive capacities. FDI could potentially help in that process, especially if international investment regimes give developing countries more 'policy space' and embrace the principle of investor social responsibility.

FDI in Developing Countries

FDI is a financial investment in a domestic enterprise by which a foreign investor gains a significant equity stake in the firm. In most national accounting systems, FDI is defined as an equity share of 10 per cent or more. Besides selling equity, enterprises finance their operations via debt, including loans from banks and other financial institutions and corporate bonds.

The major players in FDI are transnational corporations (TNCs). The world's largest 100 TNCs held nearly US$2 trillion in foreign assets at the end of the 1990s, and employed over 6 million people in their foreign affiliates. All of the top 10 and nearly 90 per cent of the top100 TNCs are from the US, Japan and the European Union (UNCTAD, 2002a). Given the predominance of TNCs, a conventional definition of FDI is a 'form of international inter-firm cooperation that involves significant equity stake and effective management decision power in, or ownership control of, foreign companies' (de Mello, 1999, p135).

FDI, in short, is more than a flow of capital. It is a cross-border expansion of production undertaken by large corporations. The internationalization of production is at the heart of the process of globalization. FDI takes place in two ways: 'mergers and acquisitions' (M&As) – that is, the purchase by TNCs of existing domestic companies, in whole or in part; and 'greenfield investment', – that is, the creation of new productive capacity.

Why and where? Determinants of FDI

Why does a TNC decide to expand production overseas rather than exporting products it makes at home? What determines which countries TNCs will invest in?

Mainstream trade theory suggests that FDI is driven by imperfections in markets for goods or factors of production, including labour and technology. To make FDI profitable, a firm must have some distinctive asset – technology, global marketing capacities or management skills – not possessed by domestic firms (Blomström and Kokko, 1996). The firm is thus able to earn a 'rent' by producing in the host community.

Because the superior technology and/or management skills of foreign firms raise the efficiency and productivity of domestic firms, at least in theory, FDI is sometimes said to be 'efficiency seeking'. In addition, FDI can be 'market seeking'. If a government restricts imports, FDI may be prompted by efforts to get under import barriers or high tariffs, or to gain preferential treatment to third-country markets. If transport costs are high, local production would promote competitiveness in local markets, especially if there are economies of scale.

Many developing countries seek to attract FDI on the basis of low labour costs. Lacking the technology and/or global marketing networks of the TNCs, developing countries conceive of FDI primarily in terms of providing capital to employ low or unskilled workers. Differences in labour costs between countries are kept large by immigration restrictions, that is, an 'imperfection' in global labour markets.

An understanding both of what drives TNCs to invest globally and what determines the location of FDI is murky. Traditionally, studies have found that the most unambiguous 'pull' factor drawing FDI to particular countries – both developed and developing – is the market size (per capita GDP) of the host economy (Chakrabarti, 2001). For the most part, it seems, TNCs invest where markets are large, either to expand markets or to earn rents, or both.

With globalization have come predictions that 'non-traditional' factors would increasingly determine the location of FDI, opening up new possibilities for developing countries. These factors include cost differences between locations, the quality of infrastructure, the ease of doing business and the availability of skills. However, a recent study found that globalization has not 'changed the rules of the game' and confirmed that market size is still the dominant driver of the distribution of FDI in developing countries (Nunnenkamp and Spatz, 2002).

There is also close to a consensus that macroeconomic and political stability are needed to attract FDI. Volatile exchange rates and high and growing trade deficits tend to be negatively correlated with FDI. Evidence on whether low (or high) labour costs attract FDI, on the other hand, is ambiguous. A review of 16 studies found that in 6 of them low wages attracted FDI, while 4 studies found FDI to be correlated with higher wages and 6 found labour costs to be insignificant (Chakrabarti, 2001). Other studies emphasize the importance of human capital, in particular the level of education, in attracting FDI.

There has been much debate in recent years about the role of environmental factors, especially differences in enforced standards, in attracting or repelling FDI. No consistent statistical evidence has been found that differences in standards affect TNC location decisions, presumably because, in most industries, environmental costs are a small component of total costs (Jaffe et al, 1995). However, case studies have found that in certain 'dirty' industries, such as leather tanning, more stringent standards in OECD countries propelled companies to shift production to countries with lower standards (Mabey and McNally, 1999).

Finally, there is the question of whether standards of treatment of foreign investors play a role in attracting FDI to particular countries. The surge in the number of bilateral investment agreements (BITs) concluded in the 1990s was fuelled – at least on the part of developing countries – by the hope that expanding the rights and protections of foreign investors would attract FDI. However, there is no evidence that it has done so (Peterson, Chapter 5). Nonetheless, with over 2000 BITs in force, investor protections have become the norm. They may not provide marginal benefits, but their absence might have marginal costs in attracting FDI.

FDI trends in the 1990s

Inflows of FDI soared to unprecedented levels during the 1990s. From 1970 to 1990, global FDI inflows averaged US$58 billion a year, or less than one-half of 1 per cent of global GDP. Between 1990 and 1995, FDI inflows averaged US$225 billion per year and surged to US$828 billion per year between 1996 and 2000. With a total of US$1.5 trillion in 2000 alone, FDI inflows were 4 per cent of global GDP (Figures 1.1 and 1.2).

Originating from North America, Europe and Japan, the FDI boom affected both developing and developed countries. Indeed, the lion's share – nearly three-quarters on average – of FDI inflows went from one OECD country to another. However, the boom was big news in developing countries because FDI inflows started from a low base. In 1990, FDI comprised only about a quarter of all capital flows into developing countries. By 2000, the share of FDI had climbed to 60 per cent (UNCTAD, 2002a, p12).

'Official flows', that is, multilateral and bilateral development aid, overseas development assistance (ODA), remained stagnant during the 1990s, with an annual flow of US$54 billion. Many analysts began to predict – or hope – that FDI would replace ODA as the primary source of global development capital.

The promise of FDI as a replacement for ODA, however, largely remains to be fulfilled. For 55 of the world's 70 poorest countries, ODA flows outstripped FDI in the late 1990s. For 42 poor countries, ODA flows were twice the size of FDI. Indeed, FDI 'dwarfed' ODA in only seven of the poorest countries[1].

Moreover, only a small part of global FDI inflows – about 30 per cent on average between 1990 and 2001 – went to developing countries. Indeed, the developing country share fell off sharply between 1997 and 2000, falling from 39 to 16 per cent.

FDI inflows are highly concentrated in ten, mostly large developing countries, led by China, Brazil and Mexico. Between 1990 and 2000, the 'top ten' garnered 76 per cent of the total FDI flowing into developing countries. The trend towards concentration seems to be intensifying: in 2001, the top ten share rose to 81 per cent (Table 1.1).

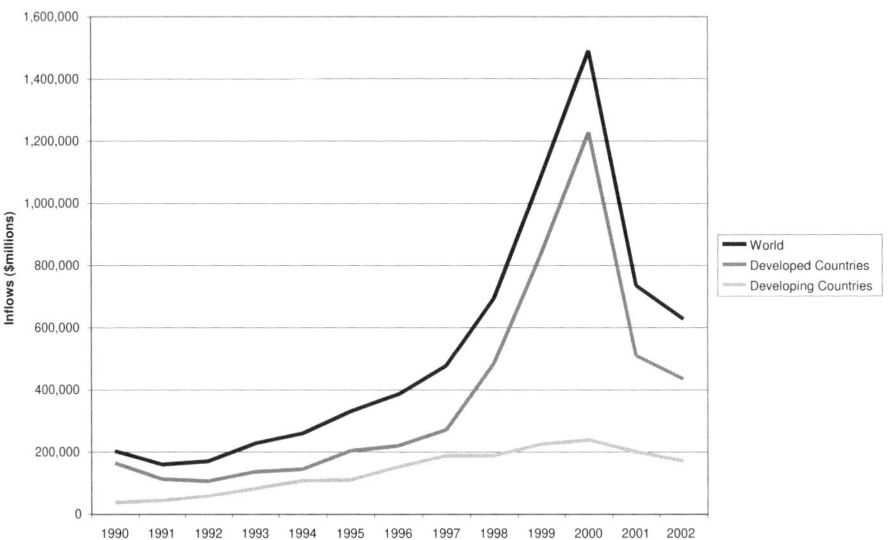

Figure 1.1 *FDI Flows in the World Economy: 1990–2002*

Source: UNCTAD, 2002a

Although they are miniscule in the global picture, FDI inflows to poor, developing countries may comprise a significant part of total investment and/or GDP in particular nations. For example, between 1996 and 1999, FDI comprised about 10 per cent of GDP in Bolivia, 26 per cent in Lesotho, and 26 per cent in Thailand (Overseas Development Institute, 2002, Figure 9). Overall, the ratio of FDI to

Table 1.1 *Ten Largest Developing Country Recipients of FDI inflows ($US billions)*

Top 10	(1990–2000) average	Top 10	2001
China*	43.4	China*	69.7
Brazil	12.0	Mexico	24.7
Mexico	10.1	Brazil	22.5
Argentina	7.2	Bermuda	9.9
Singapore	7.1	Poland	8.8
Malaysia	4.7	Singapore	8.6
Bermuda	4.7	Chile	5.5
Poland	3.7	Czech Republic	4.9
Chile	3.3	Taiwan	4.1
South Korea	3.2	Thailand	3.8
Top 10 total:	99.5		162.5
Total for Developing Countries:	130.9		200.9
Top 10 share:	76%		81%
Top 3 share:	50%		58%

*China figures include Hong Kong.
Source: UNCTAD, 2002a

GDP in developing countries rose from about 1 per cent to 3.5 per cent between 1990 and 2000 (Figure 1.2).

The 1990s FDI boom will probably prove to be a bubble, although the long-term trend is towards expansion[2]. Global FDI inflows took a nosedive in recent years, falling by over 40 per cent in 2001 and by another 21 per cent in 2002 – the biggest downturn in three decades (UNCTAD, 2003). While FDI inflows remained flat in 2003, UNCTAD predicted a new 'take off' in 2004 (UNCTAD, 2004).

Privatization wave

In both developed and developing countries, the 1990s FDI boom was led by the 'buying up' of existing local companies by foreign companies. According to UNCTAD (2000a), the share of cross-border M&As in world FDI flows increased from 52 per cent in 1987 to 83 per cent in 1999. Although most cross-border M&As occur within OECD countries, they accounted for close to 70 per cent of FDI inflows to developing countries in 1999 (UNCTAD, 2000a, p14 and Table I.5).

In developing countries, M&As were concentrated in newly privatized state-owned companies spanning water, energy, telecommunications and financial services. In Mexico, for example, the US company Citigroup acquired Banamex, Mexico's largest bank, for US$12.5 billion in 2001. The single transaction accounted for half of all FDI inflows to Mexico in that year (UNCTAD, 2000a).

In many countries, the acquisition of formerly public services by TNCs, especially water, has generated widespread concern and popular resistance. Despite promises of more efficient, reliable and equitable access to water, social

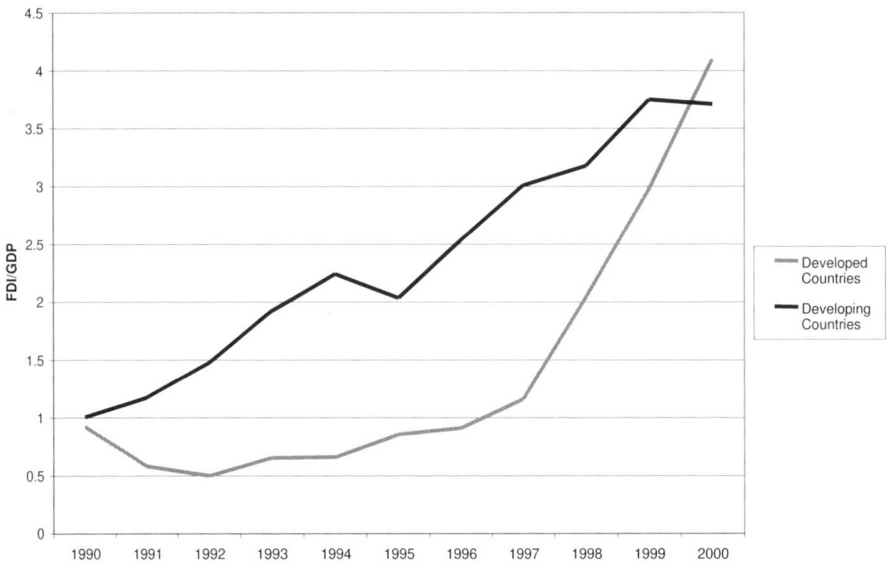

Figure 1.2 *FDI as a Percentage of GDP in the World Economy*

Source: UNCTAD, 2002a

advocates are concerned that privatized water systems under TNC management will price the poor out of the market. In Cochabamba, Bolivia, for example, a 'water war' erupted after the city's water system came under the management of an international partnership involving Bechtel Corporation. When the price for water rose by between 35 and 400 per cent, city residents took to the streets and the municipal government canceled the contract (Dolinsky, 2001)[3].

The privatization wave changed the sectoral composition of FDI in developing countries, substantially increasing the share going to the service sector. In 1999, services accounted for 37.3 per cent of FDI inflows, up from 20.7 per cent in 1988 (UNCTAD, 2000). Although shrinking in relative terms in all regions except Africa, the manufacturing sector continues to account for the largest overall share, about 55 per cent in 1999. In all regions except Latin America, the share of FDI in the 'primary' sector, mostly agriculture and mining, decreased in the 1990s and accounted for only 5.4 per cent in 1999 (UNCTAD, 2000).

Despite its small share in aggregate flows, FDI in the primary sector forms the largest share of overall inflows in particular countries, including some of the poorest. Among the 49 'least-developed countries', 3 oil-exporting countries – Angola, Equatorial Guinea and Sudan – receive nearly half of all FDI inflows. According to a recent report by UNCTAD, there is a strong link between dependence on primary commodities and poverty (UNCTAD, 2002b).

Does FDI Promote Economic Development?

The pursuit of FDI as an engine of growth is a formula prescribed by mainstream economic theory, as well as the IMF and other global development organizations. 'The overall benefits of FDI for developing country economies are well documented', claims a 2002 report undertaken for the Organisation for Economic Co-operation and Development (OECD)'s Committee on International Investment and Multinational Enterprises (OECD, 2002b, p5). Based on consultations with OECD member governments and business, labour and NGO advisors, the report, entitled *Foreign Direct Investment for Development, Maximising Benefits, Minimising Costs*, nicely sums up conventional wisdom about the promise of FDI:

> *Given the appropriate host-country policies and a basic level of development, a preponderance of studies shows that FDI triggers technology spillovers, assists human capital formation, contributes to international trade integration, helps create a more competitive business environment and enhances enterprise development. All of these contribute to higher economic growth, which is the most potent tool for alleviating poverty in developing countries.*
>
> (OECD, 2002b)

In addition, the report goes on, FDI '*may* help improve environmental and social conditions in the host country by, for example, transferring "cleaner" technologies and leading to more socially responsible corporate policies' (emphasis added, OECD, 2002b).

The more qualified endorsement of FDI's social and environmental benefits likely stems from the OECD's own commissioned work in this area, including work by one of the authors of this chapter, which shows that the environmental impacts of FDI may be positive, negative or neutral, depending on the industrial and institutional context (Zarsky, 1999; OECD, 2002a). But caution is also warranted in assessing the larger relationship between FDI and economic development. An examination of recent studies shows that, in this case too, the benefits of FDI are far from well-documented.

Efficiency spillovers: is knowledge 'contagious'?

FDI generates rents to transnational corporations by virtue of their possession of superior technology, management and/or access to global markets. According to economic theory, host communities get 'spillover' benefits of the superior asset(s). Indeed, 'efficiency spillovers', which occur through the transfer of technologies and management practices, are increasingly seen as the primary benefit of FDI.

Dubbed a 'contagion' effect, knowledge is diffused to local firms and workers, raising the efficiency, productivity and marketing skills of domestic firms (Findlay, 1978). While knowledge diffusion is postulated for TNC investment in both developed and developing countries, it is the transfer from industrialized to developing countries that promises the greatest hope for global economic development.

Efficiency spillovers can occur through several routes, including the copying of TNC technology by local firms and the training of workers who then find employment in local firms or start their own. The most important conduit, however, is the linkage between TNC affiliates and their local suppliers (Lall, 1980). TNCs generate spillovers when they:

- help prospective suppliers to set up production facilities;
- demand that suppliers meet high management and quality standards;
- develop capacities for product and process innovation – and provide training to enable them to do so;
- provide training in business management; and
- help suppliers find additional markets, including in sister affiliates in other countries.

To what extent do TNCs actually undertake these activities in developing countries? Put another way, what is the empirical evidence that efficiency spillovers exist? Studies have been of two types: 1) statistical studies that examine trends in key macro-variables, such as domestic investment (gross fixed capital formation), exports and productivity; 2) case studies of particular industries, such as autos (Moran, 1998) and electronics (Amsden and Chu, 2003).

In developed countries, limited evidence suggests that the productivity of domestic firms is positively correlated with the presence of foreign firms, although one study found no independent growth effect of FDI (Carkovic and Levine, 2002). However, some studies found the magnitude of spillovers to be very small (Lim, 2001). Moreover, tax policies and other incentives to attract FDI distort firm technology and investment choices and generate negative spillovers – a loss in the efficiency of local firms (Blonigen and Kolpin, 2002).

For developing countries, the evidence is mixed. Some studies have found clear evidence of spillover effects, while others have found limited or even negative effects (Table 1.2). An IMF study found 'overwhelming' evidence of productivity increases through technology transfer (Graham, 1995). However, a later literature review took a more nuanced view, finding that the transfer of technology by TNCS depended on a host of country- and industry-specific variables (Kokko and Blomström, 1995).

Several other studies suggest that the capture of spillovers depends on host country conditions. One found that the larger the productivity gap between foreign and domestic firms, the less likely were spillovers (Kokko et al, 1996). Moran (1998) found that export performance requirements helped Mexico to capture spillovers from investment by US car manufacturers. In their case study of Taiwan, Amsden and Chu (2003) found that spillovers were captured as a result of government industry policies, especially support for research and development for nationally owned companies.

Table 1.2 *Does FDI Generate Spillovers in Developing Countries?*

Author/Study	Year	Yes/No/ Maybe	Explanation
Aitken et al	1997	Yes	Foreign firms act as export catalysts for domestic firms (Mexico)
Aitken & Harrison	1999	No	No evidence of spillovers (Venezuela)
Amsden & Chu	2003	Maybe	Government industry policies must actively promote domestic firms (Taiwan)
Graham	1995	Yes	Increases productivity of domestic firms
Kokko & Blomström	1995	Maybe	Depends on industry and country characteristics, especially policy environment
Kokko	1994	Yes	Increases productivity of domestic exporting firms (Mexico)
Kokko et al	1996	Maybe	Productivity gap between foreign and domestic firms must not be too big (Mexico and Uruguay)
Krugman	1998	No	Domestic investors are more efficient but foreign investors have superior cash position
Lensink & Morrissey	2001	Yes	Reduces costs of R&D and promotes innovation
Moran	1998	Maybe	Liberal investment climate must encourage integration of local firms into TNC global sourcing and production network
Razin et al	1999	Maybe	Foreign investors can speculate on domestic stock prices, leading to over-investment and inefficiency.

Some studies find that, rather than generate positive spillovers, FDI generates *negative* spillovers. Krugman (1998) argues that, generally, domestic investors are more efficient than foreign investors in running domestic firms – otherwise, foreign investors would have purchased them. However, in a financial crisis, such as the crisis which swept East Asia in the late 1990s, domestic firms may be cash-constrained and be available for purchase at 'fire-sale' prices. Krugman concludes that a superior cash position, rather than efficiency-enhancing technology or management, drives FDI.

Another study argues that FDI is driven by the information advantage of foreign investors, who are able to gain– and use as leverage– inside information about the productivity of firms under their control. With their superior information, foreign firms can inflate the price of equities sold in domestic stock markets. The expectation of future stock market opportunities then leads to over-investment and inefficiency (Razin et al, 1999).

Overall, of the 11 studies reviewed for this chapter, only 4 unequivocably found that FDI generates efficiency spillovers in developing countries. Two found the opposite, while 5 found that FDI may or may not generate spillovers, depending on local productive, policy or financial conditions (Table 1.2). The evidence suggests that there is no automatic or consistent relationship between FDI and efficiency spillovers, either for developing countries as a whole or for all industries within a county. Realizing the promise of FDI to transfer technology and diffuse knowledge apparently requires 'conducive' policy, institutional and market environments.

Like the benefits of FDI itself, however, there is little consensus on what constitutes a conducive policy. Moran (1998) argues that a liberal trade and investment regime that allows TNCs maximum flexibility has the best chance of increasing the efficiency of local firms and integrating them into global supply chains. On the other hand, Moran also found that export performance requirements in Mexico reoriented TNC investment and production strategies in ways which generated local spillovers. Amsden and Chu (2003) conclude that the most important ingredient in capturing spillovers and indeed, in increasing productive capacity in 'latecomer' countries is a strong state acting to nurture domestic firms through effective, market-friendly and performance-related subsidies.

Crowding in or crowding out domestic investment?

The central promise of FDI is that it promotes economic growth, not only through efficiency spillovers but by stimulating or 'crowding in' domestic investment. Indeed, by increasing the productivity and efficiency of local firms, spillovers themselves can help to stimulate further domestic investment.

But the 'crowding in' effect of FDI on investment may be gained whether or not there are technology spillovers or even if much value beyond labour is added in local production. Assembly operations, for example, where workers put together components made elsewhere, can still drive domestic investment and growth if workers spend their increased incomes on locally produced consumer goods and services. On the other hand, if they prefer imports, investment in domestic firms is likely to stagnate and contract.[4]

On the other hand, TNCs may undermine local savings and 'crowd out' domestic investment by competing in product, service and financial markets and displacing local firms. The loss of domestic firms can undermine market competition, leading to inflated prices and lower-quality products.

TNCs can also crowd out domestic investment by borrowing in domestic capital markets, thus driving up interest rates and the cost of capital to business. High domestic interest rates may also be the result of deliberate government policies to attract foreign capital. The higher-than-global-average interest rates will also cause the exchange rate to be overvalued, further crowding out domestic firms producing for export. While foreign firms will also suffer from loss of competitiveness, the impact is cushioned by their access to foreign sources of financing. While much is made of the potential for FDI to increase foreign exchange earnings, there is a risk that it will instead contribute to crises in the balance of payments by repatriating profits and by increasing the rate of imports faster than the rate of exports[5].

Taken together, the risk is that FDI could lead to an overall contraction, rather than an increase, in domestic investment and economic growth. Indeed, in a study that generally argues for the potential benefits of FDI, Moran (1998) cautions that 'the possibility that FDI might lead to fundamental economic distortion and pervasive damage to the development prospects of the country is ever present' (p2).

What is the most likely 'face' of FDI? A host of studies over the past decade have examined the nature of macro-economic benefits and the conditions under which they are, or are not, captured (Table 1.3). Moran (1998) reports on the findings of three separate 'net assessments' of the impact of FDI covering 183 projects in some 30 countries over the past 15 years. Two studies found that FDI had a positive impact in 55 to 75 per cent of the projects they studied. But one study found that FDI had 'a clearly negative impact on the economic welfare of the host' in an astonishing 75 per cent of the projects studied (Moran, 1998, p25).

Table 1.3 *Does FDI Promote Economic Growth in Developing Countries?*

Study Author(s)	Year	Yes/No/ Maybe	Explanation
Balasubrmayam et al	1996 1999	Maybe	Requires open or neutral trade regime
Borensztein et al	1998	Maybe	Depends on education level of workforce
de Mello	1999	Maybe	Depends on degree of complementarity and substitution between FDI and domestic investment
Graham and Wada	2001	Yes	Raised per capita GDP in Chinese provinces with FDI concentration
Graham	1995	Maybe	TNC's market power can generate negative impacts
Loungani & Razin	2001	Maybe	Risks
Lim	2001	Maybe	Depends on tax incentives, regulatory & legal impediments, macroeconomic instability
Marino	2000	Maybe	Requires open trade and investment policies
Mallampally & Sauvant	1999	Maybe	Requires human resource development, information and other infrastructure
Markusen & Venables	1999	Yes	Raises productivity and exports of domestic firms; generates spillovers
Rodrik	1999	No	Reverse causality: TNCs locate, rather than drive growth, in more productive and faster growing countries

Economy-wide studies generally have found both positive and negative impacts of FDI on domestic investment. For example, a study by the Brookings Institution covering 58 countries in Latin America, Asia and Africa found that a dollar of FDI generates another dollar in domestic investment (Bosworth and Collins, 1999). On the other hand, many studies have found that the investment and/or growth impacts of FDI could be positive *or* negative, depending on a variety of variables, mostly having to do with host country policies.

One study found that the impact of FDI is significantly positive in 'open' economies, and significantly negative in 'closed' economies (Marino, 2000). Others have found that positive impacts depend on the effectiveness of domestic industry policies; and on tax, financial or macroeconomic policies. A World Bank study found that the impacts of FDI depend on the structure and dynamics of the industry, as well as host country policies (World Bank, 2003a). In its recent report on the role of FDI in development, the OECD concluded that the overall benefits of FDI, depend on 'the appropriate host country policies and a basic level of development' (OECD, 2002b, p9).

Several studies suggest that, to capture the benefits of FDI, a country must *already have reached* some kind of 'development threshold'. One found that FDI raises growth only in countries where the labour force has achieved a minimum level of education (Borensztein et al, 1998). Another found 'significant cross-country diversity' in terms of the catalytic role of FDI in developing countries and concluded that the key variables are 'country-specific factors', including institutions and policies (de Mello, 1999, p148).

Overall, of the 11 studies reviewed for this chapter, 2 found positive links between FDI and economic growth, while 1 found a negative link and 8 studies found that 'it depends'. Like efficiency spillovers, the positive benefits of FDI on domestic investment and growth depend largely on domestic policies, capabilities and institutions.

FDI AND THE ENVIRONMENT

In the last decade, a surge of regional and bilateral investment agreements have promoted the liberalization of investment regimes. These agreements expand the rights of foreign investors but, with few exceptions, articulate no environmental or social responsibilities of either investors or governments. Many in the sustainable development community are concerned that, without mandatory and enforceable guidelines, liberalization will accelerate environmental degradation (Zarsky, 1999; Mabey and McNally, 1999).

The impacts of FDI on the environment can be traced through three routes:

- environmental performance of TNCS;
- impacts of FDI-induced economic growth on the scale and composition of industry; and
- impacts on national and global environmental regulation.

In this section, we sketch the key mechanisms at play in each of these routes and review some of the theoretical and empirical literature (for a deeper look at the FDI–environment relationship, see Zarsky, 1999 and Arraya, Chapter 2, this volume).

Performance of TNCs

Two critical strategic and management decisions of TNCs affect their environmental performance. First is the choice of technology, *viz*, whether to invest in newer, cleaner 'best available' or to 'dump' older, dirtier technologies. In most industries, a range of technologies are in use. Efficiency and 'clean-ness' may be a function as much of industry sector as of company choice: some industries are more technologically dynamic than others.

The second decision has to do with management practice; that is, whether the corporate parent has implemented an effective environmental management system (EMS) and required the same of its overseas subsidiaries and suppliers. NGO advocacy campaigns have increasingly demanded that TNCs adopt 'voluntary initiatives' to go 'beyond compliance' in global operations.

One of the promises of FDI for sustainable development is that TNCs, especially from the OECD, will help to drive up standards in developing countries by transferring both cleaner technology and/or better environmental management practices. The evidence for such a trend, however, is mixed. A case study of foreign investment in Chile's mining sector in the 1970s and 1980s found that foreign companies not only performed better than domestic companies but diffused better environmental management practices (Lagos and Valesco, 1999). A volume of case studies of FDI in Latin America in the 1990s, including bananas in Costa Rica and soybeans in Brazil, concluded that FDI promotes better management practices (Gentry, 1998).

Other studies have failed to find a positive link between foreign firms and environmental performance in host countries. In statistical studies of Mexico (manufacturing) and Asia (pulp and paper), World Bank researchers found that foreign firms and plants performed no better than domestic companies. Instead, environmental performance was found to depend on 1) the scale of the plant (bigger is better); and 2) the strength of local regulation, both by government and civil society via 'informal' mechanisms (Dasgupta et al, 1998; Hettige et al, 1996).

A recent study that examined the environmental performance of TNCs in India had more nuanced findings (Ruud, 2002). On the one hand, TNCs were found generally to be transferring state-of-the-art production (although not necessarily pollution control) technologies, rather than dumping older and dirtier technologies. In addition, TNC affiliates were strongly influenced by corporate parents to improve environmental management.

On the other hand, there was no evidence that better environmental management practices were diffused by TNC affiliates to local partners, suppliers or consumers. The author concludes that there is no evidence that TNCs drive a 'race to the top' or the bottom. Rather, the chief insight is that local norms and institutions are of central importance in determining TNC practices and therefore, 'FDI inflows do not automatically create a general improvement in environmental performance' (Ruud, 2002, p116).

Many developing countries, especially the poorest, lack the capacity and/or political will to enforce environmental oversight of industry. In this context, TNCs are largely able to 'self-regulate' and have one of four choices: 1) follow local practice; 2) comply with local regulations, regardless of local practice; 3) adopt company-wide global standards based on home country standards; or 4) adopt international standards or 'best practice' norms for corporate social responsibility (CSR).

Best practice may entail the embrace of broad and encompassing norms, not only for companies themselves but also for their suppliers, such as the OECD's Guidelines for Multinational Enterprises (MNEs) (Table 1.4).

Table 1.4 *OECD's Environmental Guidelines for MNEs*

1. Establish an environmental management system, which includes:
   a) information regarding environmental, health, and safety impacts;
   b) measurable objectives and targets for improved environmental performance; and
   c) monitoring and verification of progress towards targets
2. Provide adequate and timely information on the potential environment, health and safety impacts of the activities of the enterprise; and communicate and consult with stakeholder communities.
3. Consider full life cycle impacts of production processes, goods and services.
4. Use precautionary principle.
5. Maintain accident, emergency and contingency plans.
6. Continually seek to improve environmental performance by:
   a) adopting best practice;
   b) developing products with low environmental impact, including recyclable and energy-efficient products;
   c) promoting environmental awareness by customers; and
   d) researching ways to improve environmental performance over the longer term.
7. Provide training to employees on environment, health and safety.
8. Contribute to the development of environmentally meaningful and economically efficient public policy.

Source: OECD 2000

The guidelines spell out eight good practices, including the implementation of an environmental management system and consultation with stakeholders. They also extend good practice to the supply chains of MNEs. Other approaches to best practice include implementing standards developed by industry associations, such as the chemical industry's Responsible Care initiative.

Companies make different choices, depending on company culture and the industry they are in. In the petroleum and mineral industries, case studies suggest that TNCs have tended to follow – or even to worsen – local practice (Rosenthal, 2002; Leighton et al, 2002). In many parts of the world, mining operations have generated severe environmental degradation and pollution, including the discharge of toxic substances into river systems, large volume waste disposal, the inadequate disposal of hazardous wastes, and the long run impacts of poorly planned mine closure (Sandbrooke and Mehta, 2002). Multinational oil companies have been the target of protest and criticism for widespread pollution and human rights violations in the Amazon region, Nigeria, Indonesia and, increasingly, the Caspian region.

In the high-tech sector, on the other hand, North American and European TNCs tend to adopt either company-wide standards or international best practice for environmental management and community consultation. Within the industry, however, there are 'leaders' and 'laggards' (Leighton et al, 2002).

One mechanism by which TNCs affect environmental performance in developing countries is via requirements on suppliers and sub-contractors. An increasingly popular trend is for large TNCs to require that suppliers be certified to ISO 14001, an international standard for environmental management systems.

Scale and composition effects

One of the potential, if not automatic, benefits of FDI is that it stimulates economic growth. Without adequate global and national regulation, however, economic growth is likely to accelerate environmental degradation – even if TNCs are good performers – through scale effects. The experience of East Asia, often described as an 'economic success story,' provides a tragic example. According to the Asian Development Bank, resource degradation and environmental pollution in both East and South Asia is so 'pervasive, accelerating, and unabated' that it risks human health and livelihood (Asian Development Bank, 2001, p2).

The scale impacts of economic growth on the environment derive largely from unsustainable production and consumption patterns. If FDI was channelled into sustainably produced and sustainably transported goods and services, then the overall impact – even of rapid and high growth – on the environment would presumably be neutral or low. To date, however, rapid growth, in developing and developed countries alike, has tended to be associated with an increase in unsustainable production and consumption patterns (WWF, 2002).

Potential environmental benefits of FDI may flow from changes in the structure or 'composition' of industry. In theory, FDI flows to more efficient companies and industries. Greater economic efficiency translates into greater environmental efficiency via reduction per unit output of productive inputs such as energy, water and materials, as well as reductions in wastes. The 'pollution intensity' of an economy overall, in other words, can be reduced by a change in the relative mix of industries, as well as by changes in the 'eco-efficiency' of companies within industries.

While acknowledging that environmental impacts can worsen with an increase in the rate of growth, some economists argue that, over time, economic growth generates environmental improvements. The Environmental Kuznets Curve (EKC) posits that environmental quality first worsens and then improves as per capita income (GDP) rises[6]. Reasons include the substitution of less polluting consumer goods; changes in the structure of industry; and greater political demands for environmental regulation. Early studies put the turning point at between US$3000 and US$5000 (Grossman and Kruger, 1993).

If true, the EKC suggests that, to a large extent, the pursuit of economic growth is itself a sustainable development strategy. One major concern, however, is that the environmental and resource degradation at lower levels of income often result in irreversible losses. Examples include loss of biological and genetic diversity and potable water due to degradation or destruction of old growth forests; depletion or destruction of fish stocks due to coastal degradation; and human deaths resulting from severe air pollution. Given the number of people on the planet living today at very low levels of per capita income, the potential environmental (and human) losses that must be endured before the global turnaround are staggering.

Another concern is that a positive relationship between income and environmental quality in one country or region might mask a relocation of dirty industry to another country or region, resulting in an overall neutral or even negative global environmental impact. Many East Asian studies in the 1980s and 1990s, for example, documented the correlation between improved environmental quality in Japan and the relocation of Japan's pollution-intensive industries to Southeast Asia (Mani and Wheeler, 1997).

Most importantly, a number of studies question the validity of the EKC hypothesis itself, especially for developing countries (Stern, 1998). The evidence in support of a turning point is limited to a small number of localized pollutants, primarily sulphur and particulate matter. For many other environmental problems, such as water pollution, municipal waste, carbon dioxide emissions and loss of biodiversity, no consistent evidence has been found that performance increases with higher levels of income.

Environmental regulation: stuck in the mud?

Environmental and resource management is largely the preserve of nation-states. How does FDI affect national (and sub-national) environmental regulation? There is evidence that TNCs themselves, wielding their substantial bargaining power, can help to drive local standards up – or down. In Chile in the 1970s and 1980s, foreign mining companies pressed for more coherent environmental regulation. In the Russian Far East, on the other hand, oil TNCs involved in obtaining leases for exploration and drilling off Sakhalin Island in the 1990s flouted and undermined Russia's fledgling environmental laws (Rosenthal, 2002).

The asymmetric bargaining power of TNCs regarding local governments is most troublesome in the context of the intense competition for FDI in both developed and developing countries. Given the absence of global environmental standards, would-be host governments seeking to attract FDI may be reluctant to make higher-than-average environmental demands on individual TNCs. They may even be tempted to offer lower-than-average environmental demands to enhance the attractiveness of an overall package.

This 'stuck-in-the-mud' problem, the impact of intense global competition for FDI – absent common environmental norms– is thus likely to inhibit the rise of environmental standards (Zarsky, 2002; Oman, 2000). The problem afflicts both developed and developing countries: efforts in the 1990s to put a modest tax on carbon were roundly defeated in both the US and Australia by worries that investment would move offshore.

There is some evidence that, despite regulators' fears, high environmental standards do not, in fact, deter investors and, in some cases, are even preferred by investors (Gentry, 1998). Moreover, with the rise of the global corporate social responsibility movement, TNC and host-government expectations may be changing.

Overall, an examination of all three of the channels linking FDI and the environment suggests there is no determinate trend: FDI can improve, worsen or have no impact on environmental quality. Other factors – such as government regulation, the rate of economic growth, company culture, the particular industry in which the FDI takes place and the rules that govern FDI – are key variables.

MIXED RECORD: THE MEXICAN EXPERIENCE[7]

The previous two sections suggest that the impacts of FDI on sustainable development cannot be determined at a theoretical level. Rather, it is necessary to examine FDI impacts in particular times and places, including individual countries or groups of countries with like characteristics. In this section we analyse the impacts of FDI on sustainable development in Mexico – the poster child for liberalization – in the 1990s.

For Mexico, FDI was the prize of the NAFTA regional integration process. By opening wide to foreign trade and capital flows, the Mexican government aimed to attract a large influx of FDI into the manufacturing sector. The hope was that FDI would raise the productivity and exports of manufactured goods, which would in turn stimulate domestic economic growth, investment and industrial restructuring.

Moreover, through the transfer of foreign technology and management skills, FDI-led growth would improve the environmental performance of industry. Closing a virtuous circle, sustainable growth was to remedy the severe income disparities that plague Mexico by providing better-paying jobs in manufacturing. The new jobs would absorb poor farmers, including those displaced by NAFTA's agricultural liberalization, and stem the flow of poor migrants across the border. The objective, said President Salinas, was for Mexico to 'export goods, not people' (Winn, 1992).

To achieve these goals, Mexican macro-economic and industry policies were tailored to create a climate that favoured foreign investment. Subsidies to domestic companies were removed, and inflation was reined in through high interest rates and 'economic pacts' that kept wage growth in check. The anti-inflation policy also generated an overvalued exchange rate, which made imports of productive inputs cheap.

The results have been mixed (see Gallagher and Zarsky, 2003). On one hand, Mexico successfully attracted FDI inflows. Between 1994 and 2002, Mexico received an average of US$12.3 billion of FDI inflows each year, up from only US$2.5 billion annually between 1980 and 1993 (Dussel, 2000). Indeed, for the period overall, Mexico received the third largest share of FDI flows going to developing countries, and in 2001, overtook Brazil to become second only to China (UNCTAD, 2002a).

The FDI inflows seemed to vindicate Mexico's focus on regional economic integration. Accounting for 67 per cent of the total, the US was by far the largest source of FDI. Moreover, about half of all FDI inflows went into the manufacturing sector, while another quarter went into financial services (RNIE, 2000).

Reflecting the in-pouring of FDI, exports increased by more than a factor of three between 1994 and 2002, rising from US$50 billion to US$160 billion (INEGI, 2003). A full 88 per cent of Mexico's exports were from the manufacturing sector, distinguishing Mexico from many other Latin American countries, such as Chile, which remain heavily dependent on minerals and other primary products (UNCTAD, 2002a). By 2001, Mexico had become the ninth largest economy in the world.

The success of Mexico's FDI-led integration strategy, however, has an Achilles' heel. Mexican export-oriented manufacturing plants rely heavily on imports, rather than locally sourced goods, for productive inputs (Table 1.5). While exports grew fast, imports grew faster, generating a large and persistent

Table 1.5 *Locally Sourced Inputs in Maquila Manufacturing Plants (value added as % of total)*

	1990	2002
Food and Beverage	38.6	42.9
Apparel	0.9	8.0
Footwear and Leather	6.9	2.7
Furniture and Wood Products	3.1	14.6
Chemical Products	10.2	5.5
Transportation Equipment	0.8	3.3
Machinery	4.6	2.6
Electronic Assembly	1.2	3.0
Materials and Electronic Accessories	0.01	2.2
Sporting Goods	1.1	2.2
Other	4.1	2.2
Total	4.7	3.7

Source: INEGI, 2003

current account deficit, about US$15.5 billion a year on average between 1994 and 2002 (Banco de Mexico, 2003). The manufacturing sector accounted for more than 80 per cent of the deficit.

One of the most important drivers of the current account deficit is Mexico's over-valued exchange rate, itself largely the result of the high interest, anti-inflation policy, as well as direct manipulation by Mexican authorities. High interest rates were used to attract foreign portfolio investments to manage Mexico's external debt. There is, in short, a fundamental macroeconomic contradiction in the integration strategy: while inflation was largely brought under control, the cost was a ballooning current account deficit (Nadal, 2003).

Moreover, Mexico's low-wage competitiveness has begun to slide, suggesting that the large FDI inflows of the last decade may themselves be unsustainable. From the middle of 2001 through the end of 2002, foreign-owned firms dismissed 287,000 workers (or one in five of all such workers) (INEGI, 2002). Mexican analysts worry that US (and other foreign) firms are shying away from Mexico because of sluggish growth in the US – and because of emerging opportunities in China. According to the World Competitiveness Yearbook, Mexico fell from 34th place in 1998 to 41st place in 2002 (CSIS, 2003).

Crowding out investment

How has the FDI-led global integration strategy performed in terms of its domestic linkage goals? The single most telling – and troublesome – indicator is GDP growth. Between 1994 and 2002, GDP grow at an average rate of only 2.7 per cent per year, less than half the 6.7 per cent average growth rate of the 1970s. Even in the tumultuous 1980s, GDP grew an average of 3.7 per cent per year (Table 1.6). As the editors of a sweeping study of the liberalization programme conclude, 'The strongest single indictment of Mexico's new economic model is that it has not produced robust growth' (Middlebrook and Zapeda, 2003, p25).

What accounts for this poor performance? While economists point to a variety of factors, the most important is the contraction of domestic investment. Between 1994–2002, total annual investment as a per cent of GDP averaged 19.4 per cent, the same as in the 1980s and down a bit from the 1970s (Table 1.6). However, the share of FDI in total investment more than doubled. The converse, of course, is that the share of *domestic* investment fell by a half.

Rather than stimulating new investment, FDI apparently 'crowded' – and certainly starved – out domestic investment. Anti-inflationary macroeconomic policies, including contractionary monetary policy, drove domestic interest rates sky high: commercial bank interest rates averaged 22 per cent between 1994-2002. Moreover, domestic consumer demand for manufactured goods plummeted after 1994, driven in part by falling wages. In manufacturing plants outside of the maquiladoras, real wages fell by 12 per cent 1994–2002 (INEGI, 2003; Salas and Rendon, 2000; Arroyo, 2003).

Buffetted by high interest rates, an overvalued exchange rate, and a drop in domestic demand, smaller companies were the worst hit by the poor investment

Table 1.6 *Lacklustre Domestic Performance: Investment and GDP Growth in Mexico*

	Investment as a % of GDP	FDI Share of Investment (%)	GDP Growth (%)	Growth in GDP per capita (%)
1970–1980	20.7	3.6	6.7	3.6
1981–1993	19.4	5.4	3.3	–0.3*
1994	19.4	12.0	4.5	
1995	16.1	16.8	–6.2	–7.9
1996	17.9	12.0	5.1	3.5
1997	19.5	12.3	6.8	5.2
1998	20.9	11.6	4.9	3.5
1999	21.2	11.1	3.7	2.3
2000	21.2	10.4	6.7	5.2
2001	19.4	19.3	0.5	–1.0
2002	18.9	7.9	0.0	–1.4
1994–2002	**19.4**	**12.6**	**2.7**	**1.4**

*1981–1993.
Source: World Bank (2003b); Urquidi (2003), Table 15.2

climate. As a whole, micro, small and midsize firms account for almost half of manufacturing employment. Between 1988 and 1998, the average annual growth rate for small business was only 1.2 per cent, for micro firms 2.7 per cent, and for midsize business 2.8 per cent. Large firms, on the other hand, grew by 4.2 per cent (Dussel, 2003, Table 6).

Efficiency spillovers

There is little evidence that hoped-for efficiency spillovers of FDI materialized in Mexican manufacturing. Except for a few 'bright spots,' the reliance of export-oriented firms, both domestic and foreign, on imported productive inputs meant generally that FDI generated few backward linkages to Mexican companies.

One bright spot historically is the auto industry. A case study of the automotive sector found that the integration of Mexican producers into the global sourcing and marketing strategies of multinational car companies in the 1980s generated a host of spillovers to local firms and local communities (Moran 1998, pp53–56). Another study found that the presence of foreign manufacturing firms acted to increase the export capacity of domestic firms (Aitken, Hanson and Harrison, 1997). The authors conclude that the 'export spillovers' must stem from ways in which the foreign firm acts as a channel for technology, management, distribution services, and information about foreign markets.

Broader and more recent studies, however, are less optimistic. A large statistical study covering 52 Mexican industries found no evidence that foreign presence is linked to technical spillovers, although there are positive impacts on training and demonstration. The author concludes that earlier studies found evidence only that FDI generates market access, not technical spillovers (Romo

Murillo, 2003). In the electronics industry, Mexican firms account for only about 5 per cent of the value added in production (Dussel Peters, 1999).

Indeed, Mexico's industrial structure has apparently changed little in the past 30 years, despite the radical disjuncture between liberalization policies and the import-substitution strategy which preceded it. A team of Latin American economists found that 'more than a decade of economic reform appears not to have radically changed the momentum in the makeup of manufacturing activity that had been under way since the 1970s and the oil boom . . . [T]he process of transformation and modernization has concentrated on large, export-oriented companies with access to international financing' (Mattar, Moreno-Brid and Peres, 2003, p146).

A central component of sustainable industrial development is the capacity for innovation. The skills and technical capacity to generate new ideas and products is central not only to economic growth but also to reducing the environmental impacts of industry. FDI may have done little to enhance and may even have reduced Mexico's capacity for innovation. Between 1996 and 2000, the number of patent applications by Mexican residents increased by 16 per cent, while the number of applications by non-residents increased by 120 per cent. Already miniscule, the share of Mexican resident patent applications decreased by half to only 0.7 per cent (World Bank, 2003).

Overall, the FDI-led integration strategy engendered a process of economic polarization and segmentation in Mexico. Large foreign and domestic firms that had access to international sources of financing and produced products for export were able to expand manufacturing production. Small and medium size manufacturing firms producing for the domestic market, on the other hand, were starved for capital – and for customers.

Environmental impacts

The environmental impacts of the FDI-led integration strategy were enormous. Since the 1980s, the overall level of industrial pollution in Mexico, particularly criteria air pollution[8], water pollution, and toxics, has increased faster than both population and GDP growth (Gallagher, 2003; Schatan, 2002).

Environmental degradation was fueled by the large increases in the scale of manufacturing growth and exports, rather than in the structure of industry. According to one study, every 1 per cent increase in manufacturing output correlated with a 0.5 per cent increase in pollution (Schatan, 2002). Focusing only on criteria air pollution, another study found a corresponding pollution growth rate of 0.7 per cent (Gallagher, 2003).

Despite the increase in the overall scale of pollution, there were relative environmental improvements due to 'composition effects', that is, changes in the composition of industries. The increase in pollution in the manufacturing sector was somewhat slower than the rate of growth of output, as well as of exports (Gallagher, 2002; Schatan, 2002).

The improvements were largely due to the fact that, under the integration strategy, Mexico consolidated its comparative advantage in labour-intensive (as opposed to capital intensive) assembly work and sold off state-patronized industries such as steel, cement, and pulp and paper. On the whole, labour-intensive industries such as apparel and electronics assembly are less pollution-intensive than their heavily capital-intensive counterparts in the manufacturing sector. Despite such 'bright spots,' compositional changes have been far outweighed by overall scale effects of rapid industrial growth.

In addition to increase in scale of production, environmental degradation stemmed from the social impacts generated by rapid growth, including of the export-oriented maquila assembly plants. The influx of migrants to maquila-laden locales far exceeded the infrastructure capacity of host communities, including sewage and waste management. The result has been the deterioration of water and air quality (OECD, 1998; Stromberg, 2002).

The worsening of environmental trends in Mexican manufacturing is not due to the relocation of pollution-intensive U.S. manufacturing firms. The share of the five 'dirtiest' US industries in total production fell in both Mexico and the US over the 1990s. The share of employment in dirty industries in the U.S. has remained the same, and has actually declined in Mexico (Table 1.7).

Table 1.7 *Share of 'Dirty Industry'[1] in US and Mexican Manufacturing (%)*

	1988	1994	1998
Mexico			
Production	30.1	23.1	26.5
Employment	7.9	6.3	5.9
United States			
Production	17.0	15.1	14.7
Employment	11.3	11.2	11.2

[1] Iron and steel; non-ferrous metals; industrial chemicals; pulp and paper; cement
Source: Gallagher (2003)

In some sectors, there is evidence that foreign presence has led to better environmental performance. In the steel industry, for example, Mexican steel production is 'cleaner' per unit of output than its US counterpart in terms of criteria air pollution. The reason is largely due to the age of the core technology. Newer investment (both foreign and domestic) generally involves more environmentally benign mini-mill technology rather than more traditional and dirtier blast furnaces (Gallagher, 2002).

When FDI involves the transfer of older technology, environmental performance largely depends on how well firms comply with environmental regulations, including by installing end-of-pipe pollution abatement technology. Two World Bank studies concluded that government pressure, including regulation and inspection, is a key determinant of compliance by both domestic and foreign firms in Mexico (Wisner and Epstein, 2003; Dasgupta, Hettige and Wheeler, 1998).

Figure 1.3 *Real Spending on Environmental Protection in Mexico*

Source: PROFEPA (2002)

Despite its efficacy, there are signs that Mexico's commitment to regulatory pressure wavered in the 1990s. Although spending on environmental protection grew impressively between 1988 and 1993, it tapered off by 45 per cent between 1994 and 1999 (Figure 1.3) Indeed, environmental spending in Mexico is the lowest of all OECD countries: as a percentage of GDP, the average OECD country spends three times more than Mexico on the environment (OECD, 1998).

Environmental inspection patterns mirror the trend in environmental spending. Although inspections got off to an impressive start in 1992, only 6 per cent of establishments were inspected at the highest point. Total inspections decreased by 45 per cent after 1993, and inspections in the maquila sector decreased by 37 per cent (Figure 1.4).

Rising inequality and poverty

From the perspective of most Mexicans, the overarching goal of Mexico's FDI-led integration strategy was to 'make life better,' that is to raise the standard of living, especially for the poor and middle class by providing better-paying manufacturing jobs. By the end of 2002, the promise looked like a chimera. The jobs created by the growth of the manufacturing sector have been relatively few in number, as well as low-paying and unstable.

Between 1994 and 2002, a total of only 637,000 new jobs were created in the manufacturing sector, or about 82,500 new jobs each year – compared with roughly 730,000 'new entrants' to the economically active workforce. In total, 6.5 million new workers were looking for jobs between 1994 and 2002. The

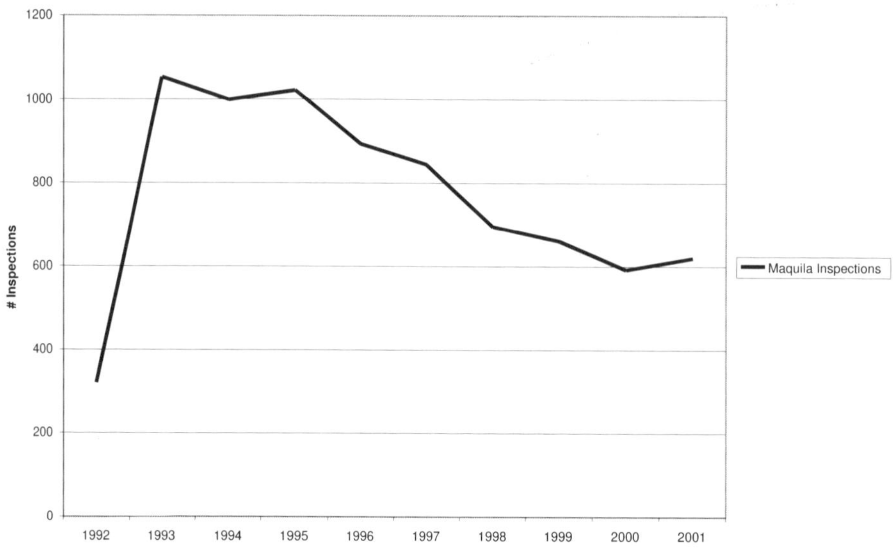

Figure 1.4 *Maquila Inspections, 1992–2001*

Source: Stromberg (2002)

manufacturing sector provided jobs for less than 12 per cent of them. Moreover, the major exporting firms and maquiladoras accounted for only 5.8 per cent of total employment in 2002 (Dussel, 2003).

There is evidence that the jobs created are of poor quality. Wages in Mexican manufacturing overall have declined by 12 per cent since 1994, despite significant increases in labour productivity, and more than half of new jobs do not provide benefits. Indeed, nearly half of employed Mexican workers are without benefits (Arroyo, 2003). Those Mexicans who cannot find jobs and end up staying in Mexico comprise the country's large and growing informal sector of the underemployed. Official estimates of the percentage of economically active Mexicans in the informal sector range from 30 to 63 per cent (INEGI, 2003).

The failure of the manufacturing sector to generate employment and raise wages has exacerbated already high levels of inequality. The share of income marshaled by the richest 10 per cent of Mexicans rose by more than 15 per cent during the liberalization years, rising from 32.8 to 38.7 per cent between 1984 and 2000. The share of the poorest 10 per cent fell slightly, from 1.7 to 1.5 per cent, while the share of the 60 per cent in the middle-income groups fell by 10 per cent (Table 1.7). By 2000, the richest 20 per cent garnered 13 times more income than all other Mexicans put together.[9]

Poverty remains widespread. Depending on the definition, between 69 and 80 per cent of Mexicans were living in poverty in 1996 (Laso, 1999). With poverty comes marginalization. Although there have been some improvements since 1995, illiteracy, the percentage of the population without a complete primary education, and the percentage of people without electricity and running water

Table 1.8 *Marginalization in Mexico*

	1995	2000 (per cent)	Average
Illiteracy among population over 15	11	9	10
Population without complete primary education	24	28	26
Housing without drainage	14	10	12
Housing without electricity	7	5	6
Housing without running water	15	11	13
Housing with dirt floor	17	15	16

Source: INEGI (2003)

are still extremely high by OECD standards (Table 1.8). Despite early hopes, Mexico continues to 'export people,' as well as goods. In the 1980s, approximately 200,000 Mexicans migrated to the US each year. In the 1990s, cross-border flows increased to some 300,000 per year (INEGI, 2003).

Conclusion: Rethinking FDI

Many developing countries, as well as the IMF and other development organizations, have placed their hopes for economic growth on attracting FDI. For them, the primary measure of success is the total value of FDI inflows.

The case study and statistical evidence examined in this chapter makes clear that FDI does not automatically or necessarily catalyze sustainable industrialization or economic growth. The economic literature itself seems increasingly to recognize that the capture of the potential benefits of FDI requires conducive conditions in host countries, including a certain level of technical and human development and the 'right' policy and institutional environment.

This chapter has also shown that in Mexico, a poster child for success in terms of attracting FDI, rapid growth of manufactured exports has not triggered a process of sustainable domestic growth. Instead, there is a 'disconnect' between the globally integrated and the domestic parts of the economy. As a result, hoped-for employment and income benefits did not materialize. Most worrisome, FDI has not stimulated backward linkages or increased endogenous capacity for innovation. In addition to its economic role, the capacity for innovation is crucial to reducing the environmental impacts generated by increasing the scale of economic activity.

The overwhelming evidence makes it easy to conclude that FDI is no 'miracle drug'. What needs fleshing out are the subtle and difficult questions that flow out of this analysis:

- What are the options for economic and social development in poorer countries?
- What kinds of local policies would best capture the potential growth benefits and efficiency spillovers of FDI?

- Are the poorest, least developed countries better off without FDI?
- How much 'room to move' do developing countries have to shape local policies towards FDI, given the constraints on national policy in regional and bilateral (and potentially global) investment agreements?
- Can voluntary TNC practices raise the probability that FDI will deliver environmental, social and economic benefits to host communities and countries?
- To best garner the potential development benefits of FDI, how should investment be governed at the supra-national level?

Fully developed answers to these questions are beyond the scope of this chapter. What our analysis does suggest, however, is that a first step is to eschew the search for a 'miracle drug' and to embrace the need to develop more fulsome, domestically oriented development strategies. Moreover, our analysis makes clear that structuring investment regimes to serve the interests and concerns of foreign investors will not necessarily deliver economic, environmental or social benefits to host communities.

The centrepiece of a more fulsome, sustainable development strategy should be the nurturance of endogenous domestic capacities for production and innovation. Rather than skew policies towards attracting *foreign* investment, macroeconomic policies should aim to enhance the overall *climate* for investment, both domestic and foreign. Rather than encouraging FDI to flow towards export platforms for the assembly of imported inputs, industry and technology policies should aim to develop local skills, local markets and solid, world-class domestic firms. With the right set of local – and global – policies, FDI could potentially help in that process.

ENDNOTES

1 Vietnam, Angola, Lesotho, Ecuador, Turkmenistan, Azerbaijan and China.
2 For developed countries, the drop-off was 49 per cent; for developing countries, it was 82 per cent.
3 In response, Bechtel sued the city under a bilateral investment agreement between Bolivia and the Netherlands, where the partnership is incorporated.
4 Such operations, however, have 'shallow roots' and are vulnerable to being relocated to other locales where labour and other production costs are cheaper.
5 This is precisely what happened in Mexico's manufacturing sector in the 1990s.
6 A landmark article by Simon Kuznets in 1955 posited that inequality first rises, then falls with increases in per capita income. Development policymakers evoked the theory for decades to argue that inequality could be ignored in the short term. More recently, empirical evidence has faded, leading economists to conclude 'there is no empirical tendency whatsoever in the inequality–development relationship' (Fields, 1995).

7 This section draws from Gallagher and Zarsky (2003).
8 Criteria air pollutants are non-toxic air pollutants such as nitrogen oxide (NOx), sulphur oxide (SOx), sulphur dioxide (SO_2), nitrogen oxide (NO_2), volatile organic compounds (VOC), hydrocarbons (HC), all particulates, and carbon monoxide (CO).
9 Authors' calculations, based on Corbacho and Schwartz (2002).

REFERENCES

Aitken, B. and A. Harrison (1999) 'Do Domestic Firms Benefit from Foreign Direct Investment?', *American Economic Review*, vol 89, no 3, pp605–618, June

Aitken, B., G. H. Hanson and A. Harrison (1997) 'Spillovers, Foreign Investment and Export Behavior', *Journal of International Economics*, vol 43, pp103–132

Amsden, A. and W. Chu (2003) *Beyond Late Development: Taiwan's Upgrading Policies*, Cambridge, Massachusetts, MIT Press

Amsden, A. (2001) *The Rise of 'The Rest': Challenges to the West From Late-Industrializing Economies*, New York, Oxford University Press

Asian Development Bank (2001) *Asian Environment Outlook*, Manila, ADB

Balasubramanyam, V. N. M. Salisu and D. Sapsford (1999) 'Foreign Direct Investment as an Engine of Growth', *Journal of International Trade and Economic Development*, vol 8, no 1, pp27–40

Balasubramanyam, V. N. M. Salisu and D. Sapsford (1996) 'Foreign Direct Investment and Growth in EP and IS Countries', *Economic Journal*, vol 106, pp92–105

Banco de Mexico (2003) www.bancomex.mx

Barkin, D. (2002) 'The Greening of Business in Mexico', in P. Utting (ed) *The Greening of Business in Developing Countries*, London, Zed Books

Blomstrom, M. and A. Kokko (1996) 'The Impact of Foreign Investment on Host Countries: A Review of the Empirical Evidence', World Bank Policy Research Working Paper, 1745

Blomstrom, M., A. Kokko and M. Zejan (1994) 'Host Country Competition, Labour Skills, and Technology Transfer by Multinationals', *Weltwirtschaftliches Archiv*, vol 130, no 3, pp521–533

Blonigen B. A. and V. Kolpin (2002) 'Technology, Agglomeration, and Regional Competition for Investment', NBER Working Paper 8862, April

Borensztein, E., J. de Gregorio, J.-W. Lee (1998) 'How does Foreign Direct Investment Affect Economic Growth?' *Journal of International Economics*, vol 45, pp115–135

Bosworth B. P. and S. M. Collins (1999) 'Capital Flows to Developing Economies: Implications for Savings and Investment', Brookings Papers on Economic Activity: 1, Washington, DC, Brookings Institution, pp143–169

Carkovic, M. and R. Levine (2002) 'Does FDI Accelerate Economic Growth?', University of Minnesota, May

Chakrabati, A. (2001) 'The Determinants of FDI: Sensitivity Analyses and Cross Country Regressions', *Kyklos*, vol 54, no 1, pp89–113

Corbacho, A. and G. Schwartz (2002) 'Mexico: Experiences with Pro-poor Expenditure Policies', IMF Working Paper No 02/12

CSIS (2003) *Economic Competitiveness in Mexico*, Washington, DC, Center for Strategic International Studies

Dasgupta, S., H. Hettige and D. Wheeler (1998) 'What Improves Environmental Performance? Evidence from Mexican Industry', Policy Research Working Paper 1877, Washington, DC, Development Research Group, World Bank

deMello, L. R. Jr (1999) 'Foreign Direct Investment-led Growth: Evidence from Time Series and Panel Data', *Oxford Economic Papers*, vol 51, pp133–151

Dolinsky, L. (2001) 'Cochabamba's Water Rebellion – And Beyond', *San Francisco Chronicle*, February 11

Dussel, E. P. (1999). La Suncontratación Como el Proceso de Aprendizaje: El Caso de la Electrónica en Jalisco (México) en la Decáda de los Noventa, Santiago, CEPAL

Dussel, E. D. (2000) *Polarizing Mexico: The Impact of Liberalization Strategy*, Boulder, Lynne Rienner

Dussel, E. P. (2003) 'Industrial Policy, Regional Trends, and Structural Change', in K. J. Middlebrook and E. Zepeda (eds), *Confronting Development: Assessing Mexico's Economic and Social Policy Changes*. Palo Alto, Stanford University Press, pp24–176

Fields, G. (1995) 'Income Distribution in Developing Countries: Conceptual, Data and Policy Issues in Broad Based Growth', in M. G. Quibria (ed), *Critical Issues in Asian Development*, Hong Kong, Oxford University Press, pp75–93

Findley, R. (1978) 'Relative Backwardness, Direct Foreign Investment', *Quarterly Journal of Economics*, vol 92, pp1–16

Gallagher, K. (2002) 'Industrial Pollution in Mexico: Did NAFTA Matter?' in C. L. Deere and D. C. Esty (eds), *Greening the Americas: NAFTA's Lessons for Hemispheric Trade*, Cambridge, MIT Press

Gallagher, K. (2003) 'NACEC and Environmental Quality: Assessing the Mexican Experience', in J. Knox and D. Markel (eds) *Greening NAFTA*, Stanford, Stanford University Press

Gallagher, K., and L. Zarsky (2003) *Sustainable Industrial Development? The Performance of Mexico's FDI-led Strategy*, Global Development and Environment Institute, Tufts University, www.ase.tufts.edu/gdae

Gentry, B. (ed) (1998) *Private Capital Flows and the Environment*, Lessons from Latin America, Cheltenham, Edward Elgar

Gentry, B. and L. Fernandez (1998) 'Mexican Steel', in B. Gentry (ed), *Private Capital Flows and the Environment: Lessons form Latin America*, Cheltenham, Edward Elgar

Graham, E. H. (1995) 'FDI in the World Economy', IMF Working Paper, wp/95/59, Washington DC.

Graham, E. M. and E. Wada, (2001) 'Foreign Direct Investment in China: Effects on Growth and Economic Performance', in P. Drysdale (ed), *Achieving High Growth: Experience of Transitional Economies in East Asia*, New York, Oxford University Press

Grossman, G. M. and A. B. Krueger, (1993) 'Environmental impacts of a North American free trade agreement', in P. Garber, *The Mexico–US Free Trade Agreement*, Cambridge, MA, MIT Press

Hanson, G. H. (2001) 'Should Countries Promote Foreign Direct Investment?' G-24 Discussion Paper 9, UNCTAD, February

Hettige, H, M. Huq, S. Pargal and D. Wheeler (1996) 'Determinants of Pollution Abatement in Developing Countries: Evidence from South and Southeast Asia', in *World Development*, vol 24, no 12, pp1891–1904

INEGI (2003) Bureau of Economic Informations. Mexico City, Instituto Nacional de Estadística Geografía e Informática (INEGI): www.inegi.gob.mx

INEGI (2000) Instituto Nacional de Estadistica Geografia e Informatica, 'Sistema de Cuentas Economicas y Ecologicas de Mexico, 1993-1999' (Determining the Economic Costs of Ecological Degradation in Mexico), Mexico City, INEGI, www.inegi.gob.mx

Jaffe, A., S. R. Peterson and P. R. Portney (1995) 'Environmental Regulation and the Competitiveness of US Manufacturing: What Does the Evidence Tell us?' *Journal of Economic Literature*, vol xxxiii (March), pp132–163

Kokko, A. (1994) 'Technology, Market Characteristics, and Spillovers', *Journal of Development Economics* vol 43, pp279–293

Kokko, A. and M. Blomstrom (1995) 'Policies to Encourage Inflows of Technology Through Foreign Multinationals,' *World Development* vol 23, no 3, pp459–68

Kokko, A., R. Tansini and M. Zejan (1996) 'Local Technological Capability and Spillovers from FDI in the Uruguayan Manufacturing Sector,' *Journal of Development Studies*, vol 34, pp602–611

Krugman, P. (1998) 'Firesale FDI,' Working Paper, Cambridge, Massachusetts Institute of Technology

Lagos, G. and P. Velasco (1999) 'Environmental Policies and Practices in Chilean Mining', in A. Warhurst (ed), *Mining and the Environment, Case Studies from the Americas*, Ottawa, International Development Research Centre. www.idrc.ca/books/focus/828/chapter3.html

Lall, S. (1980) 'Vertical Interfirm Linkages in LDCs: An Empirical Study,' *Oxford Bulletin of Economics and Statistics* vol 42, pp203–226

Leighton, M., N. Roht-Arriza and L. Zarsky (2002) *Beyond Good Deeds: Case Studies and a New Policy Agenda for Corporate Accountability*, Berkeley, California: Natural Heritage Institute, www.nautilus.org/enviro/

Lensink, R. and O. Morissey (2001) 'Foreign Direct Investment: Flows, Volatility and Growth,' paper presented at the Development Economic Study Group Conference, University of Nottingham, April 5–7

Lim, E.- G. (2001) 'Determinants of and the Relation Between Foreign Direct Investment and Growth: A Summary of the Recent Literature,' Working Paper 01/75, International Monetary Fund, November

Lougani, P. and A. Razin (2001) 'How Beneficial is Foreign Direct Investment for Developing Countries?' *Finance and Development* vol 38 no 2, International Monetary Fund, June

Mabey, N. and R. McNally (1999) 'Foreign Direct Investment and the Environment: From Pollution Havens to Sustainable Development, WWF-UK Report, August

Malampally, P. and K.P. Sauvant (1999) 'Foreign Direct Investment in Developing Countries,' *Finance and Development* vol 36 no 1, International Monetary Fund, March

Mani, M. and D. Wheeler (1997) 'In Search of Pollution Havens? Dirty Industry in the World Economy,' PRDEI, Poverty, Environment and Growth, World Bank, April

Marino, A. (2000) 'The Impact on FDI on Developing Countries Growth: Trade Policy Matters,' ISTAT (National Institute of Statistics, Université de Nice-Sophia Antipolis, France)

Markusen, J. R. and A. J. Venables (1999) 'Foreign Direct Investment as a Catalyst for Industrial Development', *European Economic Review* vol 43, pp335–356

Mattar, J., J. C. Moreno-Brid and W. Peres (2003) 'Foreign Investment in Mexico after Economic Reform', in K. J. Middlebrook and E. Zepeda, *Confronting Development, Assessing Mexico's Economic and Social Policy Challenges*, Stanford, Stanford University Press, pp123–60

Mercardo, A. (2000) 'Environmental Assessment of the Mexican Steel Industry', in R. Jenkins (ed), *Industry and the Environment in Latin America*, London, Routledge

Moran, T. H. (1998) *Foreign Direct Investment and Development, The New Policy Agenda for Developing Countries and Economies in Transition*, Washington DC, Institute for International Economics

Nadal, A. (2003) 'Macroeconomic Challenges for Mexico's Development Strategy', in K. Middlebrook and E. Zepeda (eds), *Confronting Development, Assessing Mexico's Economic and Social Policy Challenges*, Palo Alto, Stanford University Press, pp55–88.

Nunnenkamp, P. and Spatz, J. (2002) 'Determinants of FDI in Developing Countries: Has Globalization Changed the Rules of the Game? *Transnational Corporations*, vol 11, no 2

OECD (1998) *Environmental Performance Review for Mexico*, Paris, OECD

OECD (2000) *The OECD Guidelines for Multinational Enterprises*, Paris, OECD

OECD (2002a) *The Environmental Benefits of FDI*, Paris, OECD

OECD (2002b) *Foreign Direct Investment for Development, Maximising Benefits, Minimising Costs*, Paris, OECD

Oman, C. (2000) *Policy Competition for Foreign Direct Investment*, Paris, OECD

Overseas Development Institute (2002) *Optimising the Development Performance of Corporate Investment, The ODPCI Program*, Discussion Paper, August, www.odi.org.uk/pppg/activities/country_level/odpci/index.html

PROFEPA, Procuraduría Federal de Protección al Ambiente (Federal Agency for Environmental Protection) (2000) www.profepa.gob.mx

Razin, A., E. Sadka and C.Yuen (1999) 'Excessive FDI Under Asymmetric Information', National Bureau of Economic Research (NBER) Working Paper 7400

RNIE (2003) Sistema del Registro Nacional de Inversiones Extranjeras (National Registration System for Foreign Investment), Mexico City, Secretary of Economy, www.economia.gob.mx

Rodrik, D. (1999) 'The New Global Economy and Developing Countries: Making Openness Work', Policy Essay 24, Overseas Development Council, Washington, DC

Romo Murillo, D. (2002) 'Derramas Tecnologicas de la Inversion Extranhera en la Industria Mexicana,' *Comercio Exterior* vol 53, no 3 (March), pp230–43

Rosenthal, E. (2002) 'Conflicts Over Transnational Oil and Gas Development Off Sakhalin Island in the Russian Far East: A David and Goliath Tale,' in L. Zarsky (ed), *Human Rights and Environment: Conflicts and Norms in a Globalizing World*, London, Earthscan, pp96–122

Ruud, A. (2002) 'Environmental Management of Transnational Corporations in India – Are TNCs Creating Islands of Environmental Excellence in a Sea of Dirt?' *Business Strategy and the Environment* vol 11, pp103–118

Sandbrooke, R. and P. Mehta (2002) 'Rapporteurs' Report,' in OECD, *Foreign Direct Investment and the Environment, Lessons from the Mining Sector*, pp9-16, Paris, OECD

Schatan, C. (2002) 'Mexico's Manufacturing Exports and the Environment Under NAFTA,' in North American Commission for Environmental Cooperation, *The Environmental Effects of Free Trade*, Montreal, North American Commission for Environmental Cooperation

Stern, D. (1998) 'Progress on the Environmental Kuznets Curve?' *Journal of Economic Development and the Environment* vol 3, pp173–196

Stromberg, P. (2002) *The Mexican Maquila Industry and the Environment: An Overview of the Issues*, Naciones Unidas CEPAL/ECLAC, pp1–56.

UNCTAD (2000) *World Investment Report: Crossborder Mergers and Acquisitions and Development*, New York, United Nations

UNCTAD (2002a) *World Investment Report: Transnational Corporations and Export Competitiveness*, New York, United Nations

UNCTAD (2002b) *Least Developed Countries Report 2002, Escaping the Poverty Trap*, New York, United Nations

UNCTAD (2003) 'Global FDI Flows Continue to Fall', Press Release, 9 April

UNCTAD (2004) 'New take-off Predicted for FDI', Press Release, 14 April

Urquidi, V. L. (2003) 'Mexico's Development Challenges', in K. J. Middlebrook and E. Zepeda, *Confronting Development: Assessing Mexico's Economic and Social Policy Challenges*, Stanford, Stanford University Press, pp561–76.

Wackernagel, M. (2001) 'Shortcomings of the Environmental Sustainability Index', *Refining Progress*, www.anti-lomborg.com/ESIcritique.rtf.

Winn, P. (1992) *The Americas: The Changing Face of Latin America and the Caribbean*, Los Angeles, University of California Press

Wisner, P. S. and M. J. Epstein (2003) 'The NAFTA Impact on Environmental Responsiveness and Performance in Mexican Industry', *Journal of International Business Studies*, vol 44, pp1–31

World Bank (2003a) *Global Economic Prospects and the Developing Countries 2003*, Washington, DC, World Bank, www.worldbank.org/prospects/gep2003/

World Bank (2003b) *World Development Indicators*, Washington, D.C.: World Bank

WWF (2002) *Living Planet Report 2002*, www.panda.org/news_facts/publications/general/livingplanet/index.cfm

Zarsky, L. (1999) 'Havens, Halos and Spaghetti: Untangling the Relationship Between FDI and the Environment,' in OECD, *Foreign Direct Investment and the Environment*, Paris, OECD, pp47–73

Zarsky, L. (2002) 'Stuck in the Mud? Nation-States, Globalization, and the Environment', in K. P. Gallagher and J. Werksman (eds), *International Trade and Sustainable Development*, London, Earthscan, pp19–44

Chapter Two

FDI and the Environment: What Empirical Evidence Does – and Does Not – Tell Us[1]

Monica Araya

Abstract

This chapter analyses recent empirical research on foreign direct investment (FDI) and the environment in developing countries. The review focuses on the environmental effects resulting from the impact of FDI on changes in economic scale, technology and productive structure. Despite common myths about both positive and negative linkages, it finds that there is no overarching determinate relationship between FDI and the environment.

The chapter also examines multinational enterprises' choices about how to manage environmental impacts in the different countries in which they operate. It finds that a number of variables affect such choices, including firm and industry characteristics, as well as market forces, regulation, and actions by non-governmental groups. The study of *cross-border* corporate environmental management has been neglected theoretically and empirically. Hence, emerging research in this area represents a promising development in the study of FDI and the environment.

Introduction

Private capital – both local and foreign – plays a central role in a country's quest for sustainability and development (OECD, 2001a; von Moltke, 2000; French, 2000; Gentry, 1999). Conventional wisdom – especially since the 1990s – suggests that FDI is development-enhancing when it brings opportunities for infrastructure improvement, technology transfer and capacity building in host countries.

An analytical and empirical assessment is useful for identifying whether, and if so how, positive linkages between FDI and environmental protection emerge. FDI can create both benefits and risks for the environment; the outcome is often context-dependent (OECD, 1997; Zarsky, 1999; Neumayer, 2001; OECD, 2002a).

The study of pre-conditions in the host-country that makes FDI work for – not against – the environment has received increased attention in research and policy circles. But host economies will not necessarily internalize positive effects that environmentally responsible investors may generate (e.g. the arrival of environmental 'know-how'). Institutional variables, in particular, will play a key role in whether host countries actually capture the FDI-driven benefits.

In addition to the study of host-country pre-conditions, the exploration of positive FDI and environmental linkages requires deeper understanding of *cross-border* corporate environmental management. But traditionally, the research about business and the environment has focused on company and industry responses in their home-countries – not on their performance abroad. As a result, cross-border environmental management, in particular, has been overlooked theoretically and empirically. Fortunately, a number of recent analytical developments have geared in this direction trying to explain why some investors prefer globally oriented environmental management while others do not. Another question that is frequently asked is why industry associations promote beyond-compliance behaviour among its members regardless of their international operations while others do not. This research, however, is still in its early stages.

The literature on private investment and the environment has traditionally emphasized FDI over portfolio equity investment (e.g. highly mobile and short-term investments) and debt finance (e.g. commercial loans and bonds). FDI often translates into facilities such as power stations, mines and plants, which raises a number of environmental issues such as pollution, ecosystems' carrying capacity, resource use and productivity. As a result, it is this type of investment that creates the most direct, significant and observable environmental linkages.

Other types of private investment have less observable and yet important environmental repercussions. The connection between the environment and each type of private capital flows – FDI, equity investment and debt – varies in depth and character (O'Connor, 2000; OECD, 1999a; Gentry, 1998). More recently, researchers have begun to study the environmental dimension of both portfolio equity investments and debt finance (Boxes 2.1 and 2.2).

This chapter is organized as follows. Section 2 summarizes core themes of the literature on FDI and the environment, and defines the scope of the survey. Section 3 will discuss the effects of FDI on environmental quality. Section 4 analyzes the emerging literature on cross-border corporate environmental management. The final section offers key conclusions from the literature review and proposes themes that deserve further theoretical and empirical attention.

FDI and the Environment: Core Themes

The theoretical and empirical research on FDI and the environment falls generally into three clusters. Each is explored below.

Box 2.1 *Portfolio Equity Investment and the Environment: Some Key Issues*

- Portfolio equity investments are usually highly mobile and short term. The environmental implications of this investment are less clear than in the case of FDI flows. For example, initial public offerings (IPOs) – a company's first offer of stock to the public – and bond placements provide capital to companies (and thus may act like FDI), but once they are sold, they normally change hands many times in other markets (e.g. stock exchanges). ***This distance attenuates the link between the investor and the entity in which the investment is held.*** Moreover, many portfolio investors seek to maximize returns in the short term, so environmental risks (which often occur in the long term) tend to be discounted. The search for quick returns also means that portfolio investors may pull out of a sector or a country overnight, if they lose confidence in it (OECD, 1997).
- ***Accountability*** for the impacts of portfolio flows, whether environmental in nature or not, is hard to locate. By their very nature, portfolio investment risks are dispersed across a diverse array of holdings, and the transaction costs of obtaining accurate information about the nature of each investment are high (OECD, 1997).
- Some studies have revealed that financial analysts and investors did not fully understand the links between environmental performance, improved competitiveness and financial performance (Schmidheiny and Zorraquín, 1996; Gentry and Fernandez, 1997).
- Yet, the opportunities that portfolio flows present as a point of environmental policy leverage are becoming more evident (OECD, 1997):
  a. Portfolio investors hold the purse strings to more money worldwide than is available from any other type of investment source, dwarfing the resources potentially available from FDI or commercial loans.
  b. Pressure for short-term profitability in these investments may also create incentives to reduce the environmental performance of host firms.
- Analysts are increasingly assessing the relationship between shareholder value and environmental performance. Some studies suggest a positive correlation between ***good environmental results and good financial performance***, (OECD, 1999a; Gentry and Fernandez, 1997; Dowell et al, 2000).
- But the mainstream financial community remains ***sceptical*** about the portfolio equity investment–environment link, and 'when the connection is made, it is usually made in terms of environmental risks, not environmental benefits' (OECD, 1999a, p35). Demonstrating causation – not only correlation – is very important. Although King and Lenox (2001) found evidence of a positive association between lower pollution and higher financial performance, they also found that a firm's strategic position and stable attributes might cause this association. For example, there is strong evidence that firms in cleaner industries have higher market valuation, but there is no evidence that firms that increase their production in cleaner industries increase their market valuation. Thus, they argue that credible 'green' calls will require researchers to rigorously demonstrate that environmental improvements actually produce financial gain.
- On a more pragmatic note, it is worth mentioning that new tools for assessing financial–environmental linkages have emerged. For example, the 'Dow Jones Sustainability Index' launched in 1999 by the Dow Jones Indexes and the Switzerland-based Sustainability Asset Management (SAM) Group provides a benchmark for financial products based on the concept of corporate sustainability. For more information see www.sustainability-index.com.

Impacts from policy-based competition for FDI

One body of research focuses on the effects of competition for FDI and explores different scenarios. One dominant theme in this literature is whether lower environmental standards, mainly in low-income nations, may attract foreign investment from high-income countries thus creating pressure for industrial relocation (i.e. the 'pollution haven' hypothesis).

A related question is whether the competition for FDI leads to a downward pressure on environmental standards (i.e. 'race-to-the-bottom' hypothesis) and/or regulatory standstill in both capital-importing and capital-exporting countries (OECD, 2002b; Zarsky, 1999). Other studies focus on the opposite effect and test whether competition for foreign investment leads countries to improved environmental standards (i.e. 'race-to-the-top' hypothesis) because stronger environmental policies may improve competitiveness by fostering innovation and efficiency (OECD, 2002b).

Since the end of the 1990s, studies have also assessed the legal repercussions of investment protection rules in environmental policy-making. A question that has received attention in this debate is whether investment protection rules decrease the regulatory autonomy of the host-country. The analysis has predominantly focused on the investment provisions of the North American Free Trade Agreement (NAFTA) (see Cosbey, Chapter 6). Other studies evaluate the potential environmental repercussions of the draft Multilateral Agreement on Investment (MAI) negotiated under the auspices of the Organization for Economic Development and Cooperation (OECD) until 1998 (Neumayer, 2001). Researchers have also explored the potential repercussion of bilateral investment agreements on environmental regulation (see Peterson, Chapter 5).

Effects from increased FDI on environmental quality

A second body of research focuses on the effects of FDI flows on environmental quality – for example, pollution levels and natural resources depletion. The net effect will be the result of three fundamental effects from FDI: *scale effects* from increased economic activity; *technological effects* from changes in the production and abatement technology and managerial skills; and *composition effects* from changes in industry structure.

Drivers behind cross-border corporate environmental performance

The most recent body of research focuses on the determinants of foreign investors' environmental management across borders. The literature suggests the following factors: firm characteristics, type of industry, market, regulatory, and informal forces (e.g. non-governmental actions).

This chapter reviews and analyses recent empirical and analytical work on the last two clusters. Evidence of the first the hypotheses about 'pollution

Box 2.2 *Debt Finance and Environmental Performance*

Attention to the connection between debt and environmental performance has increased in part because of the effect of debt finance in 'greening' FDI. For example, commercial lending to private firms gives banks a stake in the borrowers' financial performance and provides banks with an incentive to consider environmental risks. Debt holders will be good or poor environmental performers, depending on the nature of the instruments they hold (which affects how insulated they are from variations in a company's value), or on the importance of environmental performance to the success of the enterprises in which they have invested. For example, investors in government-issued bonds are likely to be relatively uninterested in environmental concerns, because the connection between government environmental performance and the ability to repay is somewhat remote (Gentry, 1998).

The link between banks and environmental issues usually arises in the course of the ***banks' evaluation of the potential borrower's creditworthiness,*** which helps them assess borrowers' ability to repay the loan. According to a survey by Ganzi and Tanner (1997), less than half of the 51 respondents 'always' or 'usually' require that environmental due diligence be performed on lines of credits, project finance transactions or equipment financing. Frye (1998) suggests that whether a lender has an explicit policy objective of environmental protection, or whether the lender views environmental issues only in terms of minimizing losses and maximizing returns, lenders have made and continue to make important contributions to environmental protection as a necessary by-product of their efforts to identify and minimize their risks.

Among the ***advantages of lenders' involvement*** are: forced assessment of environmental impacts, third party review of the potential project's environmental aspects, improved technologies or practices, expedited cleanup, continued oversight, and insurers as additional third party (Frye, 1998). Other work (O'Connor, 2000; Gentry, 1998) suggests that an even more positive finance–environment link emerges as banks discuss ***why and how they may profit from financing investment in environmental technologies and projects.*** Although traditional infrastructure projects are still financed by multilateral banks, private infrastructure financing has been growing in recent years (e.g. water and waste services).

A recent development on the debt finance–environment front is the adoption of the ***Equator Principles*** in 2003, a voluntary set of guidelines developed by the banks for managing social and environmental issues related to the financing of development projects. The banks will apply the principles globally and to project financings in all industry sectors, including mining, oil and gas and forestry. The principles are based on the policies and guidelines of the World Bank and International Finance Corporation (IFC) and the banks that originally adopted them underwrote approximately $14.5 billion of project loans in 2002, representing approximately 30 per cent of the project loan syndication market globally in 2002. More information is available at http://www.equator-principles.com (last visited 5 November 2003).

havens', 'race-to-the-bottom,' and 'regulatory chill', has been extensively analysed over the past years (OECD, 2001a; Neumayer, 2001; Zarsky, 1999; OECD, 1997; and Jaffe et al 1995).[2]

IMPACTS OF FDI ON ENVIRONMENTAL QUALITY

This section reviews recent empirical evidence with respect to scale, structural and technological effects associated with FDI flows in developing countries.

Scale effects

Scale effects occur when investment leads to greater economic activity that places new demands for raw materials, energy, water, transportation services and leads to more waste[3]. If output is produced and delivered using unchanged technologies, scale effects are expected to be negative as a result of increased emissions and resource depletion. However, the size of these effects is the subject of considerable debate (Nordström and Vaughan, 1999) and will often depend on the particular environmental factor under investigation (OECD, 2001a).

Although scale effects are expected to be negative for the environment, the 'silver lining' is that as national income grows, the country's capacity for achieving higher environmental quality may be enhanced. Traditionally, as income increases and countries develop, environmental protection may become a higher political priority for citizens.

The posited existence of an 'inverted-U' relationship between pollution and development is known as the Environmental Kuznets Curve (EKC) (Andreoni and Levinson, 2001; Panayotou, 1997; Grossman and Krueger, 1995; Seldon and Song, 1994). There is some empirical evidence in support of the existence of an EKC, including studies confirming that pollution increases at the early stages of development and then decreases once a certain income level is reached (Dasgupta et al, 1995).

Although microeconomic evidence suggests that increased incomes augment demand for environmental quality (McConnell, 1997), consumers' willingness to pay for different categories of environmental quality is far from uniform. An extensive analysis of the EKC is beyond the scope of this survey, but it is important to underscore that the ongoing debate suggests that the EKC hypothesis may be valid for some types of environmental indicators, but invalid for other important indicators (Munasinghe, 1999; Barbier, 1997).

For example, Nordström and Vaughan (1999) conclude that the U-shaped pollution path seems to hold for several local, primarily urban, pollutants to air, and, to a lesser extent, fresh water, but does not seem to hold for pollutants that disperse into a greater geographical scope, in particular carbon dioxide emissions. Additionally, Panayotou (2000; 1997) suggests that because income levels of developing countries are nowhere close to the 'turning point' posited by the EKC, increases in pollution and resource depletion would still continue for a long time, which could lead to significant and possibly irreversible damage.

Hence, it would be incorrect to assume that environmental effects of FDI-led growth will automatically be offset as income increases. In other words, as income grows, increased willingness to pay for higher environmental quality will not happen by compelling necessity (Nordström and Vaughan, 1999).

Recent empirical research on FDI and the environment reviewed for this chapter does not assess economy-wide scale effects that result from FDI-led growth. The lack of studies is not surprising because effects are very difficult to identify and quantify. For example, what scale effects can be attributed to FDI growth as opposed to increased trade? How much of increased pollution levels and resource depletion in Country X can accurately be linked back to increased FDI flows?

On the other hand, it is precisely the potential scale effects of FDI that concern many environmental advocates, especially in extractive primary sector activities such as oil and mining. Concerns about environmental effects of FDI in developing countries with low environmental standards and fragile ecosystems have generated cases of high-profile litigation. A recent example is the suit against ChevronTexaco for environmental damages from past operations in Ecuador[4].

But despite the well-documented controversies over oil and mining, no recent statistical studies examine the importance and determinants of *scale* effects of FDI in these sectors. Instead, the case study evidence that is available focuses on environmental impacts from specific investments and their impacts on pollution levels and resource use.

As part of her assessment of corporate social responsibility (CSR) in Indonesia, Kemp (2001, p31) argues that oil and gas operations have brought environmental damage to some areas, in particular, West Papua, where people were relocated, rivers polluted and holy places destroyed. Moreover, she argues that the Indonesian government has 'brutally suppressed' protests and that visits by researchers have been tightly controlled.

Jha (1999) shows that FDI has had mixed environmental effects in India. Negative environmental impacts from foreign investors were particularly common in the 1980s, leading to a heated politics and anti-FDI stances among environmental organizations – especially after the industrial accident in Bhopal in 1984. More recently, she suggests, the environmental performance of FDI has improved but the sustainability of their activities is still debated. Jha points to a huge gap that emerged between NGO and corporate claims regarding environmental and health risks and corporate practices.

He (2002) estimated the impacts on sulfur dioxide concentration in over 80 Chinese cities form 1993 to 1999 as a result of increased FDI flows. Contrary to his expectations, he found a negative correlation between economic growth and pollution, meaning a larger scale of production was associated with a decrease in air pollution concentration. How is that possible? One of He's explanations is that technological variables (i.e. pollution abatement technology) may have offset the negative scale effects from increased FDI-growth. Such effects are discussed in the next section.

Technology effects

Technology effects emerge whenever the liberalization of investment flows facilitates improvements in the production methods and processes of investors (and local industry) in the recipient nation (OECD, 1997). For the purpose of this chapter, environmental technology is defined broadly as *both* physical equipment (product, process and pollution abatement technology) and tacit knowledge (environmental management skills or 'know-how').

Conceptually, technological effects relate to three core (and related) dynamics: a) the *arrival* of advanced environmental technology; b) the *diffusion* of the latter to the local industry by way of direct transfer (e.g. a voluntary effort on behalf of the investor such as environmental training), and c) spillovers (e.g. externalities that occur through mimetic behaviour).

The arrival of foreign technology

Foreign investors are expected to bring advanced environmental technology (OECD, 2001b). Often, technological advantages are multinational enterprises' most relevant competitive edge over domestic producers and competitors – especially in developed nations (Grossman and Helpman, 1995). Usually, the arrival of technology is embodied in the transfer of machinery, equipment, patent rights, expatriate managers and technicians from the multinational enterprise parent to the affiliate as well as training of the affiliates' local employees (e.g. on-the-job training, seminars, formal schooling and overseas education) (Blomström and Kokko, 1998). Better techniques that reduce pollution and resource depletion may minimize, and even offset, scale effects from increased economic activity. Accordingly, theory predicts that technology effects from increased FDI will be positive for the environment. Whether the technological advances remain solely within the foreign investor's facilities or influence local industry will depend on several dynamics discussed below.

The transfer of technology to the local industry

If and when the advanced environmental technology arrives in a developing country, the know-how may or may not be transferred to the local industry. When such transfer occurs, it usually responds to collaboration between foreign investors and local firms by way of joint training programmes.

Productivity spillovers

Productivity spillovers (or externalities) take place when the entry or presence of foreign investors lead to productivity and efficiency benefits in the local firms and foreign investors are not able to internalize the full value of these benefits (Blomström and Kokko, 1998). Hence, technological upgrade of local industry (equipment and knowledge) may occur even if the investor does not intend it to. For example, local companies may face incentives to voluntarily improve their environmental management as a result of linkages with foreign affiliates[5]. These improvements may be 'forced' whenever the investor establishes environmental criteria that suppliers must meet and which may allow local firms to improve their productivity. But improvements can also be voluntary. For example, the local firms may try to imitate foreign affiliates environmental technologies or hire workers with environmental expertise trained by multinational enterprises.

The prospects of clean technology diffusion, by way of direct transfer and spillovers, is a key motivation for host-nations – especially in developing countries – to attract FDI. Hence, it is necessary to look at the empirical record and assess whether and if so why, this transfer occurs[6]. The review of the literature is organized according to the three clusters discussed above.

Empirical evidence on advanced environmental technology

Eskeland and Harrison (1997) concluded that foreign companies were cleaner and had lower levels of energy use in Mexico, Venezuela and Côte d'Ivoire. Blackman and Wu (1998) also found significant support for the argument that foreign investments are cleaner. Their cases suggest that foreign investment in electricity generation in China increased energy efficiency and reduced emissions. This positive effect was driven by the focus of FDI on generating advanced technologies, better management and competitive forces.

According to Christmann and Taylor (2001), multinational ownership in China positively affects environmental compliance and ISO 14000 adoption. Rasiah (1999) points out that US, European and Japanese multinational enterprises in the electronics sector tend to use better environmental practices than East Asian firms. Size and market-orientation seem to be the most important variables explaining the differences in environmental practices in Malaysia. However, Rasiah also points out that in the past, there were cases of environmentally inferior machinery transferred from multinational enterprises to Malaysia because of lower environmental standards prevailing in the country.

A case study of Mexico (Dasgupta et al, 1998) found that foreign ownership did not affect the environmental performance of firms. In other words, foreign companies were not systematically cleaner than the local ones. Instead, other aspects such as the size of the plant and public scrutiny had a more direct influence on company performance.

Guoming et al (1999) found evidence that some foreign investors brought new technologies, better environmental practices and infrastructure unavailable in China. Ruud (2002) shows that a majority of multinational enterprises in India tend to bring cutting-edge environmental management that is consistent with environmental policies of corporate headquarters in their country of origin. In other words, their performance is less environmentally offensive than previously thought.

Eriksen and Hansen (1999) point to the activities of a Danish pharmaceutical company, Novo Nordisk, in a joint venture with the Suzhou-Hongda Group from China for the production of starch-degrading enzymes for the alcohol industry. As a result of their environmental management, untreated water is no longer discharged but processed through biological wastewater treatment plants, which reduced the organic material by 90 per cent. The authors document that Novo Nordisk plants were opened in Tiajin with state-of-the-art technology and environmental management.

Rondinelli and Vastag (1999) studied the Aluminum Company of America (Alcoa) and show that its affiliates generally use advanced environmental technologies in their developing-country operations. Andonova (2003, p199) also observes that multinational enterprises located in eastern and central Europe 'perform better than others in the adoption of formal management practices such as environmental audits and ISO 14000, which contribute to environmental improvements'.

Other studies also show that foreign investors engage in poor environmental practices. Guoming et al (1999) suggest that, especially in the past, investors producing toys, leather, footwear and plastics in China managed natural resources poorly. Rasiah (1999) also provides examples of multinational enterprises that engaged in destructive environmental practices in Malaysia. These companies engaged in chemicals production (a British subsidiary), copper mining (a Japanese-Malay company), and storage and disposal of radioactive effluents (a Japanese firm).

Empirical evidence of environmental technology transfer

Gouming et al (1999) found that some multinational enterprises transferred environmental management skills to their Chinese partners and some cooperated with the Chinese government on environmental matters. In addition, some multinational enterprises promoted technology upgrades by helping domestic industry to manufacture products using less pollution and energy (fluorine-free refrigerators and pharmaceuticals). They document improvements related to electricity generation plants, energy-efficient technology and alternative energy sources.

Warhurst (1999) conducted 25 case studies and analysed the role of FDI as a conduit for clean technology transfer in mineral extraction[7]. The studies suggest that technological collaboration between suppliers and recipients – in particular intensive training – can contribute to improved environmental performance of local firms and enhanced environmental management capacity. However, the trainee must have mechanisms to both retain capacity and to diffuse it systematically throughout the firm's operation. In the absence of such mechanisms, the environmental capacity transferred through collaboration could be lost over time, or may remain concentrated in only one part of the operation.

Clearly, technology transfer is far from automatic. The local recipients of technologies need to purposefully harness the opportunities for transfer. Another finding from the studies is that environmental advantages *per se* were insufficient to ensure the adoption of the cleaner technologies in the cases analysed. Instead, the uptake of cleaner process technologies and enhanced environmental management was more likely if the process offered cost savings.

There is evidence of direct transfer of environmental management practices from US foreign investors to companies in Mexico, and to some extent, Brazil. García-Johnson (2000) explores why export-oriented firms in the Mexican chemical industry 'imported' voluntary, corporate programmes such as Responsible Care®[8]. She found that US chemical companies operating in Mexico were pivotal in the transfer of environmental know-how to the Mexican counterparts.

A collaborative US–Mexican partnership on environmental issues mainly aimed to enhance public opinion about the chemical industry. The study shows that US and Mexican chemical companies shared information about technology and pollution prevention and that those firms unwilling to cooperate with the mission behind Responsible Care® were actually expelled from the Mexican chemical industry association.

But García-Johnson also shows why the local context matters. She suggests that market-related and ideological barriers slowed the transfer of Responsible Care® to the Brazilian chemicals industry. Brazil's dominance in the Common Market of the Southern Cone (MERCOSUR) and the sheer size of the domestic market made the Brazilian industry less concerned about the perception by the US public of its environmental performance. According to Brazilian industry leaders, the negative reputation of the chemical sector was not as pressing a problem as US and Mexican companies perceived. Furthermore, the foreign origin of Responsible Care® (a Canadian–US innovation) generated resistance in Brazil. After several years, the programme led to increased communication and cooperation among industry members but smaller, domestically oriented companies remain unenthusiastic.

There is evidence that technology transfer may not happen at all or be very weak. Ruud (2002), for example, did not find evidence that foreign affiliates transferred environmental technology to Indian firms. Foreign affiliates respond to environmental constituencies in the source country, not India. This rationale, he suggests, limits the scope for deliberate transfer and productivity spillovers (e.g. demonstration effects) because the affiliates focus on improving their environmental performance and credentials abroad, not on the host country's environmental goals and needs such as training of local industry.

Andonova (2003) presents statistical evidence on whether foreign investment (and trade) encourages Eastern and Central European firms to improve their environmental management systems. Her data challenge traditional claims of FDI technology transfer. She shows that a greater share of international capital in Central and Eastern Europe has not necessarily led to greater propensity among local industry to adopt cleaner technologies. Her findings contradict prevailing wisdom in transition economies where foreign investment is viewed as a – if not 'the' – fundamental source of modernization and technological innovation. She finds that other factors, such as local policies and politics, account for improvements in environmental management in the transition economies

Developing countries should not expect that by increasing FDI inflows to their economies, foreign investors will necessarily transform their technological bases. Which technologies and functions FDI actually transfers to a particular country will depend largely on local capabilities (UNCTAD, 1999b; UNIDO and WBCSD, 2002; see also Gallagher and Zarsky, Chapter 1).

The United Nations Industrial Development Organization (UNIDO) and the World Business Council for Sustainable Development (WBCSD) showcase examples of positive relationships between the large multinational enterprises – mainly European – and poor communities in the developing world. One lesson from the cases is that local training remains a key mechanism for transferring know-how from the foreign affiliate to the local community in developing countries. The cases presented also suggest that host-governments need to be proactive in enabling partnerships between companies, workers and local communities. This is because even if foreign companies engage in capacity building, low levels of literacy, language barriers, and lack of motivation among the recipients of know-how reduce the effectiveness of the training.

Finally, local capabilities also have an impact on whether the benefits for technological transfer are short-lived or prevail in the long term (UNCTAD, 1999b). In the short term, the immediate recipients may benefit as they achieve higher levels of productivity and/or lower costs. But in the long run, their benefits depend on how much local firms learn from the technology and are able to deepen and develop their own capabilities.

Evidence on productivity spillovers favourable to the environment

A study on the pulp and paper industry in Chile points to the convergence of foreign and local facilities (Herbert-Copley, 1998, cited in UNCTAD, 1999b). This trend occurs because supplier behaviour and the presence of consulting engineering companies in Chile have left limited room for dramatic differences regarding mill design and technologies. Moreover, export market pressure has a common influence on both foreign and Chilean firms leading to similar improvements in environmental management (e.g. decreases in the use of bleaching). This dynamic is reinforced by external factors such as lending. For example, firms that request international agency funds often face similar environmental requirements.

Whether local firms imitate the technological practices of multinational enterprises will depend on several factors, in particular, the sophistication of local skills. Traditionally, 'reverse engineering' (or copying the investor's technologies) is more likely to occur in developed economies with highly skilled labour forces (Blomström and Kokko, 1998).

Finally, backward or upstream linkages (between the affiliate and its suppliers) also may facilitate spillovers conducive to better local practices. By demanding particular quality standards, multinationals can help upstream industries to improve their technological efficiency (Blomström and Kokko, 1998). Ruud (2002) finds evidence of this dynamic in India where local firms are part of a broader logistical network and must improve their performance in order to meet certain environmental criteria. Christmann and Taylor (2001) show that domestic firms with a large percentage of sales going to multinational enterprises within China are more likely to adopt ISO 14000 than firms that are not part of such linkages.

Backward linkages do not automatically generate productivity spillovers, but in the absence of such linkages, the potential for externalities leading to better environmental management is even smaller.

Structural effects

Structural effects are associated with the adjustments within and between economies that occur when the pattern of resource use shifts (OECD, 2001a). To the extent that investment liberalization promotes efficiency among economies, structural effects are expected to be positive: goods would be produced with lower input and capital per unit of output worldwide.

FDI inward stocks have undergone a transition from manufacturing to services. According to UNCTAD (1999b), FDI destined to primary sectors, such as oil extraction, declined by half between 1988 and 1997, falling from 8.6 per cent to 4.5 per cent. In the same period, the service sector experienced a corresponding increase in both developed and developing countries.

The transition to services may be beneficial from an environmental perspective because usually services are less pollution-intensive than traditional industrial activities (OECD, 2001a; Gentry, 1998). But each type of service generates different environmental impacts (e.g. compare finance versus air transport) and more empirical analysis is necessary to fully assess the environmental repercussions of switching toward service-based economies.

A case study of tourism services concludes that the environmental effects are both positive and negative (WWF International, 2001). While such services generate income and provide incentives to protect natural resources and create infrastructure, there are problems. For example, profits often are sent back to the operating countries and companies, while the environmental impacts stay in the host developing country.

In the air transport and shipping industries, there are pressures to reduce noise and limit the chances of environmental emergencies. Financial services are also facing some environmental pressure *vis-à-vis* the types of projects that receive financing and the preconditions that need to be met. Debt finance can have significant environmental effects (Box 2.2). This idea is captured in the Equator Principles in 2003, a voluntary set of guidelines for managing social and environmental issues related to the financing of development projects. The banks will apply the principles globally and to project financing in all industry sectors, including mining, oil and gas, and forestry[9].

But structural changes in the global economy that favour the service sector in OECD countries may be driving a relocation of manufacturing industries from developed countries into rapidly industrializing economies, which could have some negative environmental implications (O'Connor, 2000). UNCTAD (1999b) suggests that outward services-based FDI has grown over the past decade at a faster rate than FDI in any other sector, increasing its share from 45 per cent in 1988 to 56 per cent in 1997. Empirical work will be required in order to assess whether manufacturing FDI has in fact shifted to developing countries in spite of the increase of service-FDI inflows. Another aspect to consider is the extent to which growth in service-FDI relates to growth in manufacturing-FDI. UNCTAD, for example (1999b), suggests multinational enterprises in primary and manufacturing industries (i.e. trading affiliates) – not just service companies – also establish service affiliates.

Net impacts from scale, technological and structural effects

We have seen that scale effects from increased FDI are likely to be negative for the environment, while technological and structural effects are expected to be positive. From an analytical perspective, what matters is the net effect, not only the individual parts. Net environmental effects of FDI will depend on a combination of macro and micro variables. Key macro factors include the investors' profile – for example, the type of industry to which it belongs and its pollution-intensity. Among the key micro issues are the management decisions that multinational enterprises make in relation to production and whether they diffuse environment-friendly technologies.

But assessing the net effects of FDI on the environment is a complex task and empirical studies of this nature are scarce. Such assessment is challenging for at least two reasons. Firstly, it will always be difficult to detach the environmental effects of domestic economic activity from the effects of activities of foreign affiliates. Secondly, FDI does not occur in a vacuum and its environmental effects cannot be easily analysed in isolation from the other economic developments. The investment–trade linkage, for example, presents several empirical challenges since foreign direct investors who are usually exporters. As O'Connor (2000) points out, trade expands the market for the investors' output and may facilitate resource extraction. And while the scale effect from trade would tend to dominate, it could be offset by increased efficiencies in extraction and processing technologies that investors bring. Links of this nature are rarely captured in the FDI-environment literature.

Cross-border Corporate Environmental Management

Foreign investors in developing countries utilize different environmental management strategies. Some develop comprehensive management strategies that seek to internalize their environmental costs; others simply comply with local environmental regulation. Some multinational enterprises direct their foreign affiliates to address environmental issues at the local level (a 'decentralized' strategy); others let the parent company make the most of the environmental decisions for global operations (a 'centralized' strategy), thus seeking to ensure similar environmental performance regardless of location.

Such analytical puzzles have only recently begun to command attention, probably as a result of the continuous internationalization of production patterns. As a result, the literature in this area is in an early stage. Moreover, data shortages further slow the study of cross-border aspects of corporate environmental management. For example, voluntary disclosure about international environmental practices of multinational enterprises is unusual, even among companies with positive environmental reporting credentials. A 2000 benchmark survey of corporate environmental reporting, for instance, found that nearly all the companies evaluated (50 multinational enterprises with leading environmental reporting practices) failed to systematically include in the reports their activities (and impacts) in the developing world (Sustainability and UNEP, 2000)[10].

In order to organize the review of the empirical studies in this area, this section examines five clusters of research on factors that Hansen (1999) proposes: 1) *firm characteristics*; 2) *type of industry*; 3) *market-forces*; 4) *regulation; and 5) non-regulatory forces*.

Firm characteristics

The size of the company – usually measured in terms of sales and employees – seems to play a significant role in the choice of environmental management systems. According to UNCTAD (1999b), bigger multinational enterprises tend to follow a centralized approach. The parent company defines an environmental management 'package' for the company and affiliates apply it regardless of location, with some adaptations that fit the host-country context. The study also suggests that smaller enterprises tend to follow decentralized strategies.

Type of industry

Hansen (1999) suggests that basic features of an industry, such as the level of concentration, collaboration and collusion, have direct impacts on the nature of cross-border environmental practices among its members. In oligopolistic industries, firms will be in a better position to offset environmental costs since they have a higher degree of market control. Additionally, higher international environmental standards are more likely in the context of close collaboration within an industry.

There is evidence that industry associations have engaged in collaborative approaches, such as the development of internal codes of conduct, guidelines, and voluntary standards (Haufler, 2001). García-Johnson (2000) shows that industrial groups played a key role in the promotion of environmental management and self-regulation in the chemicals sector. Her data support the idea that US multinational enterprises operating in Brazil and Mexico led the diffusion of Responsible Care® outside the USS.

International business associations have also played a key role in upgrading environmental management in eastern and central Europe. Andonova (2003) suggests that these groups influence both multinational enterprises and local firms. According to the OECD (1999c, cited in Andonova, 2003), by 1998 international public–private partnerships had implemented more than 900 clean-production demonstration projects in central and eastern Europe, at least one or more clean-production centres in each country, and trained more than 2500 environmental management experts in the region.

What drives certain industry associations' efforts toward convergence in environmental practices and standards overseas? According to Andonova (2003), in economies in transition, what international industry networks seek is the creation of international standards and cleaner practices as a way to level the regulatory playing field across jurisdictions, increase information flows among markets, exert greater control over new entrants, and create markets for Western technologies. In the case of the US chemicals sector, the diffusion of Responsible Care® to Mexico and Brazil was driven by a need to enhance the reputation of the chemicals sector – not just the US companies – which had been severely harmed in the aftermath of the Bhopal accident in India.

Market forces

Commercial and financial factors can both lead to improvements in environmental performance strategies. Gentry (1998) shows the positive FDI-environment synergies that emerge as a result of companies' efforts to gain competitive edge over competitors. He presents cases from the agricultural sector and shows that pressure from export consumers, combined with the need to cut production costs, and governmental programmes led to improved environmental performance in Costa Rica (i.e. environmental certification of banana exports) and Brazil (pulp and paper production). Christmann and Taylor (2001) also provide evidence that customer linkages affect the environmental approaches of exporting firms operating in China. Firms that sell a large proportion of their output to developed countries have better environmental compliance and are more likely to adopt ISO 14000 than other firms.

In India, Ruud (2002) found that market-related factors play a much stronger influence in the environmental performance of multinational enterprises than regulatory forces (i.e. local environmental laws). In particular, he found that intra-firm pressures play a particular role in promoting higher – not lower – environmental standards. He suggests that trade within different parts of the company (many of them located outside India) puts pressure toward standardization of environmental (and quality) standards. Because Indian inputs are part of broader logistical networks the company cannot compromise the quality of the products (and company reputation) by lowering the standards in India.

Regulatory forces

Regulation can play a key role in shaping corporate environmental strategies. Investors may respond to both host-country and source-country legislation.

Host-country regulation

Studies show that host-country regulations do influence investors' environmental behaviour (O'Connor, 2000; Gentry, 1998; UNCTAD, 1993). Gentry (1998) conducted a case study of 44 foreign investors in the Mexican manufacturing sector. The results show several positive technological effects, in particular, water treatment facilities, which led to higher eco-efficiency of operations more than 70 per cent of the time. Mexican regulations – including, to some extent, better enforcement – were a key motivator in the investor's decision to undertake an 'environmental investment'.

But implementation of the law in developing countries is weak and problems with enforcement are common. For example, Jha (1998) has identified weaknesses in the Indian context. Rasiah (1999) has analysed problems in Malaysia, and Gouming et al (1999) offer insights of the enforcement problems faced in China. A case study from Costa Rica illustrates a weak application of environmental regulations regarding certain investors (Gentry, 1998).

Source-country regulations

In the past, especially during the 1970s, developing-country governments called for the creation of a code of conduct for multinational enterprises. By the early 1990s, the negotiations had gone nowhere and ended officially (Aaronson, 2002; Haufler, 2001). Since then, governmental efforts to shape international investment governance have been mainly focused on liberalizing investment regimes and protecting investors in host countries.

In the absence of binding source-country rules for corporate conduct overseas, some promotion agencies in developed countries have played a complementary role. Eriksen and Hansen (1999) studied the case of the Danish investment promotion agency that sought to influence the international environmental practices of Danish investors. This agency developed a set of environmental guidelines that are mandatory for all partners (50 per cent of all Danish investment projects are in developing countries). The guidelines address several commitments: a) compliance with host country regulations; b) a 'best-practice declaration' in which deviations from the Danish environmental regulations are identified and quantified; and c) an assessment of critical environmental parameters in order to establish whether the agency can accept participation in the investment project. There is also a post-investment procedure that involves monitoring of environmental indicators.

Some source-country governments also enhance the synergies between FDI and the host countries by using development assistance to improve corporate performance (Krut and Moretz, 1999). In Denmark, the official international aid agency (Danida) has created programmes that support joint ventures between Danish investors and local industry, with a focus on transfer of technology and skills (Ericksen and Hansen, 1998). In order to have access to financial and organisational support from Danida, Danish partners must comply with a set of requirements developed by the agency. One example resulting from this programme is a joint venture between a Danish refrigeration manufacturer and a Zimbabwean company that led to building new facilities with state-of-the-art technology. Finally, a similar project from the Danish government – this time from the Ministry of Environment and Energy – encouraged Danish companies to participate in environmental projects in Malaysia and Thailand. One project financed under this initiative is a partnership between a Malay palm oil manufacturer and a Danish company that has the technology to turn palm oil wastes into energy.

Informal regulatory forces

Formal regulation is not the only tool capable of affecting corporate environmental conduct. In fact, governments in both source and host countries often lack the tools to monitor, let alone to regulate, the behaviour of these enterprises (White, 1999). This should be of little surprise, given the increasingly global pattern of international production. As of 2002, there are 64,000 multinational enterprises driving the global expansion of investment flows with more than 870,000 affiliates abroad (UNCTAD, 2003). Both source and host countries can exert various forms of non-regulatory pressure.

Source-country informal pressures

Newell (2001) has documented the rise of non-governmental efforts to influence corporate behaviour through means other than formal law – also known as 'civil regulation'. Often, the efforts initiate in source-countries. Proposals normally call for reduced environmental impacts, increased environmental disclosure, and adherence to codes of business conduct (see Buffett, Chapter 8).

Non-governmental actions such as transnational campaigns against specific corporations or products are particularly effective when the target enterprise bears a global brand[11]. The more corporate value a brand has, the more vulnerable it makes the company to public scrutiny. A hint of scandal regarding poor environmental performance may affect consumer choice and attitude in relation to the company (*The Economist*, 2001). Newell (2001) also studies the creation of NGOs such as 'Corporate Watch' and 'Oil Watch' who closely scrutinize the social and environmental performance of multinational enterprises. These and other groups also threaten companies with exposure and/or boycotts if they ignore their social and environmental obligations.

As a result of such initiatives and the increased exposure of corporate malpractice, societal scrutiny of firms – especially multinational enterprises – has increased. Clearly, scrutiny includes not only parent company behaviour, but also, and perhaps more critically, the performance of foreign affiliates. One recent example is an international coalition of over 200 NGOs that proposed 'International-Right-to-Know' legislation in the US. Such a bill would require US. companies to report *in the US* how they perform *overseas* including information on their environmental performance (International Right to Know Coalition, 2003)[12].

Other forms of source-country, informal pressure emphasize partnerships with – not boycotts against – companies. Some partnerships include governments. Often, these initiatives aim to implement globally oriented, voluntary environmental standards inside corporations. Key examples of these joint efforts are the OECD Guidelines for Multinational Enterprises (developed in the 1970s but upgraded in 2000), and the United Nations Global Compact. These international codes of conduct are voluntary and go beyond environmental issues. Even though they are voluntary, some studies suggest that in the future these mechanisms could play an important role in promoting better corporate practices across borders (Haufler, 2001; Aaronson, 2002; OECD, 2001b). Often, the main monitors of corporate commitments toward voluntary global standards are non-governmental organizations – not governments.

Because some of these non-state actors fear that companies will engage in public relations exercises (the so-called 'window dressing or 'green washing') and not substantive changes in their environmental performance, they often expose inconsistencies between corporate pledges and practices[13].

Another prominent development is the rise of 'shareholder activism' for corporate social responsibility – especially in the US and the UK. This type of activism refers to shareholders actively pressuring companies to address certain issues (in this case environmental and social concerns) through the proxy voting process (O'Rourke, 2003). There is evidence that in order to obtain access to companies and gain influence within general meetings, environmental groups have acquired a number of shares. As shareholders, they try to overturn corporate decisions or to promote activities that they find environmentally responsible (Newell, 2001). O'Rourke (2003) documents a case whereby shareholders of British Petroleum (BP) voted 'yes' to an agenda item that asked BP to halt the development of the North Slope field in Alaska and redistribute the investment to the BP Solarex (solar energy) division.

Newell (2001) also offers evidence of the UK arm of Shell International that had an uncomfortable confrontation with its institutional shareholders in 1997 because of its environmental and human rights record in Nigeria. A group of shareholders holding 1 per cent of the company led to a new report by Shell of its global health and safety activities and a new version of its Statement of General Business Principles, which now include human rights and sustainable development.

Multilateral and regional banks have also built environmental components (and conditionality, in some cases) into their lending operations, which affect investor behaviour overseas. One example is the World Bank's environmental guidelines for different sectors. The role of banks in promoting environmental protection tools is confirmed in a case study of the Russian Far East which shows that companies undertook an environmental impact assessment of large scale oil drilling only were they were pressed, mainly by multilateral finance agencies (Rosenthal, 2002).

Usually, environmental groups put pressure on lenders to suspend an investor's projects. A recent example is the project to pipe natural gas and byproducts from Peru's Camisea fields in the Amazon over the Andes to the

Pacific coast. In 2003, the US Export–Import Bank rejected a US$214 million loan-guarantee package that would have facilitated the import of US machinery and equipment for the project. The rejection was the result of intensive lobbying by environmental organizations and the completion of a bank-financed environmental and social assessment that sharply criticized the project (*EcoAméricas*, April and September 2003)[14].

Host-country informal forces

Informal forces in the host countries can also play a role in affecting foreign investors' environmental performance. There is evidence that local community pressure is playing a dynamic role (World Bank, 2000; Zarsky, 1999). This 'informal' approach to regulation seems particularly important, especially in countries where traditional regulation and law enforcement is weak.

In one assessment of the 'greening' of industry in the developing world, the World Bank (2002) highlights the role that local communities played in improving the environmental performance of Indonesia's largest pulp producer. Sari (2002) also found that local community pressure in Indonesia effectively forced the clean-up of toxic and hazardous wastes in the industrial zone of Batu Ampar.

Conclusions: What Evidence Does (and Does Not) Tell Us

This literature review has shown that researchers have made progress in the past years to develop finely textured perspectives on the relationship between FDI flows and environment. The survey also reveals that important areas of enquiry still remain scantily studied and deserve further attention. Three core lessons from this survey are presented below.

FDI and the environment: new evidence versus old myths

Traditionally, the relationship between FDI and the environment has stirred ardent emotions, especially when multinational enterprises operate in developing nations with low environmental standards, poor human rights records and fragile ecosystems. Over the years, the debate has often generated uncompromising portrayals of the interface between FDI and the environment, ranging from apocalyptic scenarios of irreversible resource depletion and relentless pollution with dire impacts on health and ecosystems, to rosy, one-dimensional predictions about the benefits of environmental technology transfer in a world where foreign investors propel efficiency and development-enhancing linkages with local industries.

The case study and statistical evidence reviewed in this chapter should help dispel common, yet misleading, myths about the environmental repercussions of foreign investment in developing nations. Clearly, the operations of multinational enterprises are not inherently and unequivocally 'bad' for the environment, as many FDI sceptics fear. Evidence suggests that FDI enables positive dynamics that benefit the environment such as environmental management standards that do not even exist in the local regulatory context. In other words, researchers have shown that some of the fears about the negative repercussions from increased FDI are understandable, yet overstated.

But the benefits are not as large as some host-countries may expect. In fact, proponents of FDI liberalization and protection, which gained the upper hand during the 1990s, often predict a flow of FDI-driven environmental benefits without empirical support. Investors *may* bring cutting edge environmental technology, which *may* be transferred to the local industry. But the empirical record suggests that these positive technological effects are often weak or even non-existent. When cutting-edge environmental technology (equipment and skills) does not arrive or is not diffused, investment-led growth does not lead to environmental improvement. Hence, contrary to common wisdom in the pro-investment community, FDI is not inherently 'good' for the environment.

Recent empirical studies confirm that the environmental repercussions of FDI largely depend on the specific context and the interactions of different actors. Moreover, corporate environmental management across borders will vary among investors depending on the characteristics of the firm and its sector as well as market, formal and informal forces.

Rethinking, yet reaffirming, roles: governments, markets and citizens

Positive FDI-environment outcomes do not happen automatically or accidentally. The main environmental opportunities associated with FDI arise from the fact that FDI may lead to higher incomes, which *could* fund pollution prevention and abatement. However, if policy and institutional failures are not addressed, higher incomes associated with FDI-induced growth may not pull environmental quality along with it fast enough. Even where there is a positive relationship between income and improved environmental quality, researchers have confirmed that this nexus may not turn out to be strong enough to prevent absolute degradation in environmental quality.

Hence, the institutional structure of the host country ends up being more important than the actual level at which environmental standards have been set. Environmental laws and requirements provide the goals, but whether environmental improvement is associated with these laws will depend on the quality of implementation.

Because implementation may be weak in developing nations, community pressure complements the role of the government in forcing environmental improvements. There is also evidence that non-governmental organizations play an important role in monitoring investors' environmental performance and exposing corporate malpractice. The studies confirm that market forces – for example, intra-firm trade – also stimulate convergent corporate environmental strategies within a multinational entity.

The analytical work in the area of informal forces is expected to increase in the future. The authors usually propose a reassessment of governmental responsibilities – not their substitution – in a way that enables communities, NGOs, and markets to exert maximum influence on polluters (World Bank, 2000; Zarsky, 1999; Gentry 1998).

Issues for further research

Studies that analyse the impacts of FDI on the environment categorize them as scale, technology, or structural effects. While this separation is useful for analytical purposes, the literature, unfortunately, is devoid of concrete results regarding net impacts – that is, the combination of the three effects. Future research in this direction would be extremely valuable.

Another query that deserves further attention is whether the structural shifts that most economies are going through, reducing the share of manufacturing and increasing the share of services (e.g. electronic commerce, tourism, financial services), is as environmentally benign as some analyses suggest.

Although corporate environmental performance in general has received increased attention, particularly in low-income countries, theoretical development in the area of cross-border environmental performance differentials remains, surprisingly, minimal. One plausible explanation is that the data necessary for studies of this nature are simply lacking, especially because environmental disclosure about operations overseas remains voluntary. As more information becomes available, further work in this area would help to shed light on the particular contribution of certain factors in both host and source countries. Such analytical exercise could also shed some light on how important are the endogenous drivers (e.g. firm characteristics) versus the exogenous ones (e.g. market, industry, regulatory forces).

Finally, FDI does not occur in a vacuum but is part of the local and the global economy. As these local and external linkages become more complex, researchers will face numerous obstacles when trying to isolate the environmental effects from FDI, let alone those accruing from the FDI-trade interface.

Clearly, the literature on FDI and the environment leaves many unanswered questions. Thus far, it is not possible to draw a decisive conclusion about the environmental repercussions of FDI in developing countries. We may never get one and, in any case, may not need one. Rather, future research may focus on specific sectors and/or specific geographical areas in an effort to discover what makes FDI work for or against the environment within a particular context. What works in Latin America may not work in China and vice versa, and what works for foreign investors in the automobile sector may be a disaster for investors in the pharmaceutical sector. In the future, more regional- and sector-based research may help us elucidate further why and when some foreign investors contribute to the environment in a positive way while others do not.

ENDNOTES

1 This chapter builds on a previous report prepared by this author for the OECD Working Party on Global and Structural Policies; 'Environmental Benefits of Foreign Direct Investment: A Literature Review' (OECD, 2002a). This chapter has been reproduced with permission from the OECD.

2 The OECD study on FDI and the environment (1997) is used as the baseline for this survey. Hence, 'recent evidence' as used in the title is defined here are research produced mainly in the period between 1997 and 2003.

3 Some debate whether and how FDI contributes to economic growth. For empirical discussions about FDI and growth, see De Mello Jr. and Ruiz (1999) who suggest that FDI is growth-enhancing depending on the degree of complementarity between FDI and domestic investment. Borensztein et al (1998) suggest that FDI contributes to growth to the extent that sufficient absorptive capability of the advanced technologies is available in the host country.

4 A recent example is the suit filed against ChevronTexaco for large-scale environmental effects of Texaco Petroleum Inc's operations in the Ecuadorian Amazon between 1971 and 1992 (*EcoAméricas*, 2003). The complaint requests that the company be ordered to pay for a thorough clean-up which could cost up to US$5 billion dollars over ten years (*Wall Street Journal*, October 29, 2003). Texaco Petroleum Inc. merged in 2002 with Chevron. The plaintiffs accuse the company of polluting groundwater, rivers and swamps in the Ecuadorian Amazon region. They allege that Texaco Petroleum Inc. recklessly dumped oil waste in more than 600 ponds over a 2,000m^2 area of rainforest and wetlands over 20 years (*Wall Street Journal*, October 29, 2003). ChevronTexaco has asked the judge to dismiss the lawsuit in Ecuador citing 'lack of credible, substantiated evidence'. A summary of the company's position is available at www.chevrontexaco.com/news/press/2003/2003-10-21_1.asp

5 See, for example, UNCTAD (2001), which focuses on promoting linkages between multinational enterprises and local firms.

6 For an overall discussion about technological transfer see UNCTAD (1999b, Chapter VII), OECD (2001, Chapter VI) and UNCTAD (2003, Chapter IV).

7 The countries analysed were Australia, Bolivia, Brazil, Chile, China, Papua New Guinea, Peru, Russia, South Africa and the US.

8 Since 1988, chemical companies have implemented Responsible Care®, a voluntary programme to achieve improvements in environmental, health and safety performance beyond levels required by governments. The programme promotes codes aiming to reduce releases to air, land and water, improvements in workplace and community safety, and expanded programmes to research and test chemicals for potential health and environmental impacts. This self-regulatory tool was developed in Canada in the aftermath of the industrial accident in Bhopal, India in 1984. The official information about Responsible Care® is found at www.responsiblecare.com. For an independent assessment see King and Lenox (2000).

9 For more information see www.equator-principles.com

10 This is a modification of the analytical framework developed by Hansen (1999).

11 For example, in 1999 Rainforest Action Network (RAN) claimed victory in a two-year campaign against Home Depot, the US home supply and building materials retail giant. After RAN organized demonstrations at Home Depot stores, hung banners outside the company's headquarters and waged letter-writing and full-page ad campaigns in national newspapers, Home Depot agreed to stop selling products made from old-growth wood. The homebuilding industry at large followed suit, saving 7.5 million acres of coastal forest in British Columbia alone (*Institutional Investor Magazine*, 2000).

12 The proposed environmental issues that multinational enterprises would have to disclose include toxic releases, air and water pollution, and natural resource extraction. For more information see the official website of the campaign: www.irtk.org/

13 A non-profit research and advocacy group 'Corp Watch' has created the 'Greenwash awards.' For information on the group and the 'awards' see www.corpwatch.org/campaigns/PCD.jsp?articleid=243

14 Environmentalists and indigenous groups fault the Camisea project for disturbing the rainforest around the drilling site, which is considered a 'hot spot' of biological diversity, and is home to the indigenous people living nearby (*EcoAméricas*, September 2003).

References

Aaronson, S. (2002) 'Global Corporate Responsibility Pressures and the Failure to Develop Universal Rules to Govern Investors and States', *Journal of World Investment*, June, vol 3, no 3, pp487–505

Andonova, L. (2003) 'Openness and the Environment in Central and Eastern Europe: Can Trade and Foreign Investment Stimulate Better Environmental Management in Enterprises?', *Journal of Environment & Development*, vol 12, no 2, pp177–204

Andreoni, J. and A. Levinson (2001) 'The Simple Analytics of the Environmental Kuznets Curve', *Journal of Public Economics* vol 80, pp269–286

Barbier, E. (1997) 'Introduction to Environmental Kuznets Curve Special Issue', *Environment and Development Economics*, vol 2, no 4, pp369–81

Blackman, A. and X. Wu (1998) 'Foreign Direct Investment in China's Power Sector: Trends, Benefits, and Barriers', *Discussion Paper 98-50*, Washington, DC, Resources for the Future

Blomström, M. and A. Kokko (1998) 'Multinational Corporations and Spillovers', *Journal of Economic Surveys* vol 12, no 2, pp1–31

Borensztein, E., J. de Gregorio and J.-W. Lee (1998) 'How Does Foreign Direct Investment Affect Economic Growth? *Journal of International Economics*, vol 45, pp115–135

Christmann, P. and G. Taylor (2001) 'Globalization and the Environment: Determinants of Firm Self-Regulation in China', *Journal of International Business Studies*, vol 32, no 3, p439–449

Dasgupta S., A. Mody, S. Roy and D. Wheeler (1995) *Environmental Regulation and Development: A Cross-country Empirical Analysis*, Washington, DC, World Bank

Dasgupta, S., H. Hettige and D. Wheeler (1998) 'What Improves Environmental Performance?: Evidence from the Mexican Industry', *Policy Research Working Paper* 1877. January, Washington, D.C., World Bank

De Mello Jr and R. Luiz (1999) 'Foreign Direct Investment-led Growth: Evidence from Time Series and Panel Data', *Oxford Economic Papers*, no 55, pp133–151

Dowell, G., S. Hart and B. Yeung (2000) 'Do Corporate Global Environmental Standards Create or Destroy Market Value?' *Management Science* vol 46, no 8 pp1059–1074

EcoAméricas (2003) 'Impacts of Gas Project at Issue in Peru', April, online version: www.ecoamericas.com

EcoAméricas (2003) 'Camisea Backers Brush-off Ex-Im Decision', September, online version: www.ecoamericas.com

EcoAméricas (2003) 'ChevronTexaco Hearings Starting Up in Ecuador', October, online version: www.ecoamericas.com

Eriksen, J. and M. Hansen (1999) *Environmental Aspects of Danish Foreign Direct Investment in Developing Countries. Managing the Environment in an Open Economy. Occasional Paper*. Cross Border Environmental Management Project, CHP, Copenhagen, Copenhagen Business School

Eskeland, G. and A. Harrison (1997) *Moving to Greener Pastures? Multinationals and the Pollution-Haven Hypothesis*. Public Economics Division, Policy Research Department, Washington, DC, World Bank

French, H. (2000) *Vanishing Borders Protecting the Planet in the Age of Globalization*, New York, W. W. Norton and Company

Frye, R (1998) 'The Role of Private Banks in Promoting Sustainable Development, from Outside the Counsel's Perspective', *Law and Policy in International Business*, vol 29, no 4, pp481–500

Ganzi, J. T. and J. Tanner (1997) *Global Survey on Environmental Policies and Practices of the Financial Services Industry: The Private Sector*, Washington, D.C., National Wildlife Federation

García-Johnson, R. (2000) *Exporting Environmentalism: US Multinationals Chemical Corporations in Brazil and Mexico*, Cambridge, MIT Press

Gentry, B (1999). 'Foreign Direct Investment and the Environment: Boon or Bane?' in OECD *Foreign Direct Investment and the Environment*, pp21–45, Centre for Co-Operation with Non-Members, Paris, OECD

Gentry, B. (1998) (ed) *Private Capital Flows and the Environment: Lessons from Latin America*. London, Edward Elgar

Gentry, B. and L. Fernandez (1997) *Valuing the Environment: How Fortune 500 CFOs and Analysts Measure Corporate Performance*, New York, United Nations Development Programme

Gouming, Z. C., Z. Yangui, G. Shunqi and J. X. Zhan (1999) *Cross Border Environmental Management and Transnational Corporations: The Case of China*, Copenhagen, UNCTAD/ Copenhagen Business School

Grossman, G. M. and E. Helpman (1995) *Technology and Trade*, Discussion Paper 1134, London, CEPR

Grossman, G. M. and A. B. Krueger (1995) 'Economic Growth and the Environment', *Quarterly Journal of Economics*, vol 110, no 2, pp353–377

Hansen, M. (1998) *Transnational Corporations in Sustainable Development: An Appraisal of the Environmental Implications of FDI in Developing Countries*, CPH, Copenhagen, Copenhagen Business School

Hansen, M. (1999) *Cross Border Environmental Management in Transnational Corporations: An Analytical Framework*, Occasional Paper No 5. Report as part of the UNCTAD/CBS project, Copenhagen, Copenhagen Business School

Haufler, V. (2001) *A Public Role for the Private Sector*, Washington, D.C., Carnegie Endowment for International Peace

He, J. (2002) 'Foreign Direct Investment and Air Pollution in China: The Case of SO_2 Concentrations in Chinese Cities', Paper Presented at Conference 'Better Air Quality in Asian and Pacific Rim Cities', Hong Kong, December 16–18, 2002

Herbert-Copley (1998) *Innovation, Regulation and Environmental Management in the Chilean and Canadian Pulp and Paper Industries*, Ottawa, Carleton University, (PhD thesis), (cited in UNCTAD, 1999b)

Institutional Investor Magazine (2000) 'The New Financial Activists,' June 1, 2000

International Right to Know Coalition (2003) *International Right to Know: Empowering Communities Through Corporate Transparency*, January, www.irtk.org

Jaffe, A. B., S. R. Peterson, and P. R. Portney (1995) 'Environmental Regulation and the Competitiveness of US Manufacturing: What Does the Evidence Tell Us? *Journal of Economic Literature*, vol 23, pp132–163

Jha, V. (1999) *Investment Liberalization and Environmental Protection: Conflicts and Compatibilities in the Case of India*, Occasional Paper No 1, Cross Border Environmental Management Project, CHP, Copenhagen, Copenhagen Business School

Kemp, M. (2001) *Corporate Social Responsibility in Indonesia: Quixotic Dream or Confident Expectation?* Technology, Business, and Society Papers, no 6, Geneva, United Nations Research Institute for Social Development

King, A. and M. Lenox (2001) 'Does it Really Pay to be Green? An Empirical Study of Firm-level Environmental and Financial Performance', *Journal of Industrial Ecology*, vol 5, no 1, pp105–117

King, A. and M. Lenox (2000). 'Industry Self-Regulation Without Sanctions: The Chemical Industry's Responsible Care Program', *Academy of Management Journal*, vol 43, no 4, 698–716

Krut, R. and A. Moretz (1999) *Home Country Measures for Encouraging Sustainable FDI: Cross Border Environmental Management Project*, Copenhagen, UNCTAD/Copenhagen Business School

McConnell, M. (1997) 'Income and the Demand for Environmental Quality', *Environment and Development Economics*, vol 4, no 2, pp383–399

Munasinghe, M. (1999) 'Is Environmental Degradation an Inevitable Consequence of Economic Growth: Tunnelling through the Environmental Kuznets Curve?', *Ecological Economics*, vol 29, pp89–109

Newell, P. (2001) 'Managing Multinationals: The Governance of Investment for the Environment', *Journal of International Development*, vol 13, pp907–919

Neumayer, E. (2001) *Greening Trade and Investment: Environmental Protection without Protectionism*, London, Earthscan

Nordström H. and S. Vaughan (1999) *Trade and Environment: Special Studies* 4, Geneva, World Trade Organization

O'Connor, D. (2000) 'Global Capital Flows and the Environment in the 21st Century' *Technical Papers*, no 161, Paris, OECD Development Centre

OECD (1997) *Foreign Direct Investment and the Environment. An Overview of the Literature*, Paris, OECD

OECD (1999a) *The Environmental Effects of International Portfolio Flows*, Paris, OECD

OECD (1999b) *Foreign Direct Investment and the Environment*, Centre for Co-operation with Non-Members, Paris, OECD

OECD (1999c) *Environment in the Transition to a Market Economy: Progress in Central and Eastern Europe and the New Independent States*, Paris, OECD

OECD (2001a) *OECD Environmental Outlook*. Paris, OECD

OECD (2001b) *Corporate Responsibility. Private Initiatives and Public Goals*. Paris, OECD

OECD (2002a) *Environmental Benefits of Foreign Direct Investment: A Literature Review* Paris, OECD

OECD (2002b) *Environmental Issues in Policy-Based Competition for Investment: A Literature Review*, Paris, OECD

O'Rourke, A. (2003) 'A New Politics of Engagement: Shareholder Activism for Social Responsibility', *Business Strategy and the Environment*, vol 12, pp227–239

Panayotou, T. (1997) 'Demystifying the Environmental Kuznets Curve: Turning a Black Box into a Policy Tool', *Environmental and Development Economics*, vol 2, no 4, pp465–484

Panayotou, T. (2000) 'Globalization and Environment', *CID Working Paper* No 53, Environment and Development Paper no 1, Boston, Center for International Development at Harvard University

Rasiah, R. (1999) *Transnational Corporations and the Environment: The Case of Malaysia*, Occasional Paper No 4, Cross Border Environmental Management Project, CHP, Copenhagen, Copenhagen Business School

Rondinelli, D. and G. Vastag (1999) 'Multinational Corporations' Environmental Performance in Developing Countries', in W. Wehrmeyer and Y. Mulugetta, *Growing Pains: Environmental Management in Developing Countries*, Sheffield, Greenleaf, pp84–100

Rosenthal, E. (2002) 'Conflicts Over Transnational Oil and Gas Development Off Sakhalin Island in the Russian Far East: A David and Goliath Tale', in L. Zarsky (ed) *Human Rights and the Environment: Conflicts and Norms in a Globalizing World*, London, Earthscan, pp965–122

Ruud, A. (2002) 'Environmental Management of Transnational Corporations in India: Are TNCs Creating Islands of Environmental Excellence in a Sea of Dirt? *Business Strategy and the Environment*, vol 11, pp103–118

Sari, A. (2002) 'Environmental and Human Right Impacts of Trade Liberalization: A Case Study in Batam Island, Indonesia', in L. Zarsky (ed) *Human Rights and the Environment, Conflicts and Norms in a Globalizing World*, London, Earthscan, pp123–146

Schmidheiny, S. and B. Gentry (1997) 'Privately Financed Sustainable Development', in Chertow M. and D. Esty (eds) *Thinking Ecologically: The Next Generation of Environmental Policy*, New Haven, Yale University Press

Schmidheiny, S. and F. Zorraquín (1996) *Financing Change*, Cambridge, MIT Press

Seldon, T. M. and D. Song (1994) 'Environmental Quality and Development: Is there a Kuznets Curve for Air Pollution Emissions?' *Journal of Environmental Economics and Management*, vol 27, supplementary issue, pp757–773

Sustainability and UNEP (2000) *The Global Reporters: First International Benchmark Survey of Corporate Sustainability Reporting*, London, Sustainability

The Economist (2001) 'The Case for Brands', September 8, 2001

UNCTAD (1993) *Environmental Management in Transnational Corporations*, New York, UNCTAD

UNCTAD (1998) *Linking Environmental and Financial Performance: A Survey of Best Practice Techniques*, Document ITE/EDS/Misc.9, Geneva, UNCTAD

UNCTAD (1999a) *Foreign Portfolio Investment and Foreign Direct Investment: Characteristics, Similarities and Differences, Policy Implications and Development Impact*, Document E/B/COM.2EM.6/2, Geneva, UNCTAD

UNCTAD (1999b) *World Investment Report* Geneva, UNCTAD

UNCTAD (2000) *World Investment Report*, Geneva, UNCTAD

UNCTAD (2001) *World Investment Report*, Geneva, UNCTAD

UNCTAD (2003) *World Investment Report*, Geneva, UNCTAD

UNIDO and WBCSD (2002) *Developing Countries and Technology Cooperation*, Vienna, United Nations Industrial Development Organization and World Business Council for Sustainable Development

Von Molkte, K. (2000) *An International Investment Regime: Issues of Sustainability*, Winnipeg, International Institute for Sustainable Development

Wall Street Journal (2003) 'ChevronTexaco Faces Big Tab for Cleanup', Marc Lifsher, 29 October, 2003, online at: www.wsj.com

Warhurst, A. (1999) *Technology Transfer and the Diffusion of Clean Technology*, Final Report to the UK Economic Social Research Council, Bath, University of Bath

White, A. (1999) 'Sustainability and the Accountable Corporation: Society's Rising Expectations of Business', *Environment*, vol 41, no 8, pp30–43

World Bank (2000) *Greening Industry: New Roles for Communities, Markets, and Governments*, Washington, D.C., World Bank and Oxford University Press,

WWF International (2001) *Preliminary Assessment of the Environmental and Social Effects of Liberalization of Tourism Services*, WWF International Discussion Paper, May, Geneva,WWF International

Zarsky, L. (1999) 'Havens, Halos, and Spaghetti: Untangling the Evidence about Foreign Direct Investment and the Environment', in OECD (1999) *Foreign Direct Investment and the Environment*, pp21–45, Centre for Co-operation with Non-Members, Paris, OECD

Chapter 3

Governing Foreign Direct Investment in Sub-Saharan Africa: Policies and Practices Reconsidered

John Mugabe

ABSTRACT

Countries in Sub-Saharan Africa (SSA) are increasingly emphasizing foreign direct investment (FDI) as a source of capital for economic change and development. Many of them have undertaken major policy, legislative and institutional reforms to attract FDI. Despite these efforts, the region as a whole has not seen a surge of FDI inflows. While FDI inflows to SSA increased during the past two decades, they remain low compared with other regions of the world. A more fundamental concern is whether such flows contribute to poverty reduction and sustainable development. Indeed, it is not just the quantity of FDI that matters but its quality – whether it contributes to the enlargement of livelihood options, respect and protection of social and labour rights, protection of the environment and overall national economic development.

This chapter focuses on the interface between FDI and sustainable development in SSA. It explores the nature of policies, laws and institutions that would ensure that FDI does not undermine prospects of achieving environmental sustainability and poverty reduction. Using a number of illustrative cases, it demonstrates that, in many African countries, there is a mismatch between the goals of FDI regimes and those of environmental and social regulations.

The chapter argues that an increase in FDI inflows would create new challenges for decision- and policy-makers in Africa. It is no longer enough for governments to reduce administrative barriers to FDI and to institute policies for economic liberalization. They have responsibility to secure and protect the environmental and socio-economic rights of citizens. The chapter concludes with a call for the explicit integration of environmental and poverty reduction considerations into FDI policies, laws and practices.

INTRODUCTION

Foreign direct investment (FDI) – investment in capital stock or assets by a firm abroad – is one of the main engines of economic globalization. In the last decade, it has surged in importance as a source of capital formation for transition and least-developed economies. FDI now accounts for almost half the private capital flows to developing countries. In 2000, developing countries accounted for approximately 24 per cent of total global FDI flows (UNCTAD, 2000a).

The rise in FDI flows to developing countries has been driven by at least two interrelated factors. Firstly, the forces of globalization, particularly the opening up of national economies through liberalization of trade and investment, have created favourable conditions for the entry of transnational corporations into the markets of developing countries. While privatization and deregulation have enlarged economic and political space for inflow of FDI, the creation and growth of equity markets has facilitated the sale of developing countries' public enterprises to foreign investors.

Secondly, rapid development and introduction of information and communication technologies have contributed to an increase in FDI inflows to developing countries. These technologies have considerably enhanced the flow of financial capital across national borders. They have also exposed national economies to scrutiny as information on domestic production opportunities, political behaviour and economic capabilities has become easily accessible globally.

This chapter focuses on Sub-Saharan Africa (SSA). The SSA region encompasses all of Africa, except for the countries of North Africa – that is, Algeria, Egypt, Libya, Morocco and Tunisia.

Generally, FDI flows to SSA have expanded only marginally and are still at levels behind those of other developing country regions. In 1999, the region accounted for only 0.7 per cent of total FDI global inflows (Odenthal, 2001). Historically, low rates of FDI inflows to SSA are explained by hostile policies, an unstable political environment characterized by civil wars and armed conflicts, lack of effective regional integration efforts, poor and deteriorating infrastructure, burdensome regulations or lack of institutional capacity to implement FDI policies, lack of institutional clarity, and limited government efforts to promote investment.

In the 1990s, most SSA countries made major efforts to increase FDI inflows by improving their investment climate. They embarked on wide-ranging policy, political and institutional reforms aimed at reducing (and, if possible removing) barriers to the entry of foreign capital, particularly FDI. Trade and investment liberalization, privatization and the creation of various incentives for foreign investment have received considerable attention from governments. Regional economic integration bodies and free trade zones have been created to enlarge the size of markets and adopt common investment regimes at sub-regional and regional levels. These efforts are based on the premise that FDI can stimulate economic growth, generate new employment opportunities, promote transfer of new technologies and contribute to environmental sustainability in the region.

The role and growing influence of transnational corporations and FDI in SSA have elicited concern and debate among activists and policy-makers about the implications of FDI for the natural environment, poverty reduction, human rights and sustainable development. One of the main concerns is that the increasing reliance on FDI, mainly through transnational corporations, will spread industrialized countries' consumerism, undermine domestic infant industry leading to underemployment, increase overexploitation of natural resources, increase pollution and on the whole undermine the region's prospects of achieving sustainable development.

Concerns are also being raised by environmental activists about foreign companies' responsiveness to their host countries' goals of environmental sustainability, social equity and the protection of citizens' human and economic rights.

It is far from clear whether domestic regulations and institutions are capable of ensuring that corporate behaviour and activities respond to public concerns regarding socio-economic equity and environmental issues. The challenge for many countries is to establish an explicit interface between policies and laws designed to encourage inflows of FDI and those for promoting environmental sustainability and socio-economic development. They need to implement policies that enhance the beneficial effects or impacts of FDI while avoiding or at least minimizing negative effects. Beyond formulating liberal investment policies and laws, governments of SSA countries should ensure that FDI practices are consistent with their overall national sustainable development objectives.

This chapter discusses recent trends in private FDI in SSA, including related policy reforms and institutional developments. It focuses on the impact of FDI on environmental sustainability and socio-economic development. It examines the nature of policies, regulations and institutions that have been established in the region to make foreign private companies responsive to sustainable development goals. Emphasis is placed on those policy and institutional innovations that would ensure that FDI is channelled and controlled in ways that contribute to the achievement of environmental sustainability and the improvement of socio-economic conditions of the poor, as well as the protection of human rights.

The main message of the paper is that, while most SSA countries have formulated and adopted FDI policies as well as legislation that contain provisions to promote sustainable development, they have not created institutional arrangements to ensure that these provisions are implemented.

The first section provides an overview of recent economic growth and social development trends in SSA. It shows that the region has achieved dismal or very low economic growth and its share of global trade is declining. Income levels have fallen and the majority of the population lives in extreme poverty. Many countries are faced with huge and increasing external debts and declining capacity to service it.

The second section describes FDI inflows to SSA, including sectoral trends and sources. The third section examines national regimes – policies, laws and institutions – for FDI. The fourth section focuses on bilateral and regional investment regimes and analyses how they are implemented to promote FDI flows to SSA.

The fifth section provides illustrative cases of the impacts of FDI on the environment, social equity and other sustainable development considerations. The cases show that FDI has often not targeted host countries' sustainable development agendas. There is often poor coordination between government agencies responsible for the implementation of FDI policies and those that are charged with environmental management and social development. FDI promotion and inflows have not deliberately targeted goals such as employment generation, technology inflow or acquisition, upgrading of domestic industries and enhancement of the status of women and rural people.

On the whole, the SSA experience suggests that FDI inflows do not automatically generate positive effects. Host countries must create appropriate conditions for the realization of their potential socio-economic and environmental benefits. The final section makes a number of suggestions to integrate sustainable development considerations into FDI policies, laws and practices in SSA.

Economic Growth and Social Trends: An Overview

Slow growth, low per capita income, increasing debt and declining capacity to service it, over-reliance on a narrow range of natural resources, and declining exports and increasing imports are persistent features of economies of SSA. In real terms, the region's GDP growth slowed from 3.2 per cent in 2000 to 2.5 per cent in 2002 (World Bank, 2003). Excluding South Africa, the region's average income per capita is estimated to be less than US$300 per year. At least 40 per cent of SSA's population lives on less than US$1 a day (World Bank, 2003). To halve poverty by 2015, SSA economies will need to grow at 7 per cent per year on average – more than twice the current growth rate.

Paralleling its low and declining per capita income, SSA's share of world trade has fallen considerably in the last two decades. In the 1970s, its share of total world trade was estimated to be 3 per cent (World Bank, 2000). The region now accounts for less than 2 per cent of world trade. It accounts for less than 1 per cent of US merchandise exports, less than 2 per cent of US imports, 3.5 per cent of total global exports and 3.7 per cent of total imports for the European Union (EU). According to the World Bank:

> *The erosion of Africa's world trade share in current prices between 1970 and 1993 represents a staggering annual income loss of US$68 billion – or 21 per cent of regional GDP. Part of this loss is reflected in the erosion of the trade share for traditional products, as well as policies that discourage private investment and diversification into products for which world demand was growing more rapidly.*
>
> (World Bank, 2003)

SSA has the world's lowest human development and poverty indicators. Average life expectancy in the region is now less than 55 years, compared to 78 years in OECD countries. Countries of the region have the highest illiteracy rates and lowest primary education enrolment. In the 1990s, per capita health expenditure in many African countries averaged about US$10; in OECD countries, it was at least US$1,000. The rapid spread of HIV/AIDS in the 1990s has significantly reduced life expectancy in Africa. The adult HIV/AIDS prevalence rate in 1999 was 8.6 per cent in SSA compared to 0.2 per cent globally. In Botswana, adult HIV/AIDS prevalence is 36 per cent and life expectancy has fallen by 20 years from 1988 to 1998 (Haacker, 2001) On the basis of 1980–1990s trends, projections of social indicators do not paint a bright picture. Life expectancy is expected to decline even further as a result of the spread and impact of HIV/AIDS.

Another factor influencing poverty and social instability in the region is the escalation and growth of conflict. The number of countries faced with internal conflicts increased from 6 in 1980 to 14 in 2000. Conflicts have led to the destruction of the region's economic, social and natural capital:

> *Widespread civil conflicts impose enormous costs, including on neighbouring countries.... Africa's conflicts ... are driven by poverty, underdevelopment, and lack of economic diversification, as well as by political systems that marginalize large parts of the population. But conflicts perpetuate poverty, creating a vicious circle that can be reversed only through special development efforts...*
>
> (World Bank, 2003)

SSA's dependency on foreign aid has increased considerably and it is now the world's most aid-dependent region. Foreign aid-financed investment has for a long time being treated as the key to unlock the region's development potential. Between 1990 and 1995, the region received at least 26 per cent of global official development finance. Almost 90 per cent of this was made on either highly concessional or grant terms.

Attempts to induce development in SSA have tended to follow a simplistic view that economic growth and the improvement of quality of life are proportional to investment, and that increasing foreign aid would increase investment, which would then increase economic growth. This aid-to-investment-to-growth dogma prevails in the economic policies and practices of many countries of the region. However, there is abundant evidence that foreign aid has not automatically stimulated increased investment and growth. An unpublished report by two World Bank researchers concludes:

> *There is no apparent correlation between growth predicted by the aid-financed investment to growth approach and the actual growth rate... Countries like Guinea-Bissau, Zambia, Zimbabwe, and Mauritania should have done well according to the aid-financed growth model; instead they had close to zero per capita growth.*
>
> (Dollar and Easterly, undated)

Between 1970 and 1993, Zambia received an increasing amount of foreign aid, including 18 adjustment loans from the World Bank and IMF. By the early 1990s, foreign aid rose to 11 per cent of the country's real GDP. This inflow of aid did not help to turn Zambia's economy around. Instead, the country continued to get poorer and is today one of the poorest countries of the world. There is ample evidence that many other African countries have experienced declining economic growth and become poorer while their reliance on foreign aid has increased.

To change SSA's economic performance and promote sustainable development, many governments of SSA countries have come to the conclusion that foreign aid should be complemented by other sources of external capital, particularly FDI. FDI is attractive to SSA countries for several reasons. Firstly, it has the potential to address the problems of low levels of investment and foreign exchange shortages. FDI inflows bring to the host country foreign exchange, supplement domestic savings and raise the level of investment. Import substituting investment can help reduce a country's import bill, while FDI in export industries will increase its foreign exchange earnings.

Secondly, FDI could be a source of new technologies, including know-how and know-why. It could stimulate the establishment of local industries to supply inputs, and transfer technologies, including skills, to domestic enterprises. FDI can also help to promote better environmental and labour management values and standards in host African countries. The inflow of FDI through mergers and acquisitions could disseminate new forms and values of corporate governance, including better methods of organizing institutions and making decisions.

FDI could also contribute to poverty reduction by reducing adverse shocks to the poor resulting from financial instability. Finally, through the payment of taxes, FDI-generated fiscal resources could support the development of a safety net for the poor. Foreign investors could also be encouraged to invest directly in community development projects, and to help improve the management and provision of social services such as water (Klein et al, 2002).

On the other hand, in the absence of strong regulatory measures, FDI and investment liberalization could lead to environmental degradation and undermine social development. It could generate pressures on the environment such as increased pollution and over-exploitation of natural resources (see Araya, Chapter 2). FDI is the largest form of private investment that most directly impacts on the environment (Gentry, 1999). It is often directed to such natural resource sectors as mining, forestry, water and to economic activities that have direct impacts on the environment. Unregulated – that is, in the absence of explicit policies and laws to integrate social and human development dimensions – FDI could widen the gap between the poor and rich in a country and undermine labour rights, particularly of the low-income earners.

The challenge facing SSA countries relates to creating and/or strengthening institutions that formulate and implement coherent policies and programmes that attract FDI while at the same time supporting economic growth and sustainable development. Such institutions should facilitate the integration of investment and environmental policies in favour of sustainable development. In this regard, there is a need to ensure inter-institutional synergy and programmatic linkages between the work of investment promotion agencies and that of environmental departments.

Foreign Direct Investment in SSA: An Overview

FDI trends, sources and destination

The experience of SSA countries in attracting long-term capital flows has been mixed. In the mid-1980s, FDI inflows rose but began to decline in the early 1990s, before recovering modestly during the mid- to late 1990s. Until the early to mid-1990s, the region received a small share of FDI relative to other developing regions (see Gallagher and Zarsky, Chapter 1). In the second half of the 1990s, its share rose markedly, reaching 4 per cent of total flows to developing countries (OECD, 2001).

In 2000, however, FDI inflows declined for the first time since the mid-1990s, dropping to US$9.1 billion from US$10.5 billion in 1999. The dip was based on a decline in FDI flows to two countries: South Africa and Angola. In the former, fewer privatization and merger and acquisition (M&A) deals caused the slowdown, while in the latter, inflows in the petroleum sector declined.

FDI inflows to SSA are highly concentrated. In the two years over 1995–1996, over 80 per cent of net FDI inflows to SSA went to just four countries: South Africa, Nigeria, Côte d'Ivoire and Angola, three of which are oil exporters (Table 3.1).

The largest single recipient of FDI in SSA is South Africa, the largest economy in the region. The country has gone through major transformations since the end of apartheid in 1994. It has joined the World Trade Organization (WTO) and concluded a number of trade and investment agreements, including free trade agreements (FTAs) with the European Union (EU) and the Southern African Development Community (SADC). Since 1994, FDI inflows to South Africa have been on an upward trend:

> *South Africa's share of total FDI to SSA reached 28 per cent during 1995–98, from virtually zero during the 1980s and early 1990s. A large share of this FDI (more than 40 per cent) in 1997 came from privatization of infrastructure para-statals such as Telkom. Part of the increase in FDI in recent years reflects the return of companies that had established operations in neighbouring countries during the apartheid period.*
>
> (Pigato, 2000)

In a few SSA countries, including Uganda and Tanzania, FDI inflows substantially increased in the 1990s. Inflows to Uganda increased from US$3 million in 1992 to US$88 million in 1994 to US$250 million in 1997. This positively correlates to a GDP growth rate of 3.2 per cent in 1992 to 5.3 per cent in 1997 (UNCTAD, 1999b, Table 1). Tanzania attracted US$193 million in 2000, compared with US$50 million in 1994, doubling its share of total flows to SSA from 1.5 to 3.3 per cent (UNCTAD, 2001a).

Table 3.1 *Net FDI Inflows in Sub-Saharan Africa Average 1996–1997 (US$millions)*

Country	Net FDI Inflows	GDP
South Africa	2313.5	129094
Nigeria	1566.0	36540
Côte d'Ivoire	305.1	10251
Angola	265.5	7396
Tanzania	154.0	6707
Uganda	148.0	6555
Namibia	109.9	3453
Ghana	101.3	6762
Senegal	92.2	4542
Mozambique	68.3	1944
Zimbabwe	66.5	8512
Zambia	64.0	4051
Mali	61.6	2532
Mauritius	46.7	4151
Cameroon	40.0	9115
Benin	31.5	2137
Guinea	20.6	3998
Chad	16.5	1603
Kenya	16.2	9899
Madagascar	12.1	3552
Congo Republic	8.5	2298
Central African Republic	5.5	954
Ethiopia	5.0	6330
Rwanda	2.4	1771
Congo, Democratic Republic	1.5	6904
Malawi	1.5	2424
Burundi	1.0	1137
Niger	1.0	1858
Sierra Leone	1.0	940
Total	***5526.9***	

Source: World Development Report, 1999 (in Morisset, 2001)

In terms of sub-regional trends, the Southern African Development Community (SADC) maintained its position as the most important sub-region for FDI inflows into SSA. Member countries of SADC are Angola, Botswana, Democratic Republic of Congo, Lesotho, Malawi, Mauritius, Mozambique, Namibia, Seychelles, South Africa, Swaziland, Tanzania, Zambia and Zimbabwe.

Between 1995 and 1999, SADC countries received about 2–3 per cent of total FDI to developing countries, and 44 per cent of FDI inflows to SSA, compared with 21 per cent in the first half of the 1990s. The community's improved attractiveness to FDI may have been principally driven by country-specific factors, but at least some FDI inflows were also motivated by the region's increasing economic integration (UNCTAD, 2001b).

Historically, France and the UK were the main sources of FDI inflows into Sub-Saharan Africa (Bennell, 1990). Today the primary sources are the UK, Switzerland, France, the US, Japan, Germany and the Netherlands. These countries account for about 90 per cent of FDI flows to Africa. According to UNCTAD (2001c), 'Japanese FDI to Africa has mostly been driven by tax reasons: 'flag-of-convenience' investment in shipping in Liberia accounts for some three-fourths of all Japanese FDI in Africa.'

Between 1994 and 1998, the region received about 15 per cent of UK FDI outflows to non-OECD countries. Between 1989 and 1995, the net income of UK's FDI in the region increased by 60 per cent. SSA received 8.5 and 8.2 per cent of non-OECD outflows from the Netherlands and Switzerland, respectively, between 1995 and 1996. US FDI outflows to SSA were estimated at 1.9 per cent of its total non-OECD outflows.

There are also increasing FDI inflows from Southeast Asia, including China, India, Malaysia, the Republic of Korea and Taiwan. Between 1994 and 1997, Malaysia contributed about 20 per cent of FDI inflows into South Africa.

Companies in SSA countries themselves, especially South Africa, Nigeria and Kenya, are the largest foreign investors in Sub-Saharan Africa. South African Breweries, for example, has major investments in Botswana, Tanzania and Zambia. In 2000, Kenya was the main African source of FDI inflows to Uganda. There were at least 117 Kenyan private firms investing in Uganda in a variety of sectors. South Africa had eight companies investing and operating in Uganda. In 2000, South Africa accounted for 40 per cent of the region's total FDI outflows.

Sectoral FDI outlook

There is scant information on the sectoral composition of FDI in SSA. However, available studies suggest that more than 50 per cent of total FDI inflows to the region target natural resource sectors. For example, in Ghana, US, Canadian and Australian firms have been interested in gold, winning more than 60 prospecting and reconnaissance licenses between 1988 and 1998. In Guinea, the Aredor mine had received more than US$130 million in foreign investment by 1996. In Tanzania, the largest sector for FDI is mining and the largest industry is gold. By 1998, total cumulative FDI in mining was estimated at US$370 million. Mining attracted 65 per cent of FDI, services 19 per cent and manufacturing 16 per cent (UNCTAD, 2001a).

More than 90 per cent of US$1.5 billion FDI inflows to Nigeria in the 1990s targeted petroleum and natural gas sectors. FDI inflows to Uganda went to the beverage, sugar, food processing, textiles and packaging activities of the manufacturing sector and in coffee and tea plantations. Outside manufacturing and agricultural sectors, liberalization of the telecommunications sector attracted considerable investment. The petroleum sector dominates FDI in Angola while in Ethiopia the hotel industry is the largest recipient.

The agricultural sector in SSA has attracted modest FDI. Some of the major projects of the 1990s include Del Monte's investment of more than US$9 million in bananas in Cameroon, Lonrho's US$7.5 million in tea estates in Tanzania, and Aberfoyle Holding's multi-million-dollar investment in palm oil in Zimbabwe.

National Policy and Legal Measures

The surge of global interest in FDI and multinational companies has been so high that many SSA governments have developed high expectations in terms of the development effects of FDI. While FDI can, indeed, contribute to national economic and social development in many ways, the engagement and performance of domestic actors are crucial. The effect of FDI largely depends on the policies of the host country. This goes beyond the mere liberalization of economies. Deliberate measures to develop human capital and physical and social infrastructure are also needed to enhance the quality of FDI that countries can attract.

Prior to the late 1980s, most SSA countries had adopted socialist development policies that led to nationalization of foreign companies and created state-owned industries. Foreign equity participation remained low throughout most of the 1970s and 1980s, and was largely confined to mineral extraction and agricultural exports. Many governments viewed multinational companies with suspicion and instituted measures to restrict their freedom of operation. Such measures included restrictions on profit remittances and capital repatriation.

Since the mid-1980s and particularly in the mid-1990s the situation has considerably changed. Many of the region's countries have focused their attention on attracting multinational companies, especially via trade and investment liberalization. The 1990s witnessed the removal of domestic barriers through widespread privatization and regulatory reform. The reforms targeted monetary, fiscal, infrastructural, trade, financial and other policies. The liberalization measures have also led to a dramatic decline of nationalization of foreign affiliates.

In addition to liberalization and related regulatory reforms, SSA countries have increased their reliance on market regimes through privatization of state-owned and managed enterprises. The privatization efforts have in large measure been stimulated by growing dissatisfaction with the performance of state-owned enterprises. For some countries (e.g. Botswana and South Africa), privatization has been relatively fast and induced competition in such sectors as agriculture and mining that had been dominated by state monopolies. However, in others (e.g. Kenya and Nigeria) it has been slow due to weaknesses in institutional and legal arrangements. In addition, high levels of corruption may have led to discriminatory decision-making that keeps away foreign investors.

On the whole, liberalization is playing a key role in attracting FDI to SSA. It allows foreign private firms to participate in privatization and in infrastructure development. Privatization of state-owned companies accounts for a large share of the FDI. It is a major source of foreign exchange earnings for many countries of SSA. Between 1990 and 1999 foreign exchange (both in the form of FDI and portfolio flows) represented about 58 per cent of total revenue generated through privatization. During this period privatization largely involved large enterprises, particularly utility industries – water, electricity, telecommunications and railways.

Angola is among the SSA countries that have developed and adopted specific or explicit FDI legislation. In 1994, the country enacted the Foreign Investment Law, Law 15 of September 23. This law sets out rules and procedures for determining and governing FDI. The Foreign Investment Bureau, renamed Foreign Investment Institute in 1996, was created by the law as the main agency responsible for screening and approving FDI. It is expected to assess all applications or proposals for FDI to determine whether they conform to the country's development priorities and policies. Article 3 of the law provides that FDI will be authorized if it does not contravene national 'strategies for economic and social development as defined by the competent sovereign agencies'. Section 1 of Article 3 requires applicants of FDI to be 'entities of recognized good repute and technical and financial capacity'.

In a 1997 paper, Harvard economist Keith Rosenn strongly criticizes Angola's FDI legislation arguing that: '[it] would make much sense to allow automatic entry of foreign investment and to make the [Foreign Investment Institute] responsible solely for attracting and assisting foreign investors rather than employing it to screen foreign investment. The market is a much more efficient screening and channelling agency' (Rosenn, 1997). According to this view, which still prevails in many development circles, developing-country governments should play a passive role in governing FDI. However, as the illustrative cases below show, it is a simplistic and dangerous view, one that misleads public policy and undermines the sustainable development aspirations of developing countries.

Botswana has had a relatively liberal economy since independence in 1966. It avoided nationalization of economic enterprises and instituted policies that encourage exploitation of its minerals, particularly copper, nickel and diamonds, through joint ventures with foreign companies. The Botswana Export Development and Investment Authority is the national agency responsible for promoting and facilitating FDI. It is responsible for formulating FDI norms and rules. The country's Constitution determines conditions under which foreign investment can be expropriated. It provides that expropriation can only occur for public policy reasons. Foreign investors are entitled to full and equal recourse to national courts. However, Botswana's mining law does not entitle investors to negotiate contractual rights in respect of license terms, except for diamond mining investors (UNCTAD, 2002a).

Ghana has adopted 'investor-friendly' policies and enacted legislation to increase its FDI inflows. In 1994 its parliament enacted the Investment Promotion Centre Act to regulate FDI in all sectors except minerals, gas and oil. This law aims at easing the entry and establishment of foreign business and attracting FDI. It created the Ghana Investment Promotion Centre to provide administrative and technical leadership on FDI matters. The law requires enterprises seeking registration in Ghana to apply for and obtain an environmental permit from the Environmental Protection Agency. However, it does not provide specific reference to standards of treatment of foreign investors and their investment. The country's constitution prohibits compulsory taking of private property without compensation. This constitutional provision is entrenched in the Ghana Investment Promotion Centre Act. Section 28 of the Act provides guarantees that foreign investment shall not be subjected to expropriation or nationalization unless it is in the national interest and for the public good. Expropriation can only be undertaken on the basis of fair and adequate compensation.

The policy and legislative reforms undertaken by Ghana stimulated major privatization initiatives that stimulated FDI inflows. For example, in 1994 the Government of Ghana sold significant shares in the biggest state mining company, Ashanti Goldfields Corporation (AGC), to South Africa's company Lonmin. In 1996, it sold 30 per cent of its shares in Ghana Telecom to Telekom Malaysia. In addition to privatization, Ghana enacted an Investment Code in 1994 to eliminate project approval and company registration procedures.

Nigeria is another country with a relatively liberal FDI regime. In 1995, it enacted two important FDI laws. Decree No. 16 of 1995 established the Nigeria Investment Promotion Commission (NIPC) and Decree No. 17 of 1995 instituted the Foreign Exchange Monitoring and Miscellaneous Provision that allows free repatriation of foreign currency, dividends, profit and capital transfers of any kind without any prior approvals by government. The former law opened up almost all sectors of Nigerian economy and liberalized the legal framework governing the ownership structure of Nigerian firms.

Tanzania is experimenting with a mix of liberal policies and laws that aim at maximizing local economic benefits from FDI. In 1990, the government instituted the National Investment Promotion and Protection Act, which established the Investment Promotion Centre (IPC) to promote, coordinate, regulate and monitor investment. It requires foreign companies and/or individuals wishing to invest in Tanzania to satisfy the Centre and the government of the 'likely contribution by the enterprise to the economic development and benefit of Tanzania' (United Republic of Tanzania, 1990, Part III, Article 13(1)).

The law places emphasis on benefits such as maximization of foreign exchange earnings and savings, enhancement of import substitution activities which achieve identifiable substantial foreign exchange savings, expansion of food production, achievement of high degree of technology transfer, creation of employment opportunities and the development of human resources, and production of goods and services which improve linkages between the various sectors of the economy (United Republic of Tanzania, 1990). It makes a general reference to the need for foreign investment to protect interests and conditions of employees as well as interests of potential consumers.

Tanzania's FDI law has provisions to protect land rights of local communities. Section 26(1) provides that:

> *land belonging to a registered village shall not be leased . . . for activities other than joint ventures with the village government or the village's cooperative societies, save that such land may be sub-leased by the village itself for small or medium scale, public or private economic activities.*

The law carves out and reserves a number of economic sectors for public and local investment. Areas reserved for public sector investment (largely by the state) include the manufacture, marketing and distribution of armaments and explosives of all types; the provision of public water for domestic and industrial purposes; and the building and operation of railways. Economic activities exclusively reserved for local private investment include retail or wholesale trade, product brokerage, operation of public relations business, ice-cream making, butcheries, barber shops and beauty salons, and tailoring of garments for the domestic market. In 1998, Tanzania relaxed regulatory control over the mining sector by amending the Tanzania Mining Act.

The mining legislation has provisions for regulating activities of mining companies and for ensuring environmental management. It requires that mandatory environmental impact assessment be conducted as a requirement for granting mining licenses. Section 38(4) (c) of the law requires that every application for a mining license be accompanied by the applicant's environmental management plan. In addition, the act requires the submission of an environmental impact assessment (EIA) on proposed mining operations conducted by independent consultants of international standing.

However, the implementation of these environmental provisions in the mining legislation is undermined by the absence of similar ones in the investment legislation. Tanzania's investment legislation does not require FDI to contribute to environmental protection and sustainability. It is silent on such requirements as environmental impact assessment to be conducted prior to approval of investment projects.

Uganda has made significant policy, legal and institutional reforms to attract FDI inflows. The government has liberalized the economy considerably and privatized a considerable number of public enterprises. The Public Enterprise and Divestiture Act governs acquisition and privatization of public enterprises. The Investment Code 1991 provides extensive protection to foreign investment. Provisions in the country's constitution and land law reinforce this protection and create incentives for FDI. The Land Act of 1998 provides for the availability of land to foreign investors under leasehold. In 1991, Uganda's parliament created the Uganda Investment Authority (UIA) to promote and facilitate investment. UIA has power to purchase, own and allocate land as leasehold or freehold tenure.

Uganda's Investment Code does not provide for explicit national treatment of foreign investors. In a number of ways, foreign investors are subject to requirements that are not imposed on nationals (UNCTAD, 2000d). In terms of expropriation, the code and the constitution of Uganda protect the interests of foreign investors. The constitution requires that in the case of expropriation, compensation at fair market value should be paid up front.

Legal instruments governing FDI in Kenya are the Foreign Investments Protection Act of 1981 (revised in 1990) and the Capital Markets Authority Collective Investment Schemes Regulations 2001 (Legal Notice No. 181 in Kenya Gazette Supplement No. 91). The Foreign Investments Protection Act is largely aimed at protecting investment for economic development purposes. It is silent on issues of social, environmental and labour rights. Kenya's Investment Promotion Centre (IPC) is responsible for promoting FDI inflows. It assists investors to obtain approvals and incentives such as tax holidays and the import of capital equipment without duties. This agency is supposed to be a source of information on investment opportunities and conditions in the country.

The Government of Kenya has established Export Processing Zones (EPZs) in which special tax privileges are provided for investment in designated sectors. Two zones – one a private sector initiative and the other run by the state – are currently in operation. To provide overall management of the initiative, the Kenyan government established the Export Processing Zone Authority (EPZA), a para-statal that regulates and promotes both the EPZs and area-based export processing. Currently, emphasis in the zones is on the production of textile products.

South Africa has instituted a wide range of policy and legislative measures for FDI. Its post-apartheid constitution adopted in 1996 protects private property rights. The country has an elaborate commercial law that offers foreign investors the same legal and regulatory environment and protection as domestic ones. The law abolished exchange controls in relation to non-residents (TISA, 2001). This law is complemented by the country's industrial strategy, which offers tax allowance and relocation costs for large investments with strong employment effects and linkage to local enterprises under the Foreign Investment Grant.

Environmental impact assessment and management considerations are also supposed to be taken into account in FDI decision-making in South Africa. In Schedule 4 of the Constitution of South Africa, 1996, the environment is treated as the foundation of the country's socio-political and economic security. National and provincial governments are expected to ensure that environmental stewardship is part and parcel of economic policy, including policies governing FDI.

Other FDI related laws of South Africa are the Diamonds Act of 1986, which regulates the possession, purchase, sale, processing and export of diamonds, and the Mine Health and Safety Act of 1996, which provides for the protection of the health and safety of employees and other persons at mines. The Minerals Act and the Mine Health and Safety Act are administered by the Department of Minerals and Energy, while the Diamonds Act is administered by the South African Diamond Board.

Sudan's FDI regime has evolved considerably since the 1950s. The first investment law of an independent government was enacted in 1956. The Granted Privilege Act was a restrictive law aimed at keeping foreign investors away from many economic activities. This law was reviewed and amended in 1974 to become the Development and Industrial Investment Encouragement Act, which aimed to encourage investment in agriculture and mining. In 1990, a new government, the National Salvation Revolution, enacted the Investment Encouragement Act of 1990 and created the Investment General Secretariat to determine entry and operations of foreign companies in the country. More legislative and institutional reforms were made in 1999, enacting the Investment Act of 1999, and entrusting the administration of FDI to the Ministry of Investment and International Cooperation.

Bilateral and Regional FDI Instruments

To complement investment liberalization and regulatory reforms, a growing number of SSA countries have signed bilateral investment treaties (BITs) with capital-exporting countries. These state–state agreements constitute one of the most important legal instruments for the protection of FDI. Through them, a capital exporting country secures legal protections and guarantees for the investments of its firms in addition to those provided by host-country national legislation.

SSA countries are treating BITs as important instruments for attracting foreign investors. The number of BITs concluded by SSA countries increased to 428 in 1999 from 149 at the end of 1989 (UNCTAD, 2000c). By 1999, the SSA countries had concluded 172 BITs with European Union countries, 108 with Asian countries, 39 with Central and Eastern European countries, 16 with Latin America and Caribbean countries and 44 between themselves (UNCTAD, 2000c).

Generally, BITs have provisions that define the scope and nature of FDI; provide for national treatment of foreign investors; define guarantees and compensation with respect to expropriation and for war and civil disturbances; provide guarantees for free transfer of funds and repatriation of capital and profits; create dispute settlement provisions; and define performance requirements (see Peterson, Chapter 5). For example, Article 12(5) of Nigeria–Netherlands BIT of 1992 states:

> *The tribunal shall decide on the basis of this Agreement and other relevant agreements between the two Contracting Parties, rules of International Law and rules of Domestic Law. The forgoing provisions shall not prejudice the power of the tribunal to decide the dispute* ex aequo et bono *[according to what is good and right] if the Parties so agree.*
>
> (UNCTAD, 2003b)

In addition to the BITs, SSA countries have placed emphasis on regional trade and investment treaties. For example, in East African countries (Kenya, Uganda and Tanzania), the Treaty for the Establishment of the East African Community is the main legal instrument for the promotion and regulation of investment. Its Article 79 aims at promoting cooperation in investment. In Article 80(1) paragraph (f) Partner States commit themselves to 'harmonize and rationalize investment incentives including those relating to taxation of industries, particularly those that use local materials and labour with a view to promoting the Community as a single investment area' (EAC, 1999).

The Southern Africa Development Community (SADC) has provisions to regulate FDI in its Trade Protocol. Article 22 aims at promoting cross-border FDI activities in the sub-region. It requires member states to adopt 'policies and implement measures within the community to promote an open cross-border investment regime, thereby enhancing economic development, diversification and industrialization'. In 1995, a SADC Finance and Investment Sector Co-ordinating Unit was established to promote sound investment policies. There is also a SADC Mining Protocol that lays out the legal basis for FDI in the sub-region's mining sector.

To give integrity to their FDI legal and regulatory regimes, many SSA countries have signed international investment agreements. For example, at least 30 SSA countries are members of the Multilateral Investment Guarantee Agency (MIGA), a member of the World Bank Group, which provides risk insurance to investors. Since its inception in 1988, MIGA has issued 82 contracts of guarantee in 18 SSA countries (DBSA, 2003). Many SSA countries have also signed the Convention on the Settlement of Investment Disputes between States.

On the whole, most SSA countries have adopted national and multilateral FDI regimes, as well as enacted legislation and created institutions to promote FDI inflows. But they have also been active in other dimensions of governance. SSA countries have instituted policies and laws to protect the natural environment, ensure respect for and protection of workers' rights, promote poverty reduction, and protect land and cultural rights of local communities (Okoth-Ogendo and Tumushabe, 1999).

Environmental policies and laws of many SSA countries have provisions to regulate FDI. For example, Kenya, Uganda, Tanzania, Ghana and South Africa have environmental legislation that explicitly requires environmental impact assessment of all FDI projects. These countries have poverty-reduction strategies, labour laws and other instruments that require FDI to target sustainable development goals. However, as the cases in the next section of this chapter illustrate, in practice, the governance of FDI has tended to ignore environmental protection, poverty reduction and protection of socio-economic rights of local communities.

Social, Economic and Environmental Impacts: Illustrative Cases

The overall social, economic and environmental impacts of private capital flows in general and FDI in particular are not easy to assess due to paucity of data.

Case studies offer snapshots, however, which suggest that FDI has had limited, and in some cases negative, impacts on sustainable development in SSA countries.

The impact of FDI largely depends on the nature and effectiveness of national investment policies and rules and associated agencies. Maximizing the benefits of FDI requires a regime of policies, rules and agencies that set minimum social, economic and environmental standards to be met by investors.

In many SSA countries there is a mismatch between FDI governance regimes and those that are aimed at promoting environmental sustainability, social equity, human rights and security of natural resources tenure. The cases below illustrate this point.

FDI and labour rights in Kenya

Recent industrial strikes in Kenya's EPZs have raised a pertinent concern about the country's FDI regime: Should the provision and protection of investor privileges compromise workers' rights? In January and February 2003, more than 10,000 employees of foreign companies in the EPZ went on strike demanding better terms of employment, including protection from exploitation and subjection to unhealthy working conditions. Media reports indicate that potential investors diverted their capital to Madagascar and Mauritius while US importers cancelled US$12 million worth of textile orders (*Daily Nation*, February 21, 2003).

The Kenyan government responded by condemning the workers and emphasizing the need to protect investment. Labour rights organizations and some local politicians, on the other hand, called for the protection of workers' rights. The minister for trade and industry described the strike as an act of hooliganism and irresponsibility by the workers. But one politician, who is also the vice-chairman of the Law Society of Kenya, claimed:

> *The government should chase away any investor who perceives Kenya as a place where cheap labour is available and whose intention is to exploit workers with impunity.*
>
> (*Daily Nation*, February 21, 2003, www.nation.co.ke)

Trade unionists claim that EPZ operations are not regulated and that investors enjoy a 'ten-year tax holiday' while workers are paid peanuts. The point here is that the country's FDI laws do not, at least explicitly, provide for the protection of labour or workers' rights.

FDI and large dams in Uganda

In 2001, the US-based AES corporation, the world's largest independent power producer, received approval to construct a US$530 million dam near Bujagali

Falls on the Nile. It acquired a US$70 million partial-risk guarantee from the International Development Agency (IDA), US$85 million financing from the International Finance Corporation (IFC), and US$125 million from the US government investment agency OPIC, as well as financing from commercial loans, the African Development Bank and its own sources.

According to Peter Woicke, IFC executive vice president and managing director of the World Bank Group for private sector development:

> *The project will provide an efficient, low-cost, and well-managed electricity generation facility that promises substantial economic benefits to Uganda. It will reduce the need for public investment in the power sector, enabling the government to deploy more funds to address critical social needs in other areas. Private consumers will greatly benefit from increased access to reliable and affordable electricity.*
>
> (IFC, 2003)

An impact assessment sponsored by AES in 1999 concluded that 820 people would be displaced. The AES did not anticipate any significant negative impacts on the people and the environment. But according to a report by the International Rivers Network (IRN), the project:

> *will permanently submerge highly productive agricultural land as well as islands supporting valuable natural habitats. The changes to the river could permanently harm fisheries. The area around Bujagali Falls supports a substantial number of subsistence and commercial fishermen, who depend on the resource for both food and income.*
>
> (Pottinger, 2000)

The project has sparked a global opposition campaign that includes more than 120 NGOs. In addition to environmental and social impacts, the NGOs are concerned about the process by which the project was conceived and approved. According to the IRN report:

> *The project has been characterized by political pressure, both from the Ugandan president and the US government, both of which favor the project. While Parliament was still in the process of evaluating the project last year (in 1999) having rejected it several times, the US government added to the already intense political pressure coming from the President of Uganda. Local newspaper accounts reveal that both the US Ambassador in Uganda and the US Secretary of Commerce contacted the Ugandan President on the project, and stated that US-Uganda relations could suffer if the dam were not approved quickly. Shortly thereafter, Parliament approved the project.*
>
> (Pottinger, 2000)

This case illustrates how diplomatic interventions of source-country governments can influence the quality and location of FDI. In the absence of strong host-country institutions, FDI policies can be determined by foreign missions ignoring local concerns and without local participation.

FDI and oil exploration in Sudan

In the absence of deliberate measures to protect community rights and the environment, FDI can undermine a country's prospects of achieving sustainable development. The exploration of oil in Sudan is a case in point.

Exploration for oil in Sudan, largely offshore in the Red Sea, began in the late 1950s. However, it was not until the 1970s that the country began extracting and exporting oil. In 1974, the US multinational company Chevron first discovered natural gas, 120km south east of Port Sudan. By 1975, Chevron had extended its oil exploration activities to southwestern Sudan. In 1980, it discovered oil in the north of Bentiu. During this period the company played a major role in sustaining the government of President Numeiri. Chevron was instrumental in lobbying the US government for financial and military support. The prospect of substantial oil revenues and the Chevron-brokered US political backing may have emboldened Numeiri in his dealings with Southern Sudan, permitting him to break the peace accord that had held the country together for nearly ten years.

In 1984, the Sudanese Peoples Liberation Army (SPLA) attacked Chevron oil operations and killed three employees, prompting Chevron to suspend and relocate some of its operations. In 1988, Chevron made attempts to resume oil exploration and production as a result of a deal it had entered into with a Baggara militia. But because of a military coup, it sold its operations to Concorp, a Sudanese construction company. Chevron had tax breaks and political risk guarantees from the US government, and was allegedly able to cover its losses of over US$1 billion.

Recent human rights reports focus on how the current Sudanese government has driven local small-scale farmers from their land in southern Sudan to allow big foreign companies to drill oil. Activities of oil companies are bound up with government human rights abuses.

Emerging Policy Issues and Recommendations

SSA countries have made considerable efforts to improve investment conditions. They have liberalized their investment regulations and instituted a wide range of incentives to attract FDI. However, they have received relatively low levels of FDI inflows. Moreover, FDI inflows have not necessarily contributed to poverty reduction and economic transformation. The cases outlined above illustrate that FDI can generate negative social, economic and environmental impacts. Positive impacts of FDI are few and centred in a handful of SSA countries.

There are at least four factors that explain the low or poor contribution of FDI to SSA's sustainable development. The first is *lack of policy coherence*. In many SSA countries, there is no coherence between FDI regimes and sustainable development programmes. FDI regulations have evolved in parallel to environmental and labour laws. For example while environmental laws of most SSA countries contain provisions to regulate FDI, most investment regimes are silent on environmental imperatives. Privatization and trade liberalization policies do not have explicit focus on poverty reduction, while poverty reduction strategies say very little on the role of FDI. In this regard, governments of SSA countries must make efforts to synchronize investment measures with policies that are aimed at promoting environmental sustainability, poverty reduction and socio-economic development.

The second factor is *poor coordination of institutions* and decision-making processes. Regulations and decisions that influence the character of FDI are largely made by trade and industry agencies, while environmental regulations are administered by departments of environment. The protection of workers is often the preserve of departments of labour. In SSA, departments of labour and those for the protection of the environment tend to be weaker and less influential than those for trade and industry. Environmental and labour rights issues are not well mainstreamed into the operations of and decision-making by trade and investment agencies. One way of addressing this limitation is to establish inter-agency committees on FDI. Such committees would be responsible for establishing sustainable development benchmarks or standards that FDI must meet, vet FDI applications on the basis of the standards, and monitor operations of foreign investors to ensure that they fulfil agreed upon sustainable development goals.

A third factor relates to policy-makers' *poor understanding of the nexus between FDI and poverty reduction*. The task of policy-makers is to coordinate policies affecting the two areas in such a way as to maximize the contribution of FDI to poverty reduction. A better understanding of the effects of FDI – what different types of FDI can and cannot do – can help policy-makers develop more effective FDI and poverty reduction strategies. They need to understand and balance effects of various policy instruments. For example, fiscal incentives for investment can influence foreign companies to use local labour and transfer technology to local enterprises, but may result in substantial foregone revenues to the government which disadvantages the poor through decreased social spending.

There is little data to demonstrate at an aggregate level how FDI impinges on poverty reduction, socio-economic change and environmental sustainability. Policy-makers in SSA do not have information and data to enable them to develop better strategies for enhancing FDI's contribution to sustainable development. One way of addressing this challenge is to develop research programmes dedicated to studying and generating data on the effects of different forms of FDI on local and national sustainable development. There are a number of areas in which more empirical research would be beneficial to policy making. These include the net impact of FDI on employment and FDI's contributions to technology transfer and creation of new skills.

The fourth factor is the *role of source countries* in influencing the character and effects of FDI. Generally, source country governments are not playing an active role in guiding and/or regulating investment to focus on poverty reduction, environmental sustainability and protection of workers' rights. The oil and Bujagali dam may illustrate this point. In the case of oil drilling by Chevron in Sudan, the US administration made no effort to ensure that the company's operations do not contribute to social and economic displacement of communities. Its intervention to influence the Government of Uganda's decisions on FDI in the Bujagali area without regard to environmental imperatives and local socio-economic aspirations raises questions as to whether the US is committed to contributing to sustainable development in developing countries.

On the whole, it is not sufficient for SSA countries to design new FDI policies and legislation. National institutions must be coordinated and should operate transparently to ensure that FDI has beneficial effects. SSA governments should establish national frameworks that set out minimum sustainable development principles and objectives that FDI must meet. Such frameworks should ensure that investor rights are balanced with specific obligations to contribute to poverty reduction, socio-economic development and promotion of environmental sustainability. These efforts should be buttressed by source-country rules that require their companies to explicitly integrate sustainable development considerations into their investment strategies and activities in SSA.

References

Allaoua, A. and M. Atkin (1993) 'Foreign Direct Investment in Africa: Trends, Constraints and Challenges', Paper Presented at the Meeting of the Ad-hoc Expert Group on the Revitalization of Investment for Africa's Development: Prospects in the 1990s and Beyond, Addis Ababa, United Nations Economic Commission for Africa

Bennell, P. (1990) 'British Industrial Investment in SSA: Corporate Responses to Economic Crisis in the 1980s', *Development Policy Review*, vol 8, no 2[Q10]

DBSA (2003) *Financing Africa's Development: Enhancing the Role of Private Finance*, Midrand, South Africa, Development Bank of South Africa

Dollar, D. and W. Easterly (undated) 'The Search for the Key: Aid, Investment, and Policies in Africa', draft paper for the Development Research Group, Washington, D.C., World Bank

Drabek, Z. (1998) 'A Multilateral Agreement on Investment: Convincing the Skeptics,' staff working paper ERAD-98-05, Economic Research and Analysis Division, Geneva, World Trade Organization

EAC (1999) *The Treaty for the Establishment of the East African Community*, Arusha, Tanzania, East African Community (EAC)

Gentry, B. (1999) 'Foreign Direct Investment and the Environment: Boon or Bane?' paper presented at OECD Emerging Market Economy Forum, The Hague, Netherlands, 28–29 January

IFC (2003) 'Uganda: World Bank's Board Responds To Uganda's Energy Needs and Approves Support For Bujagali Hydropower Project, http://web.worldbank.org/

Klein, M., C. Aaron and B. Hadjimichael (2002) 'Foreign Direct Investment and Poverty Reduction', in OECD, *New Horizons for Foreign Direct Investment*, Paris, OECD, pp51–70

Morisset, J. (2001) 'Foreign Direct Investment in Africa: Policies Also Matter,' paper presented at OECD Global Forum on International Investment, Mexico City, 26–27 November, 2001

Odenthal, L. (2001) 'FDI in SSA,' OECD Development Centre, Technical Paper no. 173, www.oecd.org/dev/publication/tp1a.htm

Okoth-Ogendo, H.W. and G. Tumushabe (1999) *Governing the Environment*, Nairobi, Kenya, ACTS Press

Oman, C. (2000) *Policy Competition for Foreign Direct Investment: A Study of Competition Among Governments to Attract FDI*, Organization for Economic Co-operation and Development (OECD), Paris, Development Centre

Pigato, M. (2000) 'Foreign Direct Investment in Africa: Old Tales and New Evidence', draft paper, Washington, D.C., World Bank, Africa Region AFTM2

Pottinger, L. (2000) 'A Case Study in Corporate Welfare', Berkeley: International Rivers Network, http://www.irn.org/programmes/bujagali/

Rosenn, K. (1997) 'Regulation of Foreign Investment in Angola', Consulting Assistance on Economic Reform II (CAER II), discussion paper no. 12, Cambridge, Harvard Institute for International Development

Streak, J. (1998) 'The Determinants of FDI and South Africa's Industrial Development Strategy: Towards a Research Agenda', draft working paper, Cape Town, School of Economics, University of Cape Town

Tandon, Y. (undated) 'The Role of Foreign Direct Investment in Africa's Human Development', Geneva, United Nations Conference on Trade and Development (UNCTAD)

Trade and Investment South Africa (TISA) (2001) 'Foreign Direct Investment in South Africa', paper presented at OECD Global Forum on International Investment, Mexico City, 26–27 November

UNCTAD (United Nations Conference on Trade and Development) (1999a) *Foreign Direct Investment in Africa: Performance and Potential*, United Nations publication UNCTAD/ITE/IIT/Misc.15, Geneva, United Nations

UNCTAD (1999b) 'Investment Policy Review: Uganda', UNCTAD/ITE/IIP Misc.7

UNCTAD (2000a) *World Investment Report 2000a: Cross-border Mergers and Acquisitions and Development Overview*, New York and Geneva, United Nations

UNCTAD (2000b) *Capital Flows and Growth in Africa*, Geneva, United Nations

UNCTAD (2000c) *Bilateral Investment Treaties: 1959–1999*, Geneva, United Nations

UNCTAD (2000d) 'Investment Policy Review: Uganda', Geneva, United Nations

UNCTAD (2001a) *Investment Policy Review of the United Republic of Tanzania*, Geneva, United Nations

UNCTAD (2001b) *World Investment Report 2001: Promoting Linkages*, Geneva, United Nations

UNCTAD (2001c) *FDI in Least Developed Countries at a Glance*, Geneva and New York, United Nations

UNCTAD (2002a) *Investment Policy Review: Botswana*, Geneva, United Nations

UNCTAD (2002b) 'Impact of International Investment Flows on Development', p3, UNCTAD/TD/B/COM.2/38, Geneva, United Nations

UNCTAD (2003a) *Dispute Settlement: Investor-State*, Geneva, United Nations

UNCTAD (2003b) *Dispute Settlement: State-State*, Geneva, United Nations

United Republic of Tanzania (1990) *National Investment (Promotion and Protection) Act No. 10, 1990*, Part III, Article 13(1)

World Bank (2003) *Global Economic Prospects 2003*, Washington, D.C., The World Bank

Chapter 4

Sustainable Development and Foreign Direct Investment: The Emerging Paradigm in Asia

Simon S. C. Tay and Iris Tan

ABSTRACT

More than ten years after Rio, sustainable development remains very much overshadowed by other bread-and-butter issues in Asia. Foreign direct investment (FDI) continues to be highly sought after by governments of developing Asian nations, negative environmental and social fallout notwithstanding. Nonetheless, a number of promising on-the-ground initiatives are aligned with the sustainability cause and greater environmental awareness marks the emergence of a new public consciousness. This chapter seeks to examine this emerging developmental paradigm in Southeast Asia and to extrapolate the implications for the introduction of a pro-sustainability international investment regime.

INTRODUCTION[?1]

We are dealing with no small thing, but with how we ought to live.

(Socrates)

Ten years after the Rio Declaration, sustainable development remains a term foreign to many in Asia. The relative obscurity of the term both reflects and indicates the uphill task the region faces in taking up the sustainability agenda.

Slow uptake in Asia is due in part to the vision enshrined within the Brundtland definition of sustainable development (Gleeson and Low, 2001). Calling for a balance between the triple concerns for environment, economic growth and human development, the Brundtland vision represents a major shift from today's developmental path in which economic growth is often achieved at the cost of environmental degradation – a short-sighted equation that bodes ill for future generations – and a widening gap between rich and poor. Many today now believe that 'the current patterns of growth... are environmentally disruptive, macro-economically counterproductive, and socially divisive with widespread unemployment and polarization between rich and poor' (Gleeson and Low, 2001).

In the years since Rio, however, the sustainability agenda has come under fire for being too wide and ambitious (*The Economist*, 2002). The success of the agenda rested on two assumptions: first, that both leaders and the masses would be willing to make difficult adjustments to current lifestyles and habits; and second, that national governments have the ability to formulate, execute and sustain an alternative developmental path.

The slow progress made in the past ten years indicates that the general picture is otherwise. Both developed and developing nations have been reluctant to adopt substantive measures conducive towards a sustainable developmental path. Fear of economic backsliding and transitional fallouts (e.g. unemployment) are key reasons everywhere.

Among the developing nations of Asia, the lack of financial muscle, weak institutions, limited technological capacities and scepticism towards the sustainability agenda further undermine the will and ability to take action[2]. At the same time, however, worsening environmental degradation and increased awareness of its consequences, increased literacy and the impacts of globalization are slowly transforming the way the man and woman in the street view the existing state of things.

In seeking to change the situation, there has been a growing focus on the role of FDI in this equation. As a source of capital and technology transfer, FDI can be a potent facilitator of sustainable development in developing countries, especially in impoverished economies which lack the financial muscle to invest in sustainable technologies, relevant research, and capacity building.

However, not all FDI flows are equal. In broad terms, FDI is of benefit to a country's development when it increases a country's export competitiveness, upgrades the skills and technological content of the export, and/or provides a good or service that would otherwise be unavailable. Conversely, FDI can have adverse effects on a country's domestic economy such as the crowding out of infant industries. It has also been identified with undesirable environmental and social fallout, such as the unsustainable extraction of natural resources and sweatshops.

In the attempts to understand the linkages between FDI, trade and development, it became increasingly clear, as UNCTAD warned, that 'the developmental impacts from improved export competitiveness cannot be taken for granted... TNCs can help raise competitiveness in developing countries and economies in transition, but tapping their potential is not easy' (UNCTAD, 2002). It also cautioned that:

> *the basic objectives of TNCs and governments are not the same: governments seek to spur* development – *within a* national *context. TNCs seek to enhance their* competitiveness *in an* international *context. Not all FDI is, therefore, always and automatically in the best interest of host*

countries... (TNCs') needs and strategies may differ from the needs and objectives of host countries.

(UNCTAD, 1999)

The idea of a legally binding regime governing international investment was first mooted during the Uruguay Round by some developed Western nations who proposed multilateral negotiations in the World Trade Organization (WTO). As capital exporting countries, they have pushed for rules, practices and agreements that focused mainly on defining, expanding and protecting investor rights – without addressing the potential negative impacts of FDI (Lal Das, undated).

With this understanding, developing nations are calling for an international investment regime that goes beyond the articulation of investor rights to articulate investor responsibilities towards host countries and to take into account the developmental needs of impoverished populations. Such calls rightly recognize FDI as an important means to an end. With appropriate channelling and wielding, FDI can contribute significantly to the sustainable paradigm in developing Asia.

However important and necessary, FDI is only the software to a complex machine. For an investment regime to be successful, the necessary hardware – including good governance, robust institutional support, grassroots and private sector support – must be present. This brings the question of compliance and enforcement, and along with it, the possibility of punitive measures.

With this in mind, this chapter examines the way the sustainability paradigm is emerging in Asia and what it implies for how Asian governments, NGOs and the public are likely to view the governance of international investment, including a pro-environment investment regime. Given the complex nature of the issue and the Asian region itself, the chapter will focus primarily on the developing nations of Southeast Asia.

As a region whose growth has been largely fuelled by FDI, with a rich but severely damaged environmental heritage, and which has experienced vividly the instability that can be wrought by unregulated FDI, Southeast Asia presents a valuable point of reference for the creation of a pro-sustainability international investment regime. Within the region, financial, political and institutional constraints on moving forward a sustainability agenda have increased in recent years, limiting governments' abilities and political will to act. A counter-trend, however, is a blossoming of social and environmental consciousness. It is from this cauldron of influences that a sustainable development paradigm is emerging.

In the following section, the chapter outlines the economic and ecological dilemmas faced by governments of developing nations, as well as their institutional and financial constraints in responding to a changing international security and economic landscape. Section 3 examines changing popular priorities and argues that in the absence of strong leadership from the state, citizens and local businesses are beginning to take initiatives to better their immediate environments and lives. Looking beyond Asia, Section 4 highlights the contribution of international environmentalism to Asia's environmental movements.

The final section examines the possibility of a pro-sustainability investment regime and argues that while such a regime will be greeted with initial apprehension and suspicion, it can find acceptability if properly crafted and, in doing so, contributes greatly to the advancement of a sustainability agenda.

ASIAN GOVERNMENTS: UNWILLING OR UNABLE?

Sceptics of sustainable development in Asia and beyond question its very paradigm: Can we really have it all? Is it truly possible to reconcile the imperatives of economic growth, social justice and environmental protection?

The US' abrupt withdrawal from the Kyoto Protocol earlier this year, citing potential harm to the US economy, suggests not[3]. The US decision was greeted with widespread disapproval from both within and outside of the country. Two conclusions can be drawn from the episode: that there is a growing environmental consciousness within the international community, and that the subjugation of economic goals for sustainable development goals remains a real source of contention and concern.

With the exception of Japan, most of Asia relied heavily on FDI as a primary engine for growth in the drive to attain the status of 'developed nation'. The burst of economic euphoria of the 1980s and early 1990s – when the term 'Asian tigers' was born and the region's skyline was dramatically transformed – came to an abrupt halt with the 1997 economic crisis. The brunt of the crisis was borne by Southeast Asia and demonstrated the destabilizing effects that can be wrought by ungoverned private capital flows.

Recognizing the vulnerabilities of their relatively open and free economies in a global economy, ASEAN member countries have since stepped up talks of regional financial cooperation to make themselves more resilient in an increasingly unpredictable macro-environment. Some, like Malaysia and Thailand, are also seeking to beef up domestic industries. Nonetheless, these are slow long-haul processes with as yet uncertain outcomes. On the whole, FDI remains an intractable part of economic rejuvenation, a task that has taken on extra urgency with the rapid rise of China and with its recognized links to the threat of terrorist networks[4].

'Do as I say, not as I do'

Proponents of a pro-environment international investment regime correctly recognize the importance of FDI to Asia's development and its potential to shape the region's developmental path. However, previous attempts to link trade to the region's environmental concerns have reaped little success. Indeed, international law and policy-making on the environment have often been characterized by a highly fractious North–South divide.

The countries of Southeast Asia have almost always been on the side of the South. Either individually or collectively under the umbrella of ASEAN, they have expressed doubt over the appropriateness of most international environmental initiatives proposed by Western countries. Similarly, the vast majority of Asian states have opposed environmental conditionalities on aid and trade, whether at the bilateral level or from multilateral agencies, such as the World Bank.

This nervousness surrounding environmentalism stems partially from the track record of many developed countries in unilaterally imposing environmental standards, which are often duplicitously designed to give preference to their domestic producers. A recent report by the World Bank lent weight to this concern when it pointed out that 'the willingness of the developed west to abandon protectionist policies has not been much in evidence' (World Bank, 2001). Developing nations are thus hesitant to embrace a call for sustainable development because their experience and fear is that such a call might disguise protectionism and a donor-driven limit to their recovery and future development (Tay, 1997).

On a related front, Southeast Asian governments also resent any moves perceived to be a disguised attempt to undermine their competitiveness or sovereignty. Such resentment was evident in the run-up to the 1992 Earth Summit when Malaysia and Indonesia took a leading role to defend their rights to continue logging trees as part of their patrimony. ASEAN also fended off Austrian attempts to unilaterally declare eco-labels for tropical timber products, and US attempts to ban shrimp imports over shrimping methods that resulted in the death of endangered turtles. The Malaysian premier, Dr Mahathir Mohammed, was a leading spokesman against trade measures to increase environmental protection, often denigrating them as 'neo-imperialism' and ways of trying to stem the rise of developing countries by imposing new restrictions on their growth.

TNCs and environmental degradation: A necessary evil?

The degree to which Asian governments value economic growth over environmental concerns can be seen in the preferential treatment traditionally given to TNCs, despite studies highlighting cases of exploitation and unsustainable practices. One example is the role of Japanese TNCs in forest, wood pulp and other wood related products (Dauvergne, 1997). Additionally, TNCs have also been found guilty of shifting substandard industrial plants and hazardous production processes to developing nations, such as Thailand, to escape health and pollution standards in their home countries (Lee and So, 1999).

Alongside this display of tolerance is the frequently raised argument that governments cannot raise environmental benchmarks for fear of provoking TNCs and foreign capital to relocate to another country with lower standards. Although empirical studies show mixed evidence of such industrial migration, it has been cited repeatedly by developing nations including Indonesia and the Philippines (Esty, 1996; Revez, 1993)[5].

Environmental degradation is widely accepted as a temporary inconvenience, or even a necessary sacrifice for a greater goal, a view supported theoretically by the Environmental Kuznets Curve (EKC)[6]. However, anecdotal evidence indicates that, with proper monitoring and administrative and legal capacities to enforce laws, it is possible for countries such as Singapore to reconcile economic growth and environmental protection. Even relatively poorer countries such as the Philippines can improve their environments through better legislation and governance (*The Economist*, July 2002).

System breakdown

> *How can we prosecute offenders if the system of prosecution is broken down and its personnel are not equipped to really do the job?*
>
> (Indonesian Environment Minister Nabiel Makarim, *Straits Times*, 2002)

Throughout much of Asia, efforts to introduce environment-related laws, policy plans and programmes have been slow and generally ineffective (Parnwell and Bryant, 1996; Hirsch and Warren, 1998; Dauvergne, 1997). The slowness stems from a combination of political, economic, social and institutional factors, including systemic corruption, weak legal systems and the lack of institutional capacity (Noda, 2002). These factors were both highlighted and augmented in the aftermath of the 1997 financial crisis when confusion and fiscal austerity reigned.

Indeed, the economic crisis had negative impacts on Southeast Asia's environment for three major reasons: 1) decreased funds for environmental protection and infrastructure and weakened regulatory agencies and efforts to ensure compliance; 2) a resurgence of environmental problems associated with poverty; and 3) attempts to restart economic growth (Tay, 2001). In this manner, environmental woes in Southeast Asia are also symptomatic of a breakdown in national institutional and financial structures.

Post-1997, ASEAN governments have been largely preoccupied with the immediate tasks of political housekeeping and resuscitating the economy. Economic recovery especially was key to social and political stability and the government's own political survival, as vividly demonstrated in the popular uprisings in Indonesia and the Philippines. In post-Suharto Indonesia especially, unfamiliarity with political plurality and political insecurity have led to a situation where parties are often preoccupied with shoring up support at the expense of governance.

Complicating the picture are recent developments on the regional and international stage, namely post-911 security threats, the resurgence of fundamentalist Islam worldwide and a changing economic landscape due to China's growing economic power. Together, these developments have been the subject of much debate and research, with a considerable amount of resources poured into provision-making. Under such circumstances, it is unsurprising that the sustainable development agenda has been pushed down the list of national priorities.

On a wider scale, Asian governments' general reluctance to embrace environmental governance, however, does not mean that they are indifferent towards signs of environmental degradation and destruction. Indeed, it would have been impossible to ignore the signs. In Southeast Asia, populations are plagued by haze resulting from Indonesia's forest fires, while much of Northeast Asia must contend with acid rain. More recently, a report released by United Nations Environment Programme (UNEP) made waves with new findings on the devastating impacts of what has been dubbed as the Asian Brown Haze, a two-mile-long cloud of toxic gases and pollutants (UNEP, 2002). Media coverage of environmental disasters caused or aggravated by human activities or unsustainable practices has increased steadily over the years, often highlighting governmental inertia in correcting the underlying causes.

The depletion rates of natural resources in water, arable land, timber and oil in Asia are also high. Within the region, 40 per cent of land that can support closed tropical forests is now devoid of forest cover, while 75 per cent of the Asia and Pacific region's marine protected areas are deemed to be under high potential threat from coastal development (World Resources Institute, 1998). Pressure on the land in Asia is the most severe in the world, with over 28 per cent of the region's land area in various stages of degradation (Asian Development Bank, 2001).

Serious water and air pollution due to burgeoning populations and industrialization also pose chronic health hazards. As an indicator, the fecal coliform level found in the region's rivers is 3 times the world average and 50 times over the level recommended by the World Health Organization (Asian Development Bank, 2001)[7]. In the case of the Asian Brown Haze, scientists from the United Nations Environment Programme believe that it contributes to acid rain, and puts hundreds of thousands of people at risk of respiratory diseases (UNEP 2002)[8]. As another indicator, residents of Hong Kong reportedly spent US$462 million on treatment of respiratory ailments, most of which were aggravated by air pollution (Reuters, 2002).

Official recognition of these environmental imperatives is slowly growing, as is the political will to do more. ASEAN nations recently signed an anti-haze treaty and the three Northeast Asian nations of China, Japan and South Korea agreed to monitor air pollution. While much more is needed to address Asia's environmental woes, these moves are significant. The anti-haze treaty is the first legal treaty among the ASEAN nations, while the Northeast Asian agreement was made among three traditionally rival nations. Although it is premature to comment on the success of the two pacts, they indicate a fundamental shift in governmental stance with regard to environmental concerns.

Cooperation not coercion

> *It seems to me there is a certain hypocrisy about rich countries telling poor countries to undertake radical reform. The kind of changes we have got to*

> *make in the west are much smaller than the kinds of reforms rich countries are asking poor countries to make all the time.*
>
> (Nick Stern, World Bank's chief economist, *The Guardian*, 2002)

Sustainable development represents an uphill task for most resource-strapped Asian governments, perhaps one so daunting that procrastination may appear preferable. It is also clear that while environmental imperatives are gaining more recognition, the economic concerns of trade and FDI remain paramount for very practical and substantial reasons.

Attempts at nudging Asian governments to do more should therefore shift from a negative 'sanctions-based' approach to a more positive one where trade, investment and environmental concerns are tied together under a positive mutually reinforcing framework. One previous attempt to do so has been the recognition of the principle of common but differentiated responsibilities, set out in the Rio Declaration's Principle 7[9].

The Rio bargain was that developing countries would recognize and work towards common environmental concerns so long as and to the extent that the developed countries made financial, technical and other forms of assistance available. Unfortunately, the Rio bargain has remained largely at the level of rhetoric, belying the early optimism it inspired. Not only did the promise of increased official development assistance (ODA) not materialize, it has decreased significantly over the years.

Nonetheless, the cooperative spirit and principles of the Rio bargain remain just as, if not more, relevant today. Its lacklustre outcome points to the need to rethink the channels and means through which North–South cooperation can take place at the higher governmental levels. It also demonstrates the need to widen the pool of players beyond governments to include a greater cross-section of society on both sides of the North–South divide.

One positive approach that is gaining currency is the greater involvement of the business and civil society communities, particularly as a source of funding and specialized knowledge. Governments can and should perform the vital functions of facilitating and encouraging such alternative channels from North to South through appropriate financial incentives, institutional capacity building, and creating a policy framework that encourages and recognizes the value of sustainable development work.

An example is the China Council for International Cooperation for Environment and Development (CCICED). A high-level non-governmental advisory board established by China's state council, its purpose is to strengthen cooperation between China and the international community in the field of environment and development, with a specific policy-work focus. Tapping into international expertise, various expert working groups (WG) composed of Chinese and foreign experts are formed around trade and environment-related issues; findings and recommendations are then channeled to the country's top officials. CCICED is run jointly by high-level Chinese officials and international experts, and is supported financially by China, the Canadian International Development

Agency (CIDA) and other international organizations. Membership is broad-based, including academics, businessmen, and representatives from multilateral agencies.

On many counts, the approach has been a successful one. In a monthly Senate Committee meeting of the Simon Fraser University – where the CCICED Secretariat Canadian Office is housed – the Senate Committee on International Activities (SCIA) found that CCICED as a project has been 'able to influence China's policy at the highest level' and that it had 'exceeded expectations'[10].

The CCICED experience demonstrates what is possible when political will, financial assistance and broad-based collaboration are brought together in a rational strategy. It is important to note, however, that strategies must be tailored to countries' circumstances. For example, where awareness and understanding of environmental issues is low and institutional capacity is lacking, educating officials on environmental issues and launching small-scale collaborative efforts with local communities may be a more appropriate starting point than a top-down approach that will be difficult to sustain under the given circumstances.

CHANGING PRIORITIES

The rapid economic transformation of Asia from the 1970s to the 1990s was marked by increasing consumerism and materialism. In the past two decades, however, there has been a proliferation of environmental NGOs and a general emergence of environmental consciousness in the region (Lee and So, 1999). This is due to the worsening scale of the environmental problems, growing pool of scientific evidence on the costs of environmental degradation, and heightened media profile, all of which have increased public awareness and concern for environment-related issues.

In grappling with the region's environmental woes and searching for a viable blueprint towards a sustainable future, the issue of good governance and its accompanying institutional infrastructure has surfaced as one of great importance. In most of Asia, however, the lack of will, institutional and financial capacities mean that actors outside of the government have a key role to play in shaping the nation's developmental path. Not only can environmental NGOs and their civil society partners give added impetus to better governance, they can also contribute by taking on important functions that governments cannot.

Reflecting Asia's economic and social diversity, the nature of NGO concerns run the spectrum of basic livelihood issues to post-materialist concerns such as over-consumption and quality of life. In Japan, Taiwan and South Korea, for example, NGOs and the general public tend to focus more on issues such as ambient air, toxic waste and environmental conservation efforts (Eder, 1996). In countries such as Thailand and the Philippines, environmental movements often stem from poverty-related concerns and the need for environmental justice (Lee and So, 1999; Nicro, 1996; Poffenberger, 1990)[11]. Often, a key issue underpinning these concerns is the need for good governance.

Pushing for better governance

> *The main challenges to sustainable development are public participation in decision-making processes and the existence of a clean and accountable government. Law enforcement is another important issue.*
>
> Mr Jhamtani, a board member of Komphailindo, the National Consortium for Forest and Nature Conservation in Indonesia (*Banagkok Post*, 2002)

Current and unfolding developments since the advent of the economic crisis in 1997 have revitalized civil society. In the crisis, these actors have grown stronger, both generally and with particular regard to the environment. Partly, this has been because of the emphasis on the need for systems of better governance and to root out cronyism, corruption and nepotism, or 'KKN' as the Indonesian reformers call it.

Corruption, cronyism and nepotism are not new to Asia. This unholy trinity has skewed decision-making processes and led to many projects that were neither rational nor viable. In many cases, big businesses have been able to monopolize and over-exploit natural resources through collusion with state agencies, to their personal gain and the misfortune of the general public. Often, the overexploitation led to severe floods, smoke haze, soil erosion, or the expropriation of indigenous lands – consequences that were borne largely by the local communities (Tay, 1999). This has been strongly evident in the case of Indonesia (Barber, 1997). It is also true of a web of legal and illegal logging that links the countries of Indo-China and Myanmar (Bryant, 1997).

Public desire for good governance has particular importance for the environment. Accountability, greater and more widespread participation in decision-making and aspects of democracy are all factors that can impact on environmental protection. In fact, environmental campaigns are sometimes seen as alternative – and relatively more legitimate – modes of expression and political mobilization than political parties for the working class, as well as others traditionally found in the opposition (Eder, 1996). This can be observed in Indonesia, Thailand and the Philippines[12]. In this manner, the calls for political change and for greater environmental concern have been mutually reinforcing, particularly against a changing political backdrop in which a reformist or avowedly democratic government had come into power in the wake of the crisis.

Even in countries that have gone without widespread reform and political upheaval there are signs of greater civil society and NGO movements, both generally and particularly for environmental concerns. In Malaysia, the influence of NGOs such as Friends of the Earth and the Third World Network have grown considerably since the late 1970s. Both groups have been involved in several high-profile cases that involved public protest or litigation in the courts against government agencies[13].

Grassroot movements: creating alternatives

In addition to demands for better governance, the trauma of the 1997 economic crisis triggered a search for alternative ways to rebuild local and national economies. In Thailand, for example, calls were made for an alternative, sustainable economic model that was premised upon native Buddhist teachings (Seneviratne, 2002; *The Sunday Times*, 26 May 2002).

Some ecologists argue that Asians are more receptive towards sustainable development due to inherent elements of Asian cultures and religions. In the Philippines, however, it is the Roman Catholic Church – a religion of Western origin – that has great influence over social beliefs and values (Lee and So, 1999). Regardless of whether the religious roots are Asian or Western, the twinning of popular religious concepts and local cultural values with the principles of sustainable development works to indigenize a social movement of Western origin. Such indigenization forms a major source of empowerment and legitimization for local activists to challenge dominant ideologies and culprits of environmental degradation in the region (Lee and So, 1999: p22).

Box 4.1 *Sufficiency Economics*

Thailand's financial mess following its spectacular economic meltdown has led to calls for an alternative, sustainable economic model from the nation's popular monarch and its influential rank of Buddhist monks. Termed 'Sufficiency Economics' by the well-loved King Bhumibol, it calls for an economic model that is built upon the three pillars of Buddhism – *dana* (giving), *sila* (morality) and *bhavana* (meditation).

Stripping away the religious exoticism, it essentially calls for a shift in priorities away from the rampant consumption of the economic heydays, away from corruption, to moderate consumption and a more holistic economic model that supports sustainable development.

Though critics have warned that the move away from conventional economic path may hamper Thailand's growth and form an excuse to reject market economy, the sufficiency movement has been able to mobilize a wide and varied cross-section of the Thai population since its conception in 1997, from Buddhist social activists, rural monks, grassroots peoples' organizations, economists, and of course, the Royal Palace. In their hands, the message of 'Sufficiency Economics' have been transplanted to various parts and sectors of the population, from a Buddhist economics unit in a university to the promotion of integrated and natural farming methods, to the setting up of community savings banks.

Source: Adapted from *The Sunday Times*, 26 May 2002; Seneviratne, 2002

Religion has been a particularly potent force in marshalling the uneducated rural populations of Indonesia, Thailand and the Philippines. Through religious institutions, the message of sustainable development and environmental protection are widely related to a cross-section of people in a language they can understand and assimilate (Lee and So, 1999). In addition, religious institutions often bring with them the moral authority invested by the people. It can be observed that the moral authority and organizational abilities of Asia's religious institutions are sometimes superior to that of the state, especially where the state is perceived to be corrupt and weak.

It is not within the scope of this chapter to assess the appropriateness of such 'homegrown' solutions, or of using religion as a vehicle for sustainable development. Nonetheless, these developments constitute a vital aspect of Asia's response to the sustainability challenge and demonstrate the ability and effectiveness with which civil groups and their partners can rally the masses to effect change.

Business communities: moving towards self-governance

In the absence of strong leadership from central governments, there has been a gradual trend towards self-initiatives by local business to better their lives and environment. An article published by the *Bangkok Post* gave an account of some of these efforts (*Bangkok Post*, 2002):

- In the Philippines, a local brewery was able to improve the air quality in its vicinity and reduce staff absenteeism within one year – simply by requiring all vehicles entering its plant to be 'certified clean', i.e. not emitting noxious exhaust fumes. Today, over 80 firms have adopted the same measure.
- In Bangkok, a group of 80 tanneries banded together to set up their own treatment plant to reduce the environmental hazards of toxic waste water.
- In Indonesia, some 70 small growers and traders of bananas formed a self-help group where members not only help each other in cultivating and marketing their produce, but also worked together to clean stretches of the Pesanggrahan river. They also replanted its banks to prevent soil erosion and yield extra income.

To a great extent, initiatives such as these are fuelled by a growing awareness of the links between environmental degradation, poor health, natural disasters such as floods and landslides and the resulting impacts on livelihood. This increase in public awareness can be traced to better education, outreach efforts by civil and environmental groups, increased media profile on environmental issues as well as that of good governance, and the spread of international environmentalism.

These initiatives by local small and medium-sized enterprises indicate a growing trend towards responsible self-governance in Asian business. Western in origin, corporate governance (CG) and corporate social responsibility (CSR) movements are gradually taking root in Asia. Private-sector initiatives, such as the Asian Corporate Governance Association and the Association for Sustainable and Responsible Investment in Asia (ASrIA) in the capitalist city of Hong Kong are emerging. While their numbers remain small, the trend is expected to continue growing in the coming years (Loh, 2001).

INTERNATIONAL ENVIRONMENTALISM

In many ways, environmentalism in Asia has been shaped and supported by its international counterparts. The rise of international environmentalism is evidenced by the prominence NGOs such as Greenpeace, the Worldwide Fund for Nature (WWF) and Amnesty International have gained over the years. As a coalition, they have been able to broaden out the environmental agenda to address the darker sides of globalization, such as labour and human rights, and the social responsibility of TNCs in host countries[14].

Their strength, moreover, is not only in pressing at the international level against the states that they think are at fault, but in their ability to pursue transnational companies that invest in such states through consumer action and in the courts of their home countries. This was the case in the Nike 'sweatshop' controversy and the lawsuit against Unocal in Mynamar. The extensive media coverage and bad press by various environmental and human right groups for both cases highlight the reputational risk that companies must now take into account for their operations.

The risk is not just moral, but also has legal and financial implications for corporations and the associated companies and firms that lend, ensure and service the corporation (Case, 1999; Speeding, 1996). A downstream effect of this development is greater recognition of environmental concerns among banks and accountants (Elkington, 1998). In 2001, the Association of British Insurers, whose members control one-quarter of the UK stock market, published new guidelines asking companies to disclose any significant risks to their short-term and long-term value stemming from social, environmental and ethical factors (Asian Business Institute, 2001).

Through means such as these, NGOs and civil society abroad have been able to take on corporate giants, often with some degree of success. This is especially valuable where local avenues for change are unavailable given victims' subordinate or marginalized position in society, and where poor conditions are accepted as a necessary tradeoff in order to make a living. Distant activism, however, can be a double-edged sword. Fear of consumer backlash have caused companies to pull out of undeveloped nations, often to the detriment of local workers. This was feared to be the case when Nike pulled out of Cambodia following a publicity row over a BBC report that one of its contract factories hired underage workers (*New York Times*, 2002)[15].

With these tools and the broader coalition between environmental and other interests, the driving forces at the international level pushing for sustainable development have been growing stronger. There are two important consequences for Southeast Asia: 1) international organizations and western governments are increasingly placing environmental and social conditions on aid and loans; 2) norms and values are filtering back and influencing leaders, business, and civil society groups in Asia.

Business not as usual

Heightened public awareness and concern about environmental and human rights issues in the West are generating increased calls for action by international organizations and western governments. International finance by the World Bank and other inter-governmental agencies often comes with conditions attached. These conditions go beyond economic terms to include environmental impact assessment and mitigation. Increasingly, social impacts and governance issues are also considered in loan approval. While not a new phenomenon, the governments of Southeast Asia had been largely unaffected by these conditionalities during the economic boom of the 1980s and early 1990s. This is no longer the case after the 1997 financial crisis.

This trend of conditioned finance is increasingly being reflected at a corporate level. Also jumping onto the politically correct bandwagons are private international finance banks, insurance companies and accounting firms realizing the need to factor in lack of proper environmental protection as possible future liabilities (French, 1998). Access to finance has become an important tool that is being wielded to affect the behaviour of developing countries and TNCs in environmental protection and sustainable development.

TNCs are increasingly being pressured by governments, multilaterals and consumers to take into account the possible fallout of their decisions and operations, at home and abroad. Reactions to this pressure have been mixed, from pro-actively taking environmental initiatives, to waging public relations campaigns, to avoiding troubled spots altogether[16]. Nonetheless, a change in corporate mindset can be discerned through the growing adoption of codes of conduct, which in an increasing number of cases, is felt to be more than a matter of public relations (Wilson, 2000)[17].

In a basic paradigm shift, some companies are reframing environmental concerns as questions of efficiency, leading to systemic efforts to reduce waste and resource use while increasing productivity (Von Weizsacker et al, 1997; Romm, 1994). Some see that environmental management methods and technology alone cannot deliver sustainability; ethical and ecological concerns must instead be incorporated into strategic management (Welford, 1995; Crosbie and Knight, 1995)[18]. This shows a striking shift in corporate mindsets, from reactive thinking that sees environmental regulations as increased costs, to proactive thinking that sees them as challenges to innovation and reasons to improve productivity.

Such a change in the West's corporate mindset could have positive implications for Asia where environmental regulations are still commonly seen by businesses and governments as unwanted costs and use of precious resources. Not only could it deliver direct benefits for the region's environment and populations, it could also help raise a country's environmental standards by importing higher ones set by the company itself.

Changing values

Influences from international NGOs and movements are filtering back to Asia via a variety of routes: the Internet, returning Asian nationals after a period of work or education abroad, interactions between Track-II institutions, and the spreading of international NGOs to Asia. The World Wide Fund for Nature, for example, has affiliates in many Asian nations. In this manner, the values and ethics espoused by these groups, as well as the tools they deploy, are introduced into Asia.

Through local affiliates, much needed research and awareness programmes are funded and carried out. Given the variety of economic, environmental, social and political conditions that exist across Asia, a 'one-size-fits-all' approach towards Asia's woes is clearly inappropriate. Often conducted collaboratively with locals, their research and activities provide some of the vital missing links needed to address the region's environmental issues.

A positive example is Project Firefight Southeast Asia (PFFSEA), an international initiative of the International Union for the Conservation of Nature (IUCN) and WWF to learn more about the underlying causes of Indonesia's forest fires. Funded by the European Union and supported by the US Forest Service, the project seeks to provide a legislative and economic basis to help policy reforms with regards to forest fires in Southeast Asia through in-depth research work. Its members include both international and local Indonesian researchers who work closely with local and regional environmental organizations[19].

BUILDING SUSTAINABLE PROSPERITY

From the US to the Ukraine, national governments in industrial, developing and transition economies, are under increasing economic and political pressure to reassess their responsibilities and capabilities and to share the mantle of governance with other players.

('Business as Partners in Development', a report by Prince of Wales Business Leaders' Forum)

The confluence of internal evolution and external influence outlined above is propelling the gradual emergence of a three-way 'partnership' for sustainable development as a future paradigm. In this tripod, the key actors – governments, foreign and local corporations and civil society – each play a vital and varied function in advancing the sustainability cause.

The environmental commitment of the three actors does not often grow in tandem and the 'leading leg' of the tripod varies from country to country. For example, in China and Singapore, governments have been active leaders in formulating a broad vision for sustainable development and laying down the necessary institutional and legal infrastructure for a national development blueprint. In most of Asia, however, civil society and increasingly, the business community are looked to for answers and solutions.

Undeniably, environmental NGOs and their civil society partners are today the most active driver for sustainable development in the Asian region. Over the years, they have extended their work beyond watchdog, lobbying and advocacy to include research and grass-root projects. Their networks have also grown increasingly wider and more sophisticated, reaching a greater cross-section of the population and across national borders.

One of the most important aspects of the growth of civil society is the availability of skill and expertise in a wide range of areas – from environmental sciences, policy and trade matters, to communications and organizational skills. There is a growing recognition – both within and outside this loose grouping – that non-governmental actors have among them valuable knowledge and means required to take up the sustainability challenge. Such recognition has not only propelled them onwards but also lends credence to overtures of collaborative efforts with governments and the private sector.

More ambiguous is the role and expectations of the private sector, especially the TNCs. Although sustainable development is gaining currency, environmentalism on the whole is still very much a poor cousin to the bread-and-butter issue of employment and economic rejuvenation. The popular uprisings against the rule of Suharto in Indonesia, Joseph Estrada in the Philippines and Chavalit Yongchaiyud in Thailand in the aftermath of the economic crisis are still fresh in Asia's memories. In this light, TNCs are still very much favoured by Asian authorities as big investors and a quick solution to unemployment, and are likely to remain an integral part of Asia's development regardless of their commitment to environmental protection.

Ambiguity notwithstanding, TNCs have been identified as an important partner in the sustainability effort because of the financial and technological resources they bring. Propelled along by the sticks wielded by consumer watchdogs, and the economic carrots of greater efficiency and the blossoming market for green products, corporate social responsibility as a growing phenomenon points to greater corporate efforts in mitigating the negative impacts of FDI – at least where corporate pursuit of profit need not be compromised.

International investment regime: fears and concerns

It is fair to say that a vision of sustainable development has taken root in various communities and groups across Asia. How best to tap the potential of FDI to turn this vision into reality remains a key question for stakeholders. As a positive indicator of things to come, fledgling attempts to introduce environmental obligations into investment negotiations are being made. In the Singapore–US Free Trade Agreement negotiations, for example, the Clinton administration pushed for the inclusion of environmental and labour standards.

Among Asian governments, the central concern with regards to any international investment regime is likely to be the potential impact on the volume of FDI inflows. A number of contentious issues – especially the issue of compliance and its costs – may cast a shadow over the inclusion of environmental obligations, such as requiring foreign investors to uphold higher environmental standards and to transfer clean technologies, as well as restricting access to natural resources like timber.

Without compliance, the proposed regime risks being rendered meaningless. Yet it is clear that for most of developing Asia, the judicial and institutional infrastructure necessary to ensure compliance is still in its formative stage. Even if governments take on the role of corporate watchdogs, the scourge of corruption and lack of political will are likely to be obstacles. Nonetheless, these can be overcome if home countries of TNCs are willing to take on the onus of ensuring or at least encouraging compliance, for example, through policies such as mandatory global, social and environmental reporting (Leighton, et al, 2002; see Chapter 8).

From an industry point of view, the costs of compliance must be weighed against the overall benefits of investing in a country. At present, Asia's main draws for foreign investors are low operational costs, cheap, well-educated and plentiful labour supply, and abundant natural resources. Proximity and access to markets are another pull factor. An investment regime that curtails foreign investors' access to natural resources, or requires investors to invest in cleaner but more expensive technologies and in training a local workforce in these new technologies may erode this competitive edge. In short, it may be more rational for some TNCs to move operations to a more developed nation.

Such a development would mean transitional fallouts in the form of unemployment, including that of satellite industries – a scenario that both governments and the public would want to avoid amid the present downturn. This is ironic because an investment regime would have the greatest potential to make a difference in a country with a poor environmental record. Still, the reality is that efforts needed to raise environmental standards can be costly and daunting.

Related to this is the issue of local businesses and fairness. Will the same rules that govern FDI be applied to local businesses? Not doing so would constitute a form of discrimination against foreign investors, especially where these investors are seeking a share of the domestic market. At the same time, however, most local businesses are likely to lack the know-how and deep pockets to make the necessary investments to improve standards.

Already, environmental groups and representatives of developing nations have expressed scepticism and mistrust of an investment regime initiated by the West, especially following the debacle of the proposed multilateral agreement on investment (MAI).[20] In an article made available by Third World Network, Mr Bhagirath Lal Das, a former Ambassador and Permanent Representative of India to the GATT and former Director of International Trade Programmes in UNCTAD, pointed out that a WTO agreement on investment is a 'no gain, only loss' proposition for developing countries. He also stated that 'past experience has shown that a process of negotiation started at the initiative of the major developed countries generally ends with agreements in accordance with their aims[21].' In a similar vein, it has also been pointed out that many developing countries are already unable to participate fully in existing negotiations due to lack of resources and unfamiliarity.

Sustainability through the tripod

The concerns outlined above appear to predict the premature death of support by Southeast Asian and other developing countries for an international investment regime. Nonetheless, we argue that it is possible to garner the support of developing nations for a pro-sustainability approach to governing investment by fulfilling two conditions. Firstly, an international investment regime must not be perceived to undermine individual state sovereignty. Secondly, it must be able to address the negative impacts of foreign investment without obstructing economic growth.

The emphasis of a pro-sustainability investment regime should be placed on strengthening and supporting the sustainability tripod where possible. For developing Asia, this can be interpreted as setting achievable sustainable development goals without undermining governments' capacities to regulate and channel FDI for maximum developmental benefit. This would cover three components:

1 Setting human developmental targets such as poverty alleviation and education.
2 Mitigating and controlling the negative economic fallout of foreign investors.
3 Promoting foreign investments that are of higher developmental value. Judicious use of industrial policy instruments and other pro-developmental policies should be endorsed during the gestation of a developing economy.

While such measures may appear contrary to the relentless move towards free trade, the economic impacts of FDI are often difficult to measure with precision and the resulting economic interaction between TNCs and host countries vary from case to case (UNCTAD, 1999). Given the great diversity of economic and market situations prevailing in developing nations, a one-size-fits-all approach in managing this process is clearly inadequate. A more pragmatic approach would be to allow individual governments leverage to steer their economies through this process.

At the same time, such a regime should seek to promote investments that are in line with or further the sustainability cause. For example, FDI projects can be graded according to their environmental-friendliness factors, likely contributions to the upgrading of human and technological resources and 'promoted' accordingly through means such as tax incentives. The rapidly growing industry of eco-tourism for one can be of particular relevance to developing nations seeking a middle-ground between economic development and environmental protection.

Importantly, the regime must also address the weaknesses in the tripod by setting requirements for transparency in the governance of both governments and corporate entities, and making provisions for capacity-building. The West can play the role of a facilitator, in the latter, for example through research funding, sharing of technological know-how and facilitating informed policy-making, such as within CCICED where informed suggestions are offered to the government for its independent perusal.

Such capacity-building measures will not only help deflect criticism of interference, but also deliver very real benefits in improving environmental governance. In addition, the regime should place the onus of ensuring compliance with environmental laws on TNCs' countries of origin. The reason for this is two-fold: the home countries of most TNCs are developed nations where environmental standards are higher, and developed nations have greater capacities to perform such monitoring functions.

Finally, it would be helpful to realize that the path of sustainable development is not completely divergent from that of economic well-being. The underlying requirements to implement a strategy for the former – good governance, institutional capacity, strong judicial system, and importantly, strategic *long-term* planning – are also conditions conducive towards a country's future economic well-being and prosperity.

ENDNOTES

1 Parts of this chapter draw from Simon Tay and Lyuba Zarsky, 'Civil Society and Environmental Governance in Asia', in *Asia's Clean Revolution: Industry, Growth and the Environment* (D. Angel and M. T Rock, eds.), Greenleaf Publishing, UK, 2000; and Simon Tay, 'Business and Sustainable Development in Asia', *University of British Columbia Business Journal*, 2000

2 The Asean State of the Environment Report 2000 cited three constraints to sustainable development in Southeast Asia: institutional limitations, inadequate manpower and technological capacities, and financial constraints.

3 The only study that US President Bush cited in announcing his reversal on CO_2 reductions, a report by the Energy Information Administration, failed to consider the inexpensive reductions in greenhouse pollution that can be achieved through energy efficiency.

4 Here, terrorist networks refer not only to international terrorist networks such as Al-Qaeda, but also to domestic terrorist groups such as the Abu-Sayyaf in the Philippines and Jemaah Islamiyah in Indonesia.

5 This is despite anecdotal evidence about foreign claims. In fact, two comprehensive government studies have shown that MNCs sometimes help raise environmental standards in host countries by importing their relatively higher standards and practices (Pangestu et al,1996).

6 The Environmental Kuznets Curve refers to the phenomenon whereby pollution increases within an impoverished economy during initial economic growth, before decreasing upon the attainment of a higher level of income. This was the case for the OECD and the newly industrialized economies in Southeast Asia.

7 The fecal coloform level is used as an indicator of the health risk from human waste in assessing water quality.

8 Scientists are also investigating links between the Asian Brown Haze and changing rainfall patterns as well as the possibility that it is reducing the amount of sunlight reaching Earth.

9 The Rio Declaration's Principle 7 states that 'States shall cooperate in a spirit of global partnership to conserve, protect and restore the health and integrity of the Earth's ecosystem. In view of the different contributions to global environmental degradation, States have common but differentiated responsibilities. The developing countries acknowledge the responsibility that they bear in the international pursuit of sustainable development in view of the pressures their societies place on the global environment and of the technologies and financial resources they command'.

10 Please refer to the following link for minutes of Senate Committee on International Activities meeting, February 2002, www.reg.sfu.ca/Senate/SenateComms/SCIA/sciaminfeb02.html

11 These movements often seek to address issues such as the lack of access by the poor to environmental resources or their suffering from the direct impact of pollution.

12 In Indonesia, environmental civil society organizations and NGOs which have tended to focus on particular issues (such as opposition to dams, or making the case for environmental conservation) in their pre-crisis days (Hirsch and Warren, 1998), became linked to broader politics and calls for political reform during and in the aftermath of the crisis. This has led to a domestic challenge to the elite's monopoly over access and ownership to natural resources. Indonesian NGOs such as WALHI, the umbrella coalition for environmental NGOs, achieved considerable prominence during the crisis, as did the Indonesian chapter of the Worldwide Fund for Nature.

13 One example is the Asian Rare Earth case in which NGOs supported a suit brought by local villagers against a company for health and other damage that arose from the improper storage and disposal of hazardous materials. The government agency that approved the company's activities was also implicated. A more recent highlight of the growing role of NGOs in Malaysia has been their participation in the controversy surrounding the building of the Bakun Dam in East Malaysia. The dam, which would impact upon traditional and indigenous lands, was approved by government authorities without an environmental impact assessment. On this basis, the court initially ordered that work be stopped and, although this has since been circumvented, the issue remains contested between government and NGOs.

14 The 1999 WTO Ministerial meeting in Seattle was disrupted by NGOs and other protesters, including those who felt that increased trade would harm the environment. The incident was one among a growing number that demonstrate the increasing ability of NGOs and civil society actors to affect large and powerful transnational companies and even block governments.

15 For more information see: http://cbae.nmsu.edu/~dboje/nike/cambodia.html

16 Unocal, for example, argues on its website that it is not responsible for any reported abuse of villagers by the Myanmar government, and that the termination of its operations there would add to the country's poverty. www.unocal.com/myanmar/index.htm

17 Examples include principles adopted by the Coalition of Environmental Responsible Economies (CERES) and the work of the World Business Council for Sustainable Development. More than two-thirds of larger US corporations now have codes of business ethics, many of which include the environment.

18 The *Financial Times' FTSE4Good Indices*, for example, cover the environment, human rights, social issues and stakeholder relations, while Dow Jones has a *Sustainability Index* that rates world companies on the triple bottom line: economic criteria; environmental performance; and social trends.

19 PFFSEA has released four reports based on its research findings. For more information, see www.pffsea.com

20 The main features of the proposed agreement are as follows: the centrepiece is a 'top down' approach to liberalization of investment regimes through the application of national treatment and MFN treatment standards to both the establishment and the subsequent treatment of investment; a broad, asset-based definition of investment; provisions on country specific reservations; standstill and roll-back obligations; provisions on transparency of domestic laws, regulations and policies; a limited set of general exceptions; standards for the protection of investments (general treatment standards and specific standards on expropriation and compensation, transfer of funds, protection from civil strife, and so forth); and dispute settlement procedures through state–state arbitration. In addition, consideration is being given to the possible inclusion of disciplines on investment incentives, performance requirements, movement and employment of key personnel, corporate practices, privatization and monopolies and state enterprises: www.wto.org/english/news_e/pres96_e/pr057_e.htm

21 See 'Pitfalls in Plurilateral Path on Investment Talks': www.twnside.org.sg/titlepitfalls.htm

References

Asian Business Institute I (2001) Social Responsibility: Risks and Opportunities, www.abi.org.uk/Display/File/85/CSR_FullReport.pdf

Asian Development Bank (2001) *Asian Environment Outlook 2001*, www.adb.org/Documents/Books/AEO/2001/default.asp

Bangkok Post (2002) 'ASEAN Groups Show What a Little Can Do', August 23, 2002

Barber, C. (1997) *Environmental Scarcities, State Capacity, Civil Violence: The Case of Indonesia*, Cambridge, Mass, American Academy of Arts and Sciences

Bryant, R. L. (1997) *The Political Ecology of Forestry in Burma, 1824–1994*, London, Hurst & Co

Case, P. (1999) *Environmental Risk Management and Corporate Lending: A Global Perspective*, Cambridge, Woordhead Publishing

Crosbie , L. and K. Knight (1995) *Strategy for Sustainable Business: Environmental Opportunity and Strategic Choice*, London and New York, McGraw Hill

Dauvergne, P. (1997) *Shadows in the Forest: Japan and the Politics of Timber in Southeast Asia*, Cambridge, MIT Press

Eder, N. (1996) *Poisoned Prosperity: Development, Modernization and the Environment in South Korea*, Armonk, NY, M.E. Sharpe

Elkington, J. (1998) 'The "Triple Bottom Line" for Twenty-First-Century Business', in J.V. Mitchell (ed.) *Companies in a World of Conflict: NGOs, Sanctions and Corporate Responsibility*, London, Earthscan

Esty, D. (1996) 'Environmental Regulation and Competitiveness', in Tay, S. S. C. and D. C. Esty (eds.) *Asian Dragons and Green Trade: Environment, Economics and International Trade*, Singapore, Times Academic Press

French, H. (1998) *Investing in the Future: Harnessing Private Capital Flows for Environmentally Sustainable Development*, Worldwatch Paper 139, Washington, D.C., Worldwatch Institute

Gleeson, B. and N. Low (2001) *Governing for the Environment: Global Problems, Ethics and Democracy*, New York, Palgrave Publishers

Hirsch, P. and C. Warren (eds.) (1998) *The Politics of Environment in South-East Asia: Resources and Resistance*, London, Routledge

Lal Das, B. (undated), 'Critical Analysis of the Proposed Investment Treaty in WTO', www.twnside.org.sg/title/ana-ch.htm

Seneviratne, K. (2002) 'Sufficiency Economics. An Alternative Buddhist Economic Path for Asia?' *Lanka Daily News*, 17 July

Lee, Y. F. and A. Y. So (1999) (eds.) *Asia's Environmental Movements: Comparative Perspectives*, Armonk, N.Y., M.E. Sharpe

Leighton, M., N. Roht-Arriaza and L. Zarsky (2002) *Beyond Good Deeds: Case Studies and A New Policy Agenda for Corporate Accountability'*, Natural Heritage Institute, Nautilus Institute, and Human Rights Advocates, July, www.nautilus.org/enviro/cap/

Loh, C. (2001) *SRI New Generation of Global Investors*, CLSA Research Paper, May

New York Times (2002) 'Let Them Sweat', 25 June

Nirco, S. et al (1996) *Environmental Non-governmental Organizations in Thailand*, Bangkok, Thailand Environment Institute

Noda, P. J. (2002) *Cross-Sectoral Partnerships in Enhancing Human Security*, Japan Center for International Exchange (JCIE), Institute of Southeast Asian Studies (ISEAS)

Pangestu, M. and B. Bora (eds.) (1996) *Priority Issues in Trade and Investment Liberalization*, Singapore, Pacific Economic Co-operation Council

Parnwell, M. and R. L. Bryant (eds.) (1996) *Environmental Change in South-East Asia: People, Politics and Sustainable Development*, Routledge, London, p387

Poffenberger, M. (1990) *Keepers of the Forest: Land Management Alternatives in Southeast Asia*, West Hartford, CT, Kumarian Press

Reuters (2002) 'Hong Kong: China's Guangdong to Clean up Bad Air', April 29

Revez, R. (1993), 'Rehabilitating Interstate Competition: Rethinking the Race to the Bottom', *New York University Law Review*, vol 67 p1210

Romm, J. L. (1994) *Lean and Clean Management: How to Boost Profits and Productivity by Reducing Pollution*, New York, Kodanshu America

Speeding, L. (1996) *Environmental Management for Business*, New York, John Wiley & Sons

Straits Times (2002) 'Minister Admits Jakarta Unable to Curb Forest Fires', July 13

Tay, S. C. (1997), 'Trade and the Environment: Perspectives from the Asia-Pacific', *World Bulletin*, vol 13, no 1–2 (Jan–Apr)

The Guardian (2002) 'A Vision of Dystopia', August 21

The Economist (2002) 'How Many Planets? A Survey of the Global Environment', July 6

UNCTAD (1999) *World Investment Report 1999: Foreign Direct Investment and the Challenge of Development*, New York, United Nations

UNCTAD (2002) *World Investment Report 2002: Transnational Corporations and Export Competitiveness*, New York, United Nations

UNEP (2002) *Impact Study: The Asian Brown Cloud: Climate and Other Environmental Impacts*, www.rrcap.unep.org/abc/impactstudy/

Von Weizsacker, E., A. Lovins and H. Lovins, (1997) *Factor Four: Doubling Wealth, Halving Resource Use*, London, Earthscan

Welford, R. (1995) *Environmental Strategy and Sustainable Development*, London and New York, Routledge

Wilson, I. (2000) *The New Rules of Corporate Conduct: Rewriting the Social Charter*, Westport, Connecticut and London, Quorum Books

World Bank (2001) *Sustainable Development in a Dynamic World*, Washington, D. C., World Bank

World Resourcese Institute (1998) *Watersheds of the World: Ecological Value and Vulnerability*, Washingon, D. C., World Resources Institute

Part 2

The Governance of International Investment

Chapter 5

All Roads Lead Out of Rome: Divergent Paths of Dispute Settlement in Bilateral Investment Treaties

Luke Eric Peterson

ABSTRACT

Despite the dramatic surge in global investment flows in recent years, no single international institution is charged with creating the rules governing these flows or resolving disputes which arise between investors and host states. Twice now, governments have rejected efforts to conclude a multilateral agreement on investment, most recently at the World Trade Organization's 5th Ministerial Conference in Cancun in September, 2003.

Instead, governments have had the most success negotiating treaties in a piecemeal, bilateral fashion. Similar in scope and content to the more well-known investment chapter of the North American Free Trade Agreement (NAFTA), although sometimes broader in their coverage, these bilateral investment treaties (BITs) open up a number of dispute-settlement mechanisms for aggrieved investors.

Unfortunately, in all but one instance these mechanisms were simply grafted in from the secretive world of international commercial arbitration. As such, they fall well short of the standards for transparency, legitimacy and accountability expected of fora where sensitive government policies will be weighed against other private interests. As evidence emerges of a surge in BITs litigation – and particularly of cases which implicate sustainable development concerns – these dispute settlement avenues are proving increasingly problematic.

It is too early in the litigation cycle to offer definitive comment on the interpretation of the substantive rights contained in these BITs and their implications, particularly for developing countries. Already, however, there are ample grounds for criticizing the procedural rules under which so-called investor-state arbitration occurs. The deficiencies in the process ensure that the resolution of highly sensitive regulatory and policy decisions may be evaluated behind closed doors and out of public view.

Introduction

When a series of investor rights and protections were inserted into NAFTA, their implications remained unclear. Since 1996, however, Chapter 11 of the NAFTA has been invoked in a series of disputes brought by investors against one of the three NAFTA states (the US, Canada and Mexico).

Most controversially, upwards of ten of these so-called investor-state disputes have been brought against government measures dealing with environmental and natural resource management, including those involving hazardous waste management, maintenance of clean drinking water, and gasoline additives (Mann, 2001b; see Chapter 6). While investment treaties can provide an important bulwark for investors against mistreatment, corruption and other forms of abuse, they may be framed in such exceedingly broad terms that they privilege investor rights at the expense of other public goods.

Several cases have generated worrying interpretations of investor rights, in particular, guarantees against expropriation, or measures 'tantamount to expropriation' without payment of compensation (Mann, 2001b). These cases have sent a chill through government regulators and the broader sustainable development community.

Despite all the attention lavished on the NAFTA investment chapter, it was rarely noticed, until recently, that these rights have an extensive family tree. BITs have been largely ignored for much of their 40-year history, in part due to the lack of an obvious institutional structure. Unlike the NAFTA or the World Trade Organization (WTO) – which has been a lightning-rod on the shores of Lake Geneva – investment treaties have been concluded typically between two treaty partners, with little fanfare or publicity.

Despite this low profile, there are now 2181 international investment treaties worldwide – overwhelmingly bilateral, but also regional or plurilateral in nature[1]. At least 173 countries, a number well exceeding the WTO's membership, are bound by at least one such investment treaty (UNCTAD, 2000). What's more, investor interest in these treaties has increased markedly in recent years.

As with the NAFTA, the vast majority of BITs have opened a Pandora's box of dispute settlement options for investors, allowing them to launch so-called investor-state disputes against host governments before international arbitration tribunals (Parra, 2001). Rather than creating new institutions suited to this task, and restricting their purview to those instances where no domestic remedy could be had, the treaties often grafted in various existing international commercial arbitration mechanisms designed (with one notable exception) for the settlement of commercial disputes, primarily between two businesses.

The half-dozen different arbitral rules surveyed in this chapter suffer from a number of the same shortcomings. They also display a handful of key differences that might be exploited by savvy investors eager to shop for rules deemed most amenable to their interests. This can be seen especially in the varying levels of transparency offered under the different arbitral rules and the extent to which subsequent review of arbitral rulings is permitted by some higher legal body.

Further scrutiny of these treaties and their dispute settlement mechanisms is important. Now that member-governments of the WTO have rejected efforts to launch multilateral negotiations on investment, these bilateral agreements contain most of the global rules which govern foreign direct investment.

Foreign investors are awakening to the opportunities latent in these long-ignored bilateral treaties. The World Bank's International Centre for the Settlement of Investment Disputes (ICSID), thought to be the busiest of the various arbitral forums, notes in a recent annual report that 'the largest number' of its cases in 2001 were brought not under the NAFTA, but under BITs (Tung, 2001). While the high-profile health and environmental NAFTA disputes have attracted the most scrutiny from the sustainable development community, these arbitrations constitute only a small portion of the cases pending at ICSID.

Major law firms are also awakening to the potential uses of these BITs – hailing them as 'a most powerful weapon' for foreign investors in the context of the Argentine financial crisis, particularly in public services such as oil and gas, electricity, water, transport and telecommunications[2].

Investors have invoked the provisions of BITs in a trickle of litigation since the late 1980s. Over the past five years, however, the 'floodgates' have opened (Parra, 2000).

This surge in litigation is so recent that the bulk of these cases is still pending; most key investor rights have yet to be fully fleshed out by the tribunals charged with interpreting the treaties (Parra, 2000). Investment law commentators have drawn attention to the striking breadth and imprecision of the rights contained in these BITs. One leading arbitration lawyer has described the treaty provisions as 'dazzlingly abstract', cautioning that 'the BITs . . . are maddeningly imprecise as to the substantive legal standard to be applied by the tribunal, and that imprecision may well open the door to vexatious litigation' (Rogers, 2000).

While the substantive legal rights have yet to be fleshed out, it is already apparent that the procedural rules designed to guide this interpretive task are inadequate. As mechanisms often designed for private commercial disputes, they do not meet the basic standards of transparency, legitimacy and accountability expected of institutions entrusted with the task of balancing private economic rights with public goods. If, as legal scholar Jeswald Salacuse has argued, these investment treaties are contributing to 'a new international law of foreign investment to respond to the demands of the new global economy,' then the institutional failings of these treaties render the fuller details of this body of law frustratingly elusive.

This chapter examines and evaluates some of the key features of BITs, their dispute settlement rules and some emerging disputes. Section 2 offers an overview of the treaties and their basic provisions, followed by an introduction to the various arbitral avenues available to investors for disputes settlement. Section 3 highlights the major procedural shortcomings of these avenues, with respect to transparency, legitimacy and accountability. Section 4 summarizes what we know about formal and informal treaty disputes and profiles two pending disputes.

BITs: Origins and Features

Most of the BITs concluded during the late 1950s and the early 1960s were between Western European and African nations. Even today, a majority of the treaties still bring together a northern and southern partner, although it is increasingly common in recent years for developing countries to sign BITs among themselves (UNCTAD, 1998). In the 1990s, BITs experienced an astonishing growth spurt. In only ten years, the numbers of BITs virtually quintupled, growing from 385 to 1857 (UNCTAD, 2000). As noted earlier, the number of these treaties is now approaching some 2200 worldwide.

The family resemblance of BITs to their more famous relatives, such as the NAFTA or the OECD's proposed Multilateral Agreement on Investment (MAI), is quite striking. BITs typically contain a series of investor protections, both absolute standards, such as guarantees to 'fair and equitable treatment' or 'full protection and security', and relative standards, such as national and most-favored nation treatment, which require that investors be treated no less favourably than domestic and third-party investors respectively (UNCTAD, 1998).

As might be expected, there are considerable variations from country to country and certainly from era to era, given that these treaties have been negotiated over a four decade period. However, a number of features are quite standard. Most BITs contain brief preambles which set narrow objectives for the treaty: typically promotion and protection of investment, as well as encouragement of economic cooperation between the two signatories (UNCTAD, 1998). In addition, most tend to offer broad definitions of investment, in part to ensure the future utility of the treaties as the nature of investment itself evolves over time (UNCTAD, 1999b).

Indeed, the definitions of both investors and investments under most BITs are broader and less nuanced than they are under NAFTA's Chapter 11 (Grigera-Naon, 2000). This ensures that a wide range of economic actors and activities qualify for coverage under the agreement, (including for purposes of invoking the investor-state dispute settlement mechanism typically contained in these agreements). However, the reach of many of the substantive provisions is often restricted to the post-establishment phase of an investment (i.e. once the investment has been made), rather than extended to the pre-establishment stage (i.e. offering non-discriminatory treatment at the entry stage) (UNCTAD, 1999a). The NAFTA and some BITs concluded by Canada and the US are notable for extending non-discrimination to the pre-establishment stage; most BITs do not.

Most BITs typically safeguard investors from direct expropriation and indirect (or 'creeping') expropriation by dictating that government measures that expropriate an investment must be enacted for a public purpose, in a nondiscriminatory manner, in accordance with due process of law, and accompanied by payment of 'prompt, adequate and effective compensation' (Parra, 2001). This provision has been of particular concern in the NAFTA context, as government regulations have been challenged as measures 'tantamount to expropriation', and therefore entitling investors to compensation (Mann and

Von Moltke, 2002). Many BITs also include provisions allowing for the transfer of monies, movement of key employees, and some protection from war and civil disturbance.

A state-to-state dispute settlement mechanism has been a feature of most BITs since the earliest days. It gave home-states a legal option beyond the traditional avenue of diplomatic negotiations between home-state and host-state. However, formal state-to-state disputes under BITs are exceedingly rare. At the time of writing, one such claim was understood to have been mounted under the Chile–Peru investment treaty (Peterson, 2003a)[3]. An investor–state dispute settlement mechanism first appeared in the late 1960s, becoming 'a regular feature' in BITs signed during the 1970s, and emerging as virtually standard by the 1980s and 1990s (UNCTAD, 1998; Parra, 2000) .

It is this investor–state mechanism that allows investors to challenge alleged violations of the treaty provisions by host states before an international arbitration tribunal, merely by following the simple steps marked out under the given arbitral rules. In most instances, modern BITs do not require the exhaustion of domestic legal remedies prior to the invocation of international arbitration. Indeed, in some instances the BITs discourage the use of local courts, by declaring that recourse to them will preclude international arbitration at a later date (Grigera-Naon, 2000; Parra, 1997).

Avenues for arbitration

The World Bank's ICSID has become the most well-known and, based on available information, most commonly invoked *institutional* avenue for dispute settlement. However, treaties often allow recourse to a number of other arbitral options, both institutional and ad hoc[4]. The ICSID is unique insofar as it was conceived specifically with investment arbitration in mind, rather than the resolution of a broader range of commercial disputes. However, its jurisdiction extends only to cases where the legal instrument in question – a treaty, national investment law or contract – explicitly provides for ICSID arbitration. Moreover, both of the parties must be party (or in the case of an investor, hail from a state which is party) to the ICSID convention.

ICSID does offer a second set of arbitration rules, the so-called Additional Facility (AF) rules, in order to accommodate disputes that involve a state (or an investor hailing from a state) that has yet to come on board the ICSID Convention. For example, the AF rules are of use to countries such as Canada and Mexico (and their investors), which have not ratified the ICSID Convention to date. Indeed, as of November 2003, only 140 countries have acceded to the ICSID Convention (by contrast, recall that 173 countries have entered into BITs).

Neither set of ICSID rules are available in cases where *both* parties to a dispute do not hail from an ICSID signatory country (Parra, 1997). For this reason, the majority of investment treaties since the 1980s have incorporated references to other (non-ICSID) arbitral avenues (Parra, 2000). Arbitration under other *institutional* rules is sometimes mentioned in more recent bilateral investment treaties, for example, the International Chamber of Commerce's

International Court of Arbitration (ICC rules) or the Stockholm Chamber of Commerce's Arbitration Institute (SCC rules) (Parra 1997; Grigera-Naon, 2000).

More often, treaties will supplement the ICSID option, not by reference to other commercial institutions – such as the ICC and SCC – but with an ad hoc arbitration process, where only a tribunal (but no supervising institution) oversees the conduct of the arbitration. Examples of ad hoc arbitrations include, those under the UN Commission on International Trade Law (UNCITRAL) rules or those arbitrated in a classical ad hoc fashion (i.e. before a panel with no prescribed rules whatsoever, apart from what the treaty explicitly prescribes) (Parra, 1997).

This chapter explores some of the features of five institutional options: International Chamber of Commerce, Stockholm Chamber of Commerce, ICSID, and the so-called ICSID Additional Facility. It also examines ad hoc options, both classical and UNCITRAL.

Attention to the last of these is limited, however, because classical ad hoc arbitration is less often mentioned in treaties. Nor, as shall be seen, does it have any rules that can be helpfully compared with the other sets; as the name implies, arbitrations on these rules are entirely ad hoc, and totally off-the-record – with the parties devising the rules of arbitration themselves.

One important implication of the inclusion of a *menu* of arbitral options in most BITs is that investors generally enjoy the ability to select their favoured arbitral option from all those listed in the treaty's menu (Parra, 1997). In effect, they may be able to 'rule-shop' for the set of arbitral rules most favorable to their interests. Thus, effective monitoring of emerging investment disputes must not only countenance all of the arbitral options discussed here, but it must also come to appreciate certain important differences between these different rules.

Monitoring of investor usage of these treaties – and an assessment of their implications – is hampered by various deficiencies in transparency, legitimacy and accountablity. This ought not be surprising, as, with the exception of the ICSID system, these arbitral rules were designed for what one sympathetic textbook characterizes as a system of 'private justice in the service of merchants' (Dezalay and Garth, 1996). While the various arbitral options differ in some respects, all fall short – to some degree – of the standard expected of institutions which are increasingly charged with resolving conflicts pitting private rights against public goods.

Transparency in BITs Arbitrations

Public registration of investor–state disputes

Under NAFTA Chapter 11, disputes must be registered with the NAFTA Secretariat once a Notice of Arbitration has been filed against the host state. No BITs, however, contain a comparable requirement that investors publicly signal their intention to launch a dispute. Indeed, unlike the NAFTA, BITs do not have a secretariat, and even in cases of plurilateral investment treaties such as the

Energy Charter Treaty (ECT), which does have a permanent secretariat, there is no requirement that investors or contracting states notify the ECT Secretariat when a dispute has been launched.

In the absence of express *treaty* requirements to register disputes brought under the treaty, public disclosure will hinge upon the particular *arbitral rules* chosen by an investor. In cases brought under either set of ICSID rules, ICSID requires that a register of all cases be kept by its secretariat, including on a docket of pending cases kept on ICSID's website. This docket lists the name of the parties involved in a dispute, the date the case was registered, and a terse description of the dispute[5].

Whenever a new dispute is launched at ICSID the public can be easily apprised of the names of the parties involved, which can then guide further investigation and enquiry into the details of the investment dispute. Although the ICSID docket does not specify whether a dispute is being brought under a treaty, a law or contract, a large majority of ICSID cases now arise out of the general consents to arbitration lodged in investment laws or treaties, rather than contract disputes (Shihata and Parra, 1999; Parra, 2002). Nevertheless, it is important to remember that not all cases on ICSID's docket will be treaty arbitrations. Generally, ICSID staff can be relied upon to clarify under what type of legal instrument a given case is being contested.

Under the other *institutional* arbitral options (usually ICC or SCC) there is no comparable requirement that new BIT cases be publicly registered. Moreover, because these institutions handle a variety of other (non-investment treaty related) international commercial disputes, they do not compile precise figures on the *number* or *proportion* of their cases that arise out of a BIT (Parra, 1997; Jolivet, 2001; Magnusson, 2001).

However, in interviews conducted in 2001–2002, officials or former officials with both institutions conceded that the number of BIT cases seen each year is currently thought to be only a small handful per institution[6]. Nevertheless, this caseload marks an increase from five years ago, when neither institution was thought to see any investment treaty-based arbitration (Grigera-Naon, 2002; Franke, 2002). Indeed, further investigation by the author has revealed evidence of at least half a dozen recent BIT arbitrations at the Stockholm Arbitration Institute (Peterson, 2003b). Other cases known to have occurred at Stockholm include: Sedelmayer *v* Russia; CCL Oil *v* Kazakhstan; and Petrobart Ltd *v* Kyrgyzstan). However, details about most of these cases are extremely scant. Moreover, it is unknown what portion of the legal iceberg remains hidden from view, as the cases that have been uncovered have been those where the parties have elected to disclose the existence of these cases.

Generally speaking then, arbitrations filed at the ICC or the SCC will be arbitrated and resolved under a cloak of confidentiality.

So-called ad hoc (non-institutional) arbitration poses an even more formidable challenge to transparency. Such arbitrations may take place anywhere, without the supervision of an arbitral forum or any requirement for public registration[7].

The ad hoc rules most commonly referenced in BITs are those of UNCITRAL, which does have a permanent secretariat devoted to the creation and promotion of arbitration rules and model laws. However, this secretariat has been given no mandate to chart the actual use of its arbitral rules by investors. Thus, when faced with an enquiry as to the prevalence of investor–state arbitrations using the UNCITRAL rules – and particularly those implicating sensitive environmental, health or other issues of public interest – a secretariat official could only confess that 'We're not monitoring this at all' (Sorieul, 2002)[8].

Senior officials with institutional forums such as the ICC or SCC are at least able to make a rough guess as to the number of BIT cases occurring under their roof – even if details and the names of the parties remain frustratingly confidential. UNCITRAL's secretariat is unable to do even this. Investigators are left to gather details of unpublicized BIT arbitrations through a variety of needle-in-a-haystack techniques, including, reading transcripts of government foreign relations committee hearings; scrutinizing the publicity materials of law firms offering legal services; or poring over the statutory filings of publicly traded companies[9,10,11].

The lack of any requirement in most of these arbitral rules that disputes be publicly registered (apart from under the ICSID rules), has worrying implications when sensitive government regulations or investments in key public services are the subject of investor challenges. There are anecdotal suggestions that some investors already 'rules-shop' for those arbitral rules that will provide the greatest level of confidentiality (Ferrari, 2001; Walde, 2002).

Indeed, as greater public scrutiny is brought to bear on the more visible ICSID process – which is an increasingly scrutinized arm of the World Bank – analysts will need to be on guard for any signs that investors are decamping for more obscure and opaque arbitral avenues (provided, of course, that such options are offered in the relevant BIT)[12]. Anecdotal evidence suggests that, while non-ICSID avenues are seeing more investor–state disputes, for the moment, they may not be well known or understood by business interests (Walde, 2002).

Publication of awards

Remarkably, when an arbitral tribunal hands down a ruling – known as an award – there is no requirement that these awards enter the public domain. Sometimes, awards will circulate in the international legal community, stripped of any identifying information. These sanitized awards are useful for the legal principles that they elucidate, but offer no information about the parties' identities and the key details of the dispute[13].

Awards may be published in their entirety only under certain circumstances. According to the ICSID rules, the centre may publish an award only where both parties give their consent. However, either party may choose unilaterally to allow the award to be published elsewhere, for instance, on a law firm website. According to one ICSID lawyer, 'In many cases, one of the parties has made the award public while in a few the award has remained confidential' (Stevens,

2000). Conversely, the UNCITRAL rules set a far more onerous standard, insofar as they provide that an award may be publicized 'only with the consent of both parties' (Article 32(5)). Commentators point to this rule as safeguarding the secrecy of proceedings even once they are concluded (Dessemontet, 1996).

The same secrecy requirement constrains parties under other *institutional* rules such as those of the SCC (Franke, 2002). This means that even those disputes centring on challenges to government health, safety, environmental or other sensitive regulations might see their awards shrouded in secrecy, unless both investor and host state give their consent to publication.

Of course, major law firms will have access to more such awards through their representation of clients (investors and governments) in some cases and also through the activities of some partners as arbitrators. The author is aware that lawyers within firms will share documents related to arbitrations in which they have been involved. While such materials often may be published in due course, there is little doubt that such materials circulate informally well in advance of their publication. Clearly, practitioners enjoy a comparative advantage when it comes to knowledge about recent developments and interpretations in this young field.

The lack of any binding rules for the publication of awards contributes to a skewed playing field. Recalling Jeswald Salacuse's comment that the development of bilateral investment treaties have contributed to 'a new international law of foreign investment to respond to the demands of the new global economy', this is, nevertheless, a body of law whose contours remain shrouded in some mystery even for its most assiduous devotees (Salacuse, 1990).

The shortcomings in these arbitral rules – including the provisions on confidentiality of awards – create further uncertainty for all levels of government that may be contemplating regulatory measures or policies that might impact upon foreign investments. It is inadequate that awards circulate sporadically – or sometimes only informally within close-knit international arbitration circles – without being readily available to the government officials and elected representatives, whose policies must take heed of the developing international legal norms on investment.

One promising development has been the practice of the US to mandate in new free-trade agreements that documents related to investment arbitrations under that agreement will need to be published (apart from confidential business information). This innovation is now being replicated in the bilateral investment treaty programmes of both the US and Canada[14].

Legitimacy in BIT Arbitrations

Selection of arbitrators

One standard feature of investor–state arbitration, no matter under which arbitral rules it occurs, is the fact that 'in contrast to court litigation, arbitration . . . affords parties the opportunity to submit their disputes to judges of their own choosing' (Parra, 1997). Under the most commonly invoked sets of arbitral rules, a panel will consist of three members; the investor customarily chooses one arbitrator, while the state chooses the second, and both parties select the third.

This feature has already been flagged in the NAFTA context as an important difference between arbitration and regular courts. As IISD's Howard Mann and Konrad von Moltke argue: 'when matters of public welfare are at stake it . . . contravenes one of the most fundamental principles of jurisprudence, namely that parties to a dispute may not pick their own judges' (Mann and Von Moltke, 2002). Indeed, there are signs that the freedom to choose one's own arbitrator can have a decisive influence on the outcome of some arbitrations. Yves Dezalay and Bryant Garth have pointed to studies that show that the selection of arbitrators in commercial arbitrations plays a key role in winning or losing:

> *The attorneys to the parties well understand that the 'authority' and 'expertise' of arbitrators determine their clout within the tribunal. The operation of the market in the selection of arbitrators therefore provides a key to understanding the justice that emerges from the decisions of arbitrators.*
>
> (Dezalay and Garth, 1996)

Because the commercial arbitration community operates as a 'club' in the words of some arbitrators, the same persons act as counsel in some cases and as arbitrators in others (Dezalay and Garth, 1996). One senior arbitrator interviewed by Dezalay and Garth (1996) admitted that the close-knit nature of this arbitration community leads to potential conflicts:

> *You're often appointed a party arbitrator by someone with whom you have worked before and you know you're going to work with him again. Does that unconsciously bias one? I think that's a difficult one. But not everybody is 100 per cent honest and you know it's a very great advantage to find someone whose character you really do know and can depend on.*
>
> (Dezalay and Garth, 1996)

As international commercial arbitration rules have come to govern investment treaty disputes that may involve challenges to sensitive government measures (for example, on environmental, health or tax rules) the inadequacies of this system become more apparent.

Although BITs may sometimes dictate that arbitrators in certain categories of disputes display certain training or expertise, this is the exception rather than the rule. One such exception is the requirement found in certain Canadian BITs, that arbitrators in 'disputes on prudential issues and other financial matters shall have the necessary expertise relevant to the specific financial service in dispute' (Agreement). Otherwise, the treaties leave it to the parties – who will invariably have their own personal interests – to ensure that arbitrators have the breadth of experience necessary to resolve the dispute.

Just as the treaties themselves rarely offer guidance when it comes to the expertise required of arbitrators, nor do the major sets of arbitral rules fill this gap. Arbitrations under the ICSID Convention simply require that arbitrators be 'of high moral character and recognized competence in the fields of law, commerce, industry or in finance who may be relied upon to exercise independent judgment' (ICSID Convention, Article 14(1))[15].

Although ICSID arbitrators are often experienced and eminent international jurists, the centre's rules do not indicate that special expertise might be valuable (or even essential) in cases where disputes touch upon sensitive governmental regulatory issues. Presumably, such disputes were never envisaged. The other commonly used arbitral rules offer even fewer criteria for prospective arbitrators – providing only that arbitrators be independent and/or impartial[16]. Moreover, as these are more opaque venues of dispute resolution, it is impossible even to access the names and assess the bona fides of arbitrators entrusted to resolve investment treaty disputes under these rules.

Access by non-parties to the proceedings

Arbitral proceedings are not generally accessible to the public or concerned groups. Thus, in the absence of any express treaty language to the contrary, arbitrations under the ICSID rules would require the consent of both investor and state in order to open up the proceeding to the participation of outside actors, such as an *amicus curiae* (i.e. friend of the court) (Stevens, 2000). This point was reinforced recently in a controversial arbitration between a multinational water services company and the government of Bolivia. In the case of Aguas Del Tunari *v* Bolivia, an ICSID tribunal has indicated to prospective intervenors that it lacks the authority to open the proceedings to non-parties, in the absence of the consent of the two parties to the dispute (Peterson, 2003c).

Nor do the UNCITRAL rules offer greater openness. They stipulate that 'Hearings shall be heard in camera unless the parties agree otherwise' (Article 25(4)). This places a significant obstacle in the way of those parties seeking greater transparency of the proceedings, insofar as they require the consent of the state and the investor – and investors, in particular, are rarely keen to see greater light shone on such proceedings. In turn, this has implications for non-party access to the proceedings.

In the arbitration between the Methanex Corporation and the US under NAFTA, Methanex opposed an application for *amicus curiae* status by the International Institute for Sustainable Development (IISD)[17]. Although the tribunal took the important step of signaling its willingness to accept a written *amicus* brief – acknowledging the 'undoubtedly public interest' in the subject matter – IISD's application was undercut somewhat by express provisions contained in the UNCITRAL arbitration rules. Thus, the recalcitrance on the part of one of the parties, Methanex, led the tribunal to find that it had no authority under the UNCITRAL rules (which require in-camera hearings) to allow participation by other non-disputing parties in the *oral* portion of the proceedings (Mann, 2001a).

In another NAFTA case, involving the Canadian government and Pope and Talbot Company, the Canadian government sought *not* to advocate the participation of other actors in the hearings but simply to divulge transcripts of those hearings to interested third parties. The tribunal in that case also ruled against such disclosure, on the grounds that the UNCITRAL arbitral rules expressly require that hearings be held in-camera[18]. Subsequently, after further negotiation between Canada and the investor – and a threatened lawsuit by Canada pursuant to its own access to information legislation – agreement was reached between the parties to over-ride this portion of the UNCITRAL rules[19].

While heartening, the decision to over-ride in this case does not obviate the need to obtain future consensus between both parties, before the express provision requiring in-camera hearings will be over-ridden – a point which was underlined by the tribunal in the aforementioned Aguas Del Tunari *v* Bolivia case. In a similar vein, the ICC rules also expressly provide that proceedings shall take place in private, unless the parties and the arbitral tribunal agree otherwise (Article 21 (3)).

Although the SCC rules do not expressly mandate that the proceedings be closed to the public, the secretary-general of the Stockholm Arbitration Institute indicates that it would require the *unanimity* of the two parties to agree to open the proceedings up to the participation of other actors (Franke, 2002). Thus, the rules designed to discourage transparency of the proceedings (particularly that hearings be held in-camera), have knock-on implications for interested parties seeking to intervene and participate in the resolution of investment disputes, which brings into question the very legitimacy of the process.

ACCOUNTABILITY IN BITS ARBITRATIONS

Lack of *stare decisis* doctrine of precedent

Arbitration was conceived as a method of alternative dispute resolution (ADR) between two parties (i.e. an alternative to domestic court proceedings). In the NAFTA context, Howard Mann has observed that the one-off nature of arbitrations gives rise to concerns that 'the absence of a consistent interpretation of Chapter 11 may lead to the loss of government certainty and public understanding of the obligations governments face' (Mann, 2001b). Even the international commercial arbitration community recognizes that uncertainty plagues the process, as can be glimpsed in the suggestion that investors choose the same arbitrators for disputes that implicate similar facts, lest different arbitrators reach inconsistent decisions on the same (or virtually the same) facts (Obadia, 2001).

However, unlike the NAFTA and recent free-trade agreements signed by the US with Chile and Singapore, standard BITs do not require the consolidation of related cases into a single proceeding, as would often happen in a domestic court system (Parra, 1997)[20]. The alternative, as ICSID Deputy Secretary-General Antonio Parra concedes, is one where a state measure affecting a number of different foreign investors could give rise to multiple arbitrations and where 'the scope for inconsistent decisions in regard to essentially the same issues is obvious' (Parra, 1997).

Other practitioners concede that the one-off nature of arbitration means that common issues may have to be re-litigated in each new proceeding, which can lead to increased costs, inconsistent results, or both[21]. While this represents a continual revenue stream for commercial arbitrators, it signals a potential stream of uncertainty for governments. From the perspective of sustainable development policy-making, the prospect of multiple arbitrations – running in parallel or consecutively – sets up the very real situation where sensitive government regulations or measures will be scrutinized by a number of tribunals (under one or many different bilateral investment treaties with the host state) which could reach different, and even contradictory, conclusions.

This scenario has already come to pass in relation to two UNCITRAL arbitrations brought against the Czech Republic in the late 1990s challenging essentially the same government conduct (in one case the dispute was mounted by the affected company, and in another by its major shareholder). The cases of CME *v* Czech Republic and Ronald Lauder *v* Czech Republic arose out of CME's 1990s investment in the Czech Republic's first nationwide private television station[22]. CME was frozen out of its role as the provider of programming, when a separate Czech sister company, which was required by law to hold the TV licence, renounced its relationship with CME.

When CME, and its major shareholder Mr. Lauder, challenged its treatment at the hands of the Czech authorities (specifically the Czech Media Council), two separate tribunals handed down contradictory opinions as to the Czech Republic's liability for the treatment of the foreign investor (Peterson, 2003d). In one case, brought pursuant to the US–Czech BIT, a London-based tribunal held that the Czech Republic was almost wholly vindicated, while in the other dispute mounted under the Dutch–Czech BIT, a Stockholm-based tribunal held that the government violated various key BIT guarantees. A subsequent damages ruling by the Stockholm tribunal handed down a record award for some US$360 million in damages (Peterson, 2003e).

Respected arbitrators have since warned that the lack of any mechanism for consolidation of related proceedings under BITs threatens to undermine the legitimacy of the arbitration process itself (Peterson, 2003f). Concerns have been raised in particular about a growing succession of treaty claims brought against the Argentine Republic by foreign investors harmed during Argentina's financial crisis. At the time of this writing, upwards of 30 such claims had been mounted at ICSID alone – with an unknown number of other claims understood to have been mounted under less-transparent rules.

Although ICSID has made some effort to encourage parties to appoint the same arbitrators to adjudicate these claims, many of them are being heard by different groups of arbitrators – and are proceeding on different schedules, depending on when they were first registered. Arbitration lawyers have conceded that there is scope for conflicting or divergent rulings to be handed down in these Argentine claims (Peterson, 2003g).

The potential for conflicting rulings seriously complicates the efforts of host-states and their regulators to assess how they may remain in compliance with their own treaty commitments. In this instance – and in the face of a reluctance on the part of investors to use domestic legal systems – a single multilateral framework which required consolidation of disputes under a single panel might be preferable to the current morass of diverging avenues.

It should be noted, however, that there is no guarantee that any future multilateral regime would supplant the hundreds of existing BITs and their myriad arbitration options unless the political will for this was present. Indeed, the US has signaled its opposition to any move on the part of the WTO to overwrite existing BITs (Peterson, 2003h). In this sense, a multilateral pact might only add a further level of complexity to the web of international investment rules, without addressing the concerns raised here.

For the time being, the multiplicity of dispute settlement avenues, the lack of any mandatory requirements to consolidate similar cases, and the absence of a binding rule of a doctrine of precedent (*stare decisis*) governing investment treaty arbitration means that such arbitrations are sometimes akin to a 'crap-shoot'. Poorer developing countries seem unlikely candidates for rolling the dice in an effort to seek further new elaborations of these elusive treaty commitments.

It is well known that litigious investors will pursue multi-pronged strategies designed to create 'added cost and uncertainty' for the host state (Bishop et al, 2001). ICSID has estimated that the average investor–state arbitration alone will cost US$220,000 in arbitrator's fees alone. In 2002, ICSID issued a new schedule of fees which saw arbitrators' daily fees increase from US$1,100 per day per arbitrator, to US$2,000, which will increase significantly this average cost of ICSID proceedings[23]. Costs for non-ICSID forms of arbitration tend to be even higher, as the World Bank defrays many of the administrative costs associated with ICSID arbitrations.

The figures cited do not include legal counsel fees, which may be much higher, nor any financial damages awarded by the tribunal (Shihata and Parra, 1999). For example, in the NAFTA Metalclad case it has been estimated that the investor spent some US$4 million in arbitrators and legal fees[24]. The Czech Republic has spent a reported US$10 million (it is unclear if this figure includes arbitrator's fees) in defending the earlier-mentioned broadcasting claims.

These substantial costs make contestation of an arbitral claim an unattractive option for poorer developing countries. Moreover, uncertainty about the rules of precedence adhering from one case to the next – when coupled with the notorious secrecy which surrounds the legal argumentation deployed in some arbitrations – makes it difficult for host states to ascertain the nature of their substantive obligations under a BIT. The prospect for a chilling effect on domestic regulation or policy-making affecting foreign investors would seem likely.

Scope for post-award review

The choice of arbitral rules dictates what recourse the parties have after a tribunal hands down an award. Arbitrations under the ICSID Convention are unique insofar as they are 'insulated by that convention from the control of national legal systems' (Parra, 1997)[25]. To the extent that they fall under the sphere of the ICSID Convention, panel decisions that have been arbitrated under the ICSID rules are not subject to review by domestic courts (Grigera-Naon, 2000).

Recourse can only be had internally – within the ICSID system – and will be limited to five specific grounds listed in the ICSID Convention (Parra, 1997). These grounds for annulment do not amount to a full review of the decision on its merits, as might be typically available for court decisions in domestic legal systems. Moreover, the annulment proceeding, as with the original ICSID proceeding will take place out of public view.

By contrast, arbitrations under other rules – specifically, ICC, SCC, classical ad hoc, UNCITRAL and ICSID AF – may be subject to one or more forms of review, (for example, under the law of the place where the arbitration was sited, and/or in the place where enforcement is sought) (Grigera-Naon, 2000). If, for example, the arbitration appears to have violated some mandatory provision of the law of the place of arbitration, then a party might appeal to a local court to annul the award (Parra, 1997). However, the breadth of such review should not be over-emphasized, particularly as an increasing number of jurisdictions are adopting model laws which severely restrict the level of control which may be exercised over arbitral awards by domestic courts (Grigera-Naon, 2000)[26].

Where the victorious party seeks enforcement of an award pursuant to the New York Convention on the Enforcement of Foreign Arbitral Awards – which now has more than 100 state signatories – host states can resist enforcing the award on a handful of grounds set out in that convention. According to Antonio Parra:

> *These grounds include invalidity of the arbitration agreement; failure to give the losing party a fair hearing; excess of authority of the arbitrators; improper constitution of the arbitral tribunal or other irregularities in the conduct of the proceeding; invalidity of the arbitral award at the place of its rendition; non-arbitrability of the subject matter of the dispute in the country in which enforcement is sought; and failure of the award to conform with the public policy requirements of that country.*
>
> (Parra, 1997)[27]

On the face of things, these amount to an intriguing range of grounds – although commentators caution that controls by domestic courts are tending to be circumscribed over time. A complex body of legal literature grapples with these issues as they arise in various national jurisdictions (Grigera-Naon, 2000; Schwartz, 1994). As arbitral awards are rendered – and then challenged in domestic legal systems – the extent to which domestic courts can over-ride arbitral decisions will come into focus.

Apart from the complex substantive issues raised in the review of awards by domestic courts, there is also at least one obvious procedural distinction to be highlighted between the different arbitral rules. This post-award review process can represent another way in which the details – and perhaps even the very existence – of specific investor–state arbitrations may come to public attention (Dessemontet, 1996). When investors take their treaty claims to commercial arbitration venues such as the Stockholm Arbitration Institute, which keeps no public docket of claims, the existence of such claims has only come to public notice when one of the parties has challenged the arbitral award in a domestic court or sought to enforce that award[28]. Several high-profile investor–state arbitrations under the NAFTA (which were *not* arbitrated under the ICSID Convention rules), have been reviewed in domestic courts in Canada. These judicial reviews opened the cases up to far greater public scrutiny than was previously seen.

One such case is the controversial Metalclad case under NAFTA, which had been arbitrated under the ICSID Additional Facility rules[29]. In the Metalclad case, the Mexican government's treatment of the Metalclad Corporation's waste treatment facility was found to have violated the NAFTA's provisions on expropriation and minimum international standards of treatment, and the government was ordered to pay Metalclad nearly US$17 million (Mann, 2001b).

However, as the arbitration was legally sited in Vancouver, British Columbia, this opened the possibility for the Mexican government to challenge the award before the Supreme Court of British Columbia. That court partially overturned the substance of the award on the grounds that the tribunal had decided matters 'beyond the scope of the submission to arbitration'[30]. But at the same time, the court left intact what it called the tribunal's 'extremely broad definition' of expropriation, defining it as 'covert or incidental interference with the use of property which has the effect of depriving the owner, in whole or in significant part, of the use or reasonably-to-be-expected economic benefit of property'[31].

Despite the court's inability to overturn the tribunal's interpretation of the law on this particular point, the court's review was notable from the procedural perspective, however, for having opened the dispute up to wider public scrutiny. Indeed, the entire court hearing was broadcast live over the Internet by the Vancouver Independent Media Center[32]. Both the transcripts of the hearings and the final judgment of the court were also published and widely circulated after the judicial review proceedings.

Clearly then, the specific arbitral rules that investors elect to choose will have clear implications not only for post-award review, but also for the transparency of that process. Arbitrations under the ICSID rules will be reviewed only within the ICSID system and will be closed to public scrutiny, whereas reviews under other sets of arbitration, will fall to domestic court systems and their (often more transparent) procedural rules.

In terms of the substantive review undertaken by domestic courts, this will differ from jurisdiction to jurisdiction, and ought to be investigated by researchers in order to assess whether treaty-based challenges to sensitive government regulations show any greater signs of success under one or the sets of arbitral rules – of particular interest will be a future comparison of the evolving ICSID jurisprudence on annulment and the practice of domestic legal systems in enforcing or annulling arbitral awards. Already, there is a literature developing in the wake of the controversial Metalclad case, which questions whether awards in some of the high-profile NAFTA arbitrations which implicate important public policy issues, should be viewed far less deferentially by reviewing courts than would awards in more straight-forwardly 'commercial' disputes (Brower, 2001; Thomas, 2002; Brower, 2002; Tollefson, 2002).

Having now surveyed some of the features of the arbitral rules commonly included in investment treaties, we can turn to an effort to assess the extent to which investors are using investment treaties to challenge sustainable development policy making or other sensitive government measures.

Emerging Disputes Under BITs

Informal disputes

Efforts to monitor the volume of investor disputes under BITs are complicated by the fact that not all uses of these treaties will occur in a *formal* arbitral capacity. Increasingly, the treaties are recognized to have great utility in informal contexts – often as a deterrent – whereby investors refer to the treaty, and the threat of arbitration thereunder, in the hope of diverting a new or proposed government measure (Mann, 2001b). Armed with these BITs, investors enjoy an expansive opportunity to lobby away from the public eye, as, apart from under the ICSID rules, there are typically no treaty requirements to divulge the existence of even *formalized* legal disputes to the general public.

Practicing lawyers do admit that they hear rumours of investors applying informal pressure upon host states – while brandishing an investment treaty as a potential legal stick. One more public instance of this saber-rattling was seen in Canada under the NAFTA, where the Philip Morris company had threatened on several occasions to challenge restrictions on packaging of cigarettes under the terms of Chapter 11 of NAFTA. Canadian officials backed away from plans to impose plain packaging after Philip Morris hired a former US Trade Representative to advocate on their behalf (Appleton, 1998).

More recently, documents have fallen into the public domain that detail Philip Morris' warning to the Canadian government over its proposed ban on 'mild' and 'light' labels (Public Citizen, 2002). In general, however, such informal usage is impossible to monitor. When coupled with the dismal transparency offered by most arbitral rules, it is possible that many uses of these treaties – both formal and especially informal – will occur with minimal disclosure of the details and legal argumentation, or may go unnoticed altogether.

When related to investment treaties, such informal threats are more worrying than they might be in relation to other laws or legal norms, precisely because the substantive implications of these treaties are not yet fully fleshed out. Thus, litigious investors may point to 'precedents' in arbitrations under the NAFTA with some confidence – recognizing that under-resourced host-states may not prefer to be the ones saddled with anteing up the capital required to further flesh out these untested treaty commitments in a formal arbitration.

Formal disputes

ICSID, which is the most transparent of the arbitral avenues canvassed here, is the best starting point to examine emerging disputes. More rigorous investigation of the other more opaque arbitral processes will be necessary in future, along with sweeping reforms to open those avenues to public scrutiny.

In its 2001 annual report, ICSID noted that its caseload has continued to grow at a 'record pace' (Tung, 2001). And ICSID's caseload has continued to set new records in successive years. In 2001, the centre registered 12 investor claims which were brought pursuant to a BIT. The following year, the centre recorded 15; while in 2003 it registered an unprecented 29 treaty-based arbitrations (Peterson, 2004).

According to the deputy secretary-general of ICSID, many of these claims are no longer run-of-the-mill commercial disputes. As Antonio Parra has noted:

> *The cases now more typically concern claims over events such as civil strife in the state, alleged expropriations or denials of justice by it, and actions of its political subdivisions. Reflecting the times, several of the cases concern privatizations and several others may be said to involve environmental disputes.*
>
> (Parra, 1999)

Interestingly, a number of known BITs cases deal with water privatization (several of which are described in further detail below): Compañía de Aguas del Aconquija S.A. and Vivendi Universal *v* the Republic of Argentina[33]; Azurix Corp. *v* the Republic of Argentina[34]; Aguas del Tunari *v* Bolivia and three by subsidiaries of the Suez company against Argentina[35]. Other recent ICSID disputes relate to environmental zoning rules[36], permitting for hazardous waste sites[37]and alleged mistreatment of a diamond mining operation in the Democratic Republic of Congo[38].

Not all these disputes will necessarily implicate sensitive health and safety, human rights or environmental concerns. However, the framework under which they will be arbitrated makes it difficult – and sometimes virtually impossible – to know when they do so. Provided that the investor and host government wish, legal claims and documentation will remain confidential in BIT claims. The two disputes below have been singled out, in part, because some information is available to suggest that they may involve questions of considerable public interest.

Azurix Corp. v Republic of Argentina[39]

In 1999, the Azurix Corporation, a spin-off of the Enron Corporation, successfully bid US$438.6 million in order to obtain a 30-year concession to run the newly privatized water systems in the province of Buenos Aires (Perrin, 2000). The company courted trouble with the government when customers began to complain of poor water pressure. A larger controversy erupted in the spring of 2000 when the government was forced to warn half a million customers to avoid drinking the local water and to minimize exposure to showers and baths, due to an outbreak of toxic bacteria in the local water supply. A local public health chief was quoted in the news media as saying: 'I've worked here for 25 years and this is the worst water crisis I've ever seen here' (Perrin, 2000).

According to filings with the US Securities and Exchange Commission, Azurix countered that problems with water quality, 'for the most part are due to failures by the province to deliver infrastructure that it committed to deliver under the concession contract'[40].

Azurix Buenos Aires terminated its own concession contract with the government of Buenos Aires on October 5, 2001. Around the same time, Azurix filed a claim under the US–Argentina BIT, alleging that the regulatory actions of Argentina and its political subdivisions had violated the guarantees against expropriation and fair and equitable treatment and 'security and protection'. The firm is seeking more than US$550 million in compensation (Peterson, 2002). An arbitration tribunal has been selected and the case is proceeding behind closed doors.

Aguas del Tunari S. A. v Republic of Bolivia[41]

A long-term water-supply contract between a consortium led by the US-based Bechtel Corporation and Cochabamba, Bolivia's third largest city, gave the consortium exclusive rights to all the water in the area, including in formerly community-held wells (Finegan, 2002). Subsequent increases in local water rates – some bills doubled and amounted to a quarter of monthly incomes – and the legal expropriation of all public water supplies, triggered widespread unrest in Cochabamba and across the country. These protests led to violence and the eventual declaration of martial law. Authorities warned company executives that their safety could not be guaranteed and they fled Cochabamba.

Currently, the government and the consortium disagree as to whether Aguas Del Tunari abandoned its concession or was forced out. One thing is certain: Aguas Del Tunari is seeking to recoup its losses via an arbitration under the terms of a bilateral investment treaty signed between Holland and Bolivia. Shortly after signing the Cochabamba concession, the consortium moved its legal headquarters from the Cayman Islands to Holland. This suspicious-looking gesture has been decried by various campaigners as a form of treaty shopping[42].

A civil society campaign has been launched to open up the arbitration and to ensure that affected stakeholders may participate in the proceedings (Center for International Environmental Law, 2002). However, in a letter from the tribunal to would-be intervenors in the case, the president of the tribunal, Professor David Caron, indicated that the body lacked the authority to open the proceedings to the public, to disclose documents related to the dispute, or to join interested parties to the proceeding – without the consent of the two arbitrating parties.

However, the tribunal did not prejudice the possibility that it might enjoy the authority to seek oral testimony or written arguments from other interested parties at some later date. Professor Caron merely noted in his letter that 'the tribunal is of the view that there is not at present a need to call witnesses or seek supplementary non-party submissions at the jurisdictional phase of its work', leaving to one side the question of whether the tribunal enjoys such a power.

Given the considerable media attention already devoted to the Cochabamaba dispute, it seems fair to surmise that the formal arbitration will attract a considerable deal of notoriety for the ICSID. One unintended outcome could be to encourage investors to choose more obscure arbitral rules in future – such as those described herein – that do not divulge the existence of formal disputes to the public.

Conclusion

Doubtless, many lawyers, investors and signatory countries – and, one hopes, the sustainable development policy community – will be watching closely (or to the extent possible, due to transparency shortcomings) as the 'dazzlingly abstract' investor rights contained in these BITs are finally 'put to an extensive test' in arbitrations like the ones described above. Those countries which have yet to affix their signatures and ratification to these still poorly understood agreements – and have been made to feel sometimes that developments are passing them by – might yet come to be saluted for their foresight in having kept their feet firmly planted on the sidelines while the international legal obligations of host states to investors are slowly worked out on a case-by-case basis in arbitration. Such foresight may prove all the more laudable given that a recent World Bank study has raised doubts about the capacity of these treaties to stimulate new flows of foreign direct investment (FDI) (Hallward-Driemeier, 2003).

For the present, much more work needs to be done to monitor traffic on the various arbitral avenues in order to assess the implications of emerging disputes upon sustainable development policy-making. Indeed, until a greater proportion of the current raft of litigation works its way through the system, it will be difficult to assess what sort of *substantive* reform might be needed of the existing BITs provisions and how that reform can be best carried out.

Nevertheless, we can already identify some of the *procedural* shortcomings of BITs' dispute settlement mechanisms. A number have been highlighted herein, and doubtless others will emerge during subsequent efforts to monitor disputes under these treaties. Already it is clear that a number of the most obvious procedural weaknesses could have been avoided if the governments which negotiated these treaties had used more precise treaty language to override those portions of the arbitral rules that detract from basic standards of legitimacy, transparency and accountability[43].

For instance, the rules guiding the selection of arbitrators, could, as in cases touching upon financial matters, also require special expertise of arbitrators where sensitive health, environmental or human rights issues are implicated. Likewise, obstacles to the participation of other parties, such as *amicus curiae*, could be over-ridden by express treaty provisions.

Treaty parties could also design dispute settlement institutions with the legitimacy to handle the scrutiny of sensitive government regulations and the balancing of competing public and private interests which this requires (Pastor, 2001). Notably, when the US Congress granted trade promotion authority (fast-track) to the Bush Administration in 2002, it imposed a number of conditions on future investment provisions contained in free-trade agreements negotiated by the US Administration. This has led the administration to alter its future negotiating position, so that it requires new treaties to contain dispute settlement provisions which require the release of documents, allow for *amicus curiae* interventions in oral proceedings and hold tribunal proceedings which are open to the public (*International Trade Daily*, 2002).

These procedural innovations are slated to be replicated in the US's investment treaty programme. However, the US example has not been followed by most nations which continue to negotiate investment treaties –and increasingly free-trade agreements with investment chapters.

Moreover, literally hundreds upon hundreds of existing bilateral treaties have not been designed (or reformed) with such attention to detail. One future opportunity for sweeping reform of the existing treaties could come in the form of negotiations on a multilateral agreement on investment (Peterson, 2001). A multilateral pact could, in theory, represent a potential opportunity for improving upon the flaws which continue to emerge in these bilateral templates. However, Western governments with extensive bilateral treaty programmes have not shown enthusiasm for such an idea, with the US indicating that it would not sacrifice the high levels of investor protection found in its current BITs in order to accede to a multilateral agreement (Peterson, 2003c).

Thus, the moment for a multilateral agreement would not appear to be a propitious one. As has been argued here, only further resolution of pending cases will reveal to what extent the substantive BITs provisions prove to be a threat to sensitive government policies. If governments were to agree to negotiate a multilateral pact in the short term, it seems unlikely that negotiators would be well placed to identify those substantive portions of the BITs that should be replicated, and those which should be reformed or phased out.

Just as critically, it is doubtful whether sufficient understanding of the relationship between foreign investment and sustainable development currently exists to permit negotiators to craft an agreement that not only guards against strategic litigation against sensitive government measures, but which goes further and encourages those types of investments that are urgently needed to promote genuinely sustainable development.

ENDNOTES

1 These figures are current at July 1 2003, and based upon UNCTAD's database of treaties at: http://unctad.org/en/subsites/dite/fdistats_files/fdistats.htm
2 See 'The Argentine Crisis – Foreign Investor's Rights', January 2002. Available online at www.freshfields.com/places/latinamerica/publications/
3 It must be noted that individual country practices, and even individual treaties, will differ as to the exact nature and scope of the investor–state dispute settlement mechanism.
4 While ICSID seems to be the most popular forum, the confidentiality under other arbitral rules makes it difficult to accurately gauge ICSID's market-share of investor–state arbitration.
5 See www.worldbank.org/icsid/cases/pending.htm
6 Grigera-Naon (2002) estimates that 1 per cent of the ICC's some 500 cases per year are BIT cases. Franke (2002) estimates that there are 1, 2 or 3 cases a year at the SCC.
7 See, for example, the Asean Agreement for the Promotion and Protection of Investments, discussed in Parra (1997).
8 Of course, as noted above, NAFTA disputes using the UNCITRAL rules would presumably be caught thanks to another filter, contained in the treaty itself: the requirement that Notices of Arbitration be publicly registered with the NAFTA Secretariat.
9 See, for example, the testimony of Ronald Lauder before the Subcommittee on European Affairs, Committee on Foreign Relations, US Senate, (Lauder, 2000).
10 See, for example, the 'International Dispute Resolution' portion of the website of Patton Boggs LLP which details a BITs dispute launched on behalf of a US Oil investor in Kazakhstan.
11 For example, PSEG Energy Holdings Inc (2002), a US energy company, reveals in its filings with the US Securities and Exchange Commission (SEC), dated March 11 2002, that it is challenging an Argentine law affecting its electricity distribution investments in Argentina.
12 Some have raised the possibility that the ICSID, as the most visible of the arbitral avenues, could experience the same sort of public opprobrium as the GATT did in the early 1990s when it handled sensitive trade and environment disputes. See Sands (2000). Quoted with permission of the author.
13 See, for instance, the newly launched Stockholm Arbitration Reports available online at www.chamber.se/arbitration/english/
14 The reason being that the innovations in trade agreements (which must be approved by the US Congress) were occasioned by a deal brokered between the executive and legislative branches of government in return for the latter's acquiescing to the former's use of so-called fast-track trade negotiation authority.

15 Article 14(1) ICSID Convention.
16 Articles 9, 10, UNCITRAL Rules; Article 17, SCC Rules; Article 7, ICC Rules.
17 For background and documents relating to this intervention see: www.iisd.org/pdf/trade_methanex_background.pdf
18 The tribunal also warned that such disclosure would also be in violation of an undertaking on the part of Canada in a confidential order, agreed at the outset of the arbitration. See 'Decision and Order by the Arbitral Tribunal in NAFTA UNCITRAL Investor-State Claim Pope & Talbot, Inc. and Government of Canada', March 11 2002, at paragraphs 15 and 18.
19 This agreement is reflected in the consequent Amended Procedural Order on Confidentiality no 5, September 17 2002, available online at: www.nafta claims.com
20 New investment treaties negotiated by the US and Canada also provide for consolidation of related claims.
21 See the arbitration website of the law firm Mayer, Brown, Rowe & Maw at: www.interarbitration.net/introduction/toarbitrate.asp
22 Ronald S. Lauder *v* the Czech Republic and CME *v* the Czech Republic. These two cases mark two of the only BIT cases using UNCITRAL rules which have come to public notice, due in large measure to the investor's efforts to generate negative publicity for the Czech Republic. The tribunal awards are available on the website of the Czech Finance Ministry: www.mfcr.cz/scripts/hpe/default.asp
23 ICSID Schedule of Fees, July 1 2002, available online at: www.worldbank.org/icsid/schedule/main-eng.htm
24 For information about Metalclad's costs, see note 18 in Thomas, 2002
25 The grounds are 'that the arbitral tribunal was improperly constituted; that it manifestly exceeded its powers; that one of its members was corrupt; that there was a serious departure from a fundamental rule of procedure; or that the award failed to state the reasons on which it was based'.
26 Grigera-Naon cites the UNCITRAL Model Law on Commercial Arbitration.
27 See also Grigera-Naon (2000) regarding the increasing practice of treaties requiring that awards be rendered in New York Convention states.
28 See, for example, the case of Swembalt AB *v* Latvia, which has only come to light thanks to its having been taken up in domestic courts. A brief discussion of one such domestic court proceeding is contained in the Stockholm Arbitration Institute's 2002 Annual Report: www.sccinstitute.com/_upload/shared_files/scc_ann_report_2002_eng.pdf
29 Metalclad Corporation *v* United Mexican States, ICSID Case No. ARB (AF)/97/1.
30 The United Mexican States *v* Metalclad Corporation, 2001 BCSC 664, at 79. For a legal analysis of this decision see Mann (2001b).
31 2001 BCSC 664, at para 99
32 http://vancouver.indymedia.org/

33 ICSID Case No. ARB/97/3.
34 ICSID Case No. ARB/01/12.
35 Aguas Provinciales de Santa Fe, S. A., Suez, Sociedad General de Aguas de Barcelona, S. A. and Interagua Servicios Integrales de Agua, S. A. *v* Argentine Republic (Case No. ARB/03/17), Aguas Cordobesas, S. A., Suez, and Sociedad General de Aguas de Barcelona, S. A. *v* Argentine Republic (Case No. ARB/03/18), Aguas Argentinas, S. A., Suez, Sociedad General de Aguas de Barcelona, S.A. and Vivendi Universal, S. A. *v* Argentine Republic (Case No. ARB/03/19).
36 Lucchetti S. A. and Lucchetti Peru, S. A. *v* Republic of Peru (Case No. ARB/03/4).
37 Técnicas Medioambientales Tecmed, S. A. *v* United Mexican States (Case No. ARB(AF)/00/2).
38 Miminco LLC and others *v* Democratic Republic of the Congo (Case No. ARB/03/14).
39 ICSID Case No. ARB/01/12.
40 SEC Quarterly Report, November 19 2001, available online at: www.sec.gov/Archives/edgar/data/1080205/000095012901504206/0000950129-01-504206.txt
41 ICSID Case No. ARB/02/3.
42 See the views of campaigning groups expressed in a piece for Project Censored: www.projectcensored.org/stories/2001/1.html
43 Although the NAFTA Chapter 11 does not go far enough, its Article 1120(2) provides a model insofar as it expressly provided that the rules of arbitration applied 'except to the extent modified' by the treaty.

References

Agreement (undated) Agreement Between The Government of Canada and the Government of Barbados for the Reciprocal Promotion and Protection of Investments, available online at: www.dfait-maeci.gc.ca/tna-nac/fipa_list-e.asp

Appleton, B. (1998) Testimony before the British Columbia Legislature Special Committee on the MAI, Hansard, September 30.

Azurix Corporation (2001), SEC Quarterly Report, November 19, www.sec.gov/Archives/edgar/data/1080205/000095012901504206/0000950129-01-504206.txt

Bishop, R., D. Doak, D. Sashe and C. S. Miles (2001) 'Strategic Options When Catastrophe Strikes the Major International Energy Project, *Texas International Law Journal*, vol 36, no 4, summer

Bridges Weekly Trade News Digest (2002) 'Developing Country Concerns Emerge at WTO Investment Group', vol 6, no 31, September 18

Brower, C. H. II (2001) 'Investor–State Disputes Under NAFTA: The Empire Strikes Back', *Columbia Journal of Transnational Law*, vol 40, no 1

Brower, C. H. II (2002) 'Beware the Jabberwock: A Reply to Mr. Thomas', *Columbia Journal of Transnational Law*, vol 40, no 3

Center for International Environmental Law (2002) 'Three Hundred Citizen Groups call on Secret World Bank to Open Up Bechtel Case Against Bolivia', www.ciel.org/Tae/Bechtel_Bolivia_Aug02.html

Cytrar II Citizen Submission on Enforcement Matters, 14/02/201 www.cec.org/citizen/submissions/details/index.cfm?varlan=english&ID=58.

Dessemontet, F. (1996) 'Arbitration and Confidentiality', *American Journal of International Arbitration*, vol 7, nos 3 & 4

Dezalay, Y. and B. G. Garth (1996) *Dealing in Virtue: International Commercial Arbitration and the Construction of a Transnational Legal Order*, Chicago, University of Chicago Press

Ferrari, F. (2001) Former legal officer, UNCITRAL Secretariat, professor, University of Bologna, personal communication with author, August 1

Financial Times (2000) 'Rise in Bilateral Treaties to Guard Investors', December 19

Finnegan, W. (2002) 'Letter from Bolivia, Leasing the Rain: the Race to Control Water Turns Violent', *The New Yorker*, April 8

Franke, U. (2002) Secretary-general of Stockholm Arbitration Institute, personal communication with author, July 5

Freshfields Bruckhaus Deringer (2002) 'The Argentine Crisis – Foreign Investor's Rights', January, www.freshfields.com/places/latinamerica/publications/

Grigera-Naon, H. (2000) 'The Settlement of Investment Disputes Between States and Private Parties: An Overview from the Perspective of the ICC', *The Journal of World Investment*, vol 1, no 1, July

Grigera-Naon, H. (2002) Former secretary-general, International Court of Arbitration, personal communication with author, June 12

Hallward-Driemeier, M. (2003) 'Do Bilateral Investment Treaties Attract Foreign Direct Investment? Only a Bit... and They Could Bite', *World Bank Policy Research Working Paper 3121*, May

IISD (2001) Backgrounder on Methanex case, www.iisd.org/pdf/trade_methanex_background.pdf

Inside US Trade (2002a) Letter to Ambassador Zoellick from ECAT, NAM, NFTC, and USCIB, June 18

Inside US Trade (2002b) 'US Seeks Prospective WTO Rules on Regional Accords', November 1, p15

International Center for the Settlement of Investment Disputes (2002) Schedule of Fees, July 1, www.worldbank.org/icsid/schedule/main-eng.htm

International Institute for Sustainable Development (IISD) (2001) 'Investment – Avoiding a Dangerous Minefield for the WTO,' viewpoint, www.iisd.org/pdf/2001/trade_qatar_viewpoint3.pdf

International Trade Daily (2002) 'United States Tables Proposal on Investment in Chile Talks', October 3

Jolivet, E. (2001) General Counsel of ICC International Court of Arbitration, personal communication with author, March

Lalive, P. (1986) 'Some Threats to International Investment Arbitration', *ICSID Review*, vol 1, no 1, spring

Lauder, R. (2000) Testimony before the Subcommittee on European Affairs, Committee on Foreign Relations, US Senate, Washington, D.C., June 29

Magnusson, A. (2001) Assistant secretary-general, Stockholm Arbitration Institute, personal communication with author, March.

Mann, H. (2001a), 'Opening the Doors, at Least a Little: Comment on the Amicus Decision in Methanex *v* United States', *RECIEL* vol 10 no 2

Mann, H. (2001b), *Private Rights, Public Problems*, Winnipeg, International Institute for Sustainable Development, www.iisd.org/trade/pubs.htm

Mann, H. and K. von Moltke, (1999) 'NAFTA's Chapter 11 and the Environment: Addressing the Impacts of the Investor–State Process on the Environment', IISD working paper

Mann, H. and K. von Moltke, (2002) 'Protecting Investor Rights and the Public Good: Assessing NAFTA's Chapter 11', Winnipeg, International Institute for Sustainable Development, www.iisd.org/trade/pubs/htm

Mayer, Brown, Rowe & Maw, 'International Arbitration', www.interarbitration.net/introduction/toarbitrate.asp

Nauman, Talli 'Cytrar Parent Firm Files World Bank Complaint Against Mexico, www.us-mex.org/borderlines/updater/2000/oct24CYTRAR.html

Obadia, E. (2001) 'ICSID, Investment Treaties and Arbitration: Current and Emerging Issues', *ICSID News*, Fall

Parra, A. (1997) 'Provisions on the Settlement of Investment Disputes in Modern Investment Laws Bilateral Investment Treaties and Multilateral Instruments on Investment', *ICSID Review* vol 12, no 2, Fall

Parra, A. (2000) 'ICSID and Bilateral Investment Treaties', *ICSID News*, vol 17, no 1, Spring

Parra, A. (2001) 'Applicable Substantive Law in ICSID Arbitrations Initiated Under Investment Treaties', *ICSID Review*, vol 16, no 1, Spring

Parra, A. (2002), Deputy secretary-general, ICSID, personal communication with author, July 10–11

Pastor, R. (2001) *Toward a New North American Community*, Washington D.C., Institute for International Economics

Patton Boggs LLP, 'International Dispute Resolution', www.pattonboggs.com/practice areas/a-z/27.html

Perin, M. (2000) 'Azurix Water Bugs Argentina', *Houston Business Journal*, May, http://houston.bizjournals.com/houston/stories/2000/05/08/tidbits.html

Peterson, L. E. (2001) 'Challenges Under Bilateral Investment Treaties Give Weight to Calls For Multilateral Rules', *World Trade Agenda*, October 21, www.iisd.org/trade/pubs.htm

Peterson, L. E. (2002) 'Dusted-off Trade Treaties Ensure There Is No Such Thing as a Free Riot', *The Guardian* (UK), May 6

Peterson, L. E. (2003a) 'Peru Launches Unprecedented State-to-State Arbitration in Dispute with Chile', *INVEST-SD News Bulletin*, March 28, www.iisd.org/pdf/2003/investment_investsd_march_2003.pdf

Peterson, L. E. (2003b) 'BIT Cases going to Swedish Arbitration Institute; Volume and Details Remain Elusive', *INVEST-SD News Bulletin*, July 13

Peterson, L. E. (2003c) 'Bolivian Water Privatization Dispute Will Continue Behind Closed Doors', *INVEST-SD News Bulletin*, February 7 & 14

Peterson, L. E. (2003d) 'Czech Broadcasting Dispute Heading Towards Final Damages, and Appeal in a Swedish Court', *INVEST-SD Bulletin*, February 21

Peterson, L. E. (2003e) 'Czech Republic Hit With Massive Compensation Bill in Investment Treaty Dispute', *INVEST-SD Bulletin*, March 21

Peterson, L. E. (2003f), 'Well-known Arbitrator Warns of "Crisis of Legitimacy" in International Arbitration', *INVEST-SD Bulletin*, November 21

Peterson, L. E. (2003g) 'Latest Arbitration Against Argentine Emergency Financial Measures', *INVEST-SD News Bulletin*, March 7

Peterson, L. E. (2003h) 'US Administration Warns WTO on Inviolability of its Bilateral Investment Treaties', *INVEST-SD News Bulletin*, May 9

Peterson, L. E. (2004) 'World Bank Arbitration Facility Sees Another Record Year of Investor–State Claims', *INVEST-SD News Bulletin*, 2 January, www.iisd.org/pdf/2004/investment_investd_jan5_2004.pdf

PSEG Energy Holdings Inc. (2002) US Securities and Exchange Commission (SEC) filing, March 11, www.sec.gov/Archives/edgar/data/1089206/000095013602000647/file001

Public Citizen (2002) Harmonization Alert, March–April, vol 2, no 9, www.publiccitizen.org/documents/harmmar1.PDF

Rogers, W. D. (2000) 'Emergence of the International Center for Settlement of Investment Disputes (ICSID) as the Most Significant Forum for Submission of Bilateral Investment Treaty Disputes', presentation to Inter-American Development Bank Conference, October 26–27

Salacuse, J. (1990) 'BIT by BIT: The Growth of Bilateral Investment Treaties and Their Impact on Foreign Investment in Developing Countries', *International Law*, vol 24, no 675

Sands, P. (2000) 'Arbitrating Environmental Disputes', Draft remarks at the annual ICSID/ICC/AAA Colloquim, November 10, Washington D.C., Quoted with permission of the author

Schwartz, E. A. (1994) 'The Domain of Arbitration and Issues of Arbitrability: The View from the ICC', *ICSID Review*, vol 9, no 1, Spring

Shihata, I. and A. Parra (1999) 'The Experience of ICSID', *ICSID Review*, vol 14, no 2, Fall

Sorieul, R.(2002) UNCITRAL Secretariat, personal communication with author, June 13

Stevens, M. (2002) 'Arbitration and Investment Disputes – Are We Heading in the Right Direction?', *ICSID News*, vol 19, no 1

Stevens, M. (2000) 'Confidentiality Revisited', Presentation to the 16th ICSID/American Arbitration Association/ICC Court Colloquium on International Arbitration, reprinted in *ICSID News*, Spring.

Thomas, J. C.(2002) 'A Reply to Professor Brower', *Columbia Journal of Transnational Law*, vol 40, no 3

Tollefson, C. (2002) 'Metalclad *v* United Mexican States Revisited: Judicial Oversight of NAFTA's Chapter 11 Investor State Claim Process', *Minnesota Journal of Global Trade*, vol 11, Summer

Tung, K. Y. (2001) 'Introduction by the Secretary General', ICSID, 2001 Annual Report, www.worldbank.org/icsid/pubs/2001ar/4.htm

UNCTAD (1998) Bilateral Investment Treaties in the Mid-1990s, UNCTAD/ITE/IIT/7

UNCTAD (1999a) 'Admission and Establishment', Series on Issues in International Investment Agreements, New York and Geneva, United Nations

UNCTAD (1999b) 'Scope and Definition', Series on Issues in International Investment Agreements, New York and Geneva, United Nations

UNCTAD (2000a) 'Taking of Property', Series on Issues in International Investment Agreements, United Nations, New York and Geneva

UNCTAD (2000b) Bilateral Investment Treaties 1959-1999, UNCTAD/ITE/IIA/2.

Vesely, V. (2001) Former official with ECT Secretariat, personal communication with author, August 15

Walde, T. (2002) Director, Center for Energy Petroleum and Mineral Law & Policy, University of Dundee, personal communication with author, May

Walde, T. and S. Dow (2000) 'Treaties and Regulatory Risk in Infrastructure Investment: The Effectiveness of International Law Disciplines versus Sanctions by Global Markets in Reducing the Political and Regulatory Risk for Private Infrastructure Investment,' *Journal of World Trade* vol 34, no 2

Chapter 6

The Road to Hell? Investor Protections in NAFTA's Chapter 11

Aaron Cosbey

ABSTRACT

NAFTA's (North American Free Trade Agreement) Chapter 11 was designed to protect North American investors from mistreatment at the hands of governments and thus to accelerate intra-regional investment. But it has proven more problematic than anyone imagined, triggering high-profile challenges by corporations against domestic environmental, health and safety measures. The challenges, in turn, have generated a storm of criticism by environmental and other public interest groups.

This chapter describes and analyses problems with the procedural and substantive provisions in Chapter 11 for the protection of foreign investors. These problems include the lack of transparency, accountability, and legitimacy in the investor–state dispute settlement process; the broad definition of 'investors'; and the overly broad interpretations of host state obligations in areas such as expropriation, non-discrimination, and minimum standards of treatment.

As a package, the Chapter 11 measures constitute a powerful mechanism to protect foreign investors. However, these tools have too often been used – in ways unintended by the drafters of the agreement – to attack or threaten public policy regulations that might incidentally harm investors' economic interests.

The chapter concludes by examining four potential solutions to these problems, each of which has its own shortcomings: 1) interpretive statements; 2) exceptions to the Chapter 11 obligations; 3) amendments to clarify the substantive provisions; and 4) reform of the arbitral institutions, UNCITRAL and ICSID.

INTRODUCTION

NAFTA's Chapter 11 was forged in the fires of good intention, designed to protect investors of the three NAFTA countries from mistreatment at the hands of governments and thus to accelerate investment among them, presumably for the benefit of all. But like the proverbial 'road to hell paved with good intentions', it has proven to be more problematic than anyone imagined during the pre–1995 negotiations. Chapter 11 has given rise to a number of high-profile challenges brought by corporations against environmental, health and safety measures taken by the three governments, providing fuel for the anger of myriad civil society organizations opposed to trade and investment liberalization.

This chapter examines the protection of investors of NAFTA parties investing in other NAFTA parties. NAFTA's Chapter 11 provisions on investor protection have a rich parentage in the many pre–1994 bilateral investment treaties (BITs), and before them in the early Commerce, Friendship and Navigation Treaties of the 19th century.

Chapter 11, however, singles itself out as an interesting case study for several reasons. It is the most open of any of the existing models (although critics argue forcefully that it still has far to go), meaning the various legal rulings are available for public scrutiny and analysis. Since the myriad other bodies of investment law do not, as a rule, release such documents, analysing the growing body of Chapter 11 case law is one of the only ways to gain insight into the implications of these other agreements.

Moreover, NAFTA is one of the 'modern' investment agreements, offering a greater degree of investor protection than afforded by the previous generation of agreements. As such, it is a good laboratory in which to examine the pros and cons of the standard elements of the modern BITs and regional investment agreements – elements which are likely to be the starting point of future investment agreements both bilaterally and in regional agreements such as the Free Trade Area of the Americas.

This chapter analyses Chapter 11 through the lens of its impacts on the environment, especially on regulatory capacity for environmental management. NAFTA's investor protection regime has, in recent years, weathered a great deal of criticism from the environmental and social justice communities (Mann, 2001; Tollefson, 2002; Greider, 2001). The central argument is that the regime has gone from being a protective shield for defending corporations against unfair treatment, to a sword used by those corporations to attack legitimate government regulation in the public interest, notably in areas such as public health and the environment. The process by which claims are lodged and pursued has also been widely criticized as being closed to public scrutiny, although this situation is now changing.

Section 2 outlines concerns with respect to the Chapter 11 process of dispute resolution, focusing on deficits of legitimacy, accountability and transparency. Section 3 turns to the five key substantive provisions of Chapter 11 – obligations that host countries have accepted in their treatment of investors from the other NAFTA parties. In each case it discusses the concerns voiced with respect to the environmental impact the provisions might entail, the discussion being informed by the cases to date.

In light of the preceding analysis, the final section of the chapter explores four options that have been proposed to address Chapter 11's shortcomings: an exception for environment, health and safety; interpretive statements; amendment of the NAFTA; and reform of the arbitral institutions UNCITRAL (United Nations Commission for International Trade Law) and ICSID (International Center for the Settlement of Investment Disputes).

Chapter 11's Dispute Settlement Process

In what is known as an investor–state dispute mechanism, NAFTA Chapter 11's dispute settlement process allows private parties (investors) to directly initiate arbitration with host states. This procedure contrasts with the process of trade law disputes, for example in the WTO, which are strictly state-to-state.

Chapter 11 allows parties to arbitrate cases under any of three pre-existing arbitration mechanisms: ICSID, the ICSID Additional Facility, and UNCITRAL (see Chapter 5). An investor initiates a case by submitting to the government involved a notice of intent to submit a claim to arbitration – a document that lays out the grounds for its case. Thereafter, the investor may submit its claim to any of the above venues, provided that the state involved is a signatory and that at least six months have passed since the events giving rise to the claim.

Until recently, investment arbitration was considered to be a private commercial matter between two disputants. Present institutions are still geared towards this concept. However, the majority of the Chapter 11 cases to date have had implications that go far beyond commercial impacts to such public policy objectives as the protection of the environment and public health and safety, in which more than the two disputants will share a legitimate interest (Mann and von Moltke, 2002). Two tribunals to date have been petitioned to grant friends of the court status to non-disputing, non-parties and both have agreed that the disputes go beyond purely commercial spats, one stating that 'there is an undoubtedly public interest in this arbitration' (Methanex Corp *v* the United States of America, 2001).

Rulings in such cases amount to a determination of the balance between competing public policy objectives, with final results that impact on the public welfare. In one pending case, for example, the right of the investor to import its product must be balanced against the right of the public to limit its exposure to suspected carcinogens (Crompton Corp *v* Canada, 2001). This type of balancing is done on a regular basis by a number of domestic institutions in all three NAFTA parties, including the judiciary and various governmental bodies. There is, however, a striking contrast in the attributes of these well-developed institutions and the commercial-model arbitration conducted under Chapter 11. The former are carefully constructed so as to operate with legitimacy, accountability and transparency, qualities that are – except for some transparency provisions in the case of ICSID – utterly lacking in the latter.

As to legitimacy, the Chapter 11 dispute process is lacking in several respects. First, each litigant is able to choose one of the three arbitrators and potentially to collaborate on the choice of the third – a situation that invites biased choice. Second, and in a directly related vein, the arbitrators themselves are not generally drawn from a permanent roster of arbitrators but from the international commercial arbitration bar. This is particularly the case for the third arbitrator selected as president of the panel. As a result, arbitrators can be deciding cases on one file while arbitrating on behalf of clients in other files facing similar legal issues. Decisions they make as arbitrators may impact the positions of their own clients, or of colleagues in their firms or through other contacts. The point here is not that the arbitrators lack personal integrity but rather that the system for selecting arbitrators is inherently flawed when issues of public and private rights are involved. The old maxim that justice must be blind is clearly not at play here.

As regards accountability, the investor–state dispute process allows only a very limited form of review, and the standard for review in such cases is much higher than that set for domestic appeals. In the end it is not an appeal process; the review cannot rule on simple errors of fact or law, or substitute a decision for the one made by the tribunal. The widely acknowledged value of the World Trade Organization's (WTO's) permanent appellate body in giving consistency and predictability to the process should be seen as instructive.

Moreover, both legitimacy and accountability are impossible where there is no transparency. On this score, even Chapter 11's strongest supporters agree that change would be beneficial. As befits a purely commercial dispute mechanism, there is no provision for mandatory public access to the litigation documents. ICSID cases must at least be notified in a public registry available on the ICSID website (ICSID), but UNCITRAL lacks even this basic requirement. There is an obligation on the NAFTA secretariat to keep a public register of notices of intent to arbitrate, but compliance with this obligation has been patchy at best. However, there is no requirement to inform the public when an investor signals its intention to arbitrate a case.

There have been promising signs of change on this score. Most prominent was the set of statements emerging from the October 7, 2003, meeting of the NAFTA trade ministers – the Free Trade Commission (Mann, 2003). These included a joint statement of suggested guidelines for considering petitions for *amicus curiae*, or friend of the court, status. A non-party might seek such status in order to intervene in the proceedings of a particular case. The statement outlines the FTC's recommendations for how a tribunal might decide whether to accept or reject such petitions, which have, in the past, been controversial. However, while the FTC has the power to issue binding interpretations of Chapter 11's substantive provisions, its power over the tribunals' proceedings is limited; its guidance on this matter is not legally binding, but does carry some weight.

A second important outcome of the October 2003 meeting is a pair of statements from Canada and the US indicating that they will push for public hearings in all Chapter 11 cases – a commitment that Mexico apparently was not ready to countenance (*US Trade Representative*, 2003). Again, this is not a legally binding decision. Indeed, previous tribunals have ruled that proceedings may not be opened to the public without the consent of both arbitrating parties (that is, the investor must also agree). But it does mean that in every case against them the two governments are now committed to push for such openness.

It should be emphasized that the shortcomings surveyed above are not criticisms of the right to an investor–state process per se. The history of investment protection shows that it is probably best not left up to governments, who may respond only to bigger players, and whose decisions whether to proceed with any given claim will always be tied up in the politics of the moment (Vandevelde, 1992). But taken together they are an indictment of an inadequate process for the balancing of private rights and public goods in the investment context.

The Substantive Provisions

NAFTA's Chapter 11 contains a number of provisions that oblige the host country to accord certain types of treatment for investments from its NAFTA partners. These provisions include the following:

- Protection from direct or indirect expropriation (Article 1110).
- National treatment obligations (Article 1102).
- Most-favoured nation obligations (Article 1103).
- Prohibition of performance requirements (Article 1106).
- Obligations for minimum international standards of treatment (Article 1105).

Together, these provisions and others in the chapter constitute an accord among the NAFTA governments on what constitutes fair treatment of investors from the other NAFTA countries. The specifics of each of these provisions are examined in more detail below, but as background it is worth first elaborating on the *scope and coverage* of the obligations. That is, these provisions restrict the types of measures that can be imposed on investments. To fully understand the impacts of the provisions, we must first understand how NAFTA defines both 'measures' and 'investments'.

The definitions are unusually broad. The measures covered by Chapter 11 include 'any law, regulation, procedure, requirement or practice'. This covers most conceivable acts of government (at all levels from federal to municipal), from lawmaking to zoning codes, and even extending to cover the actions of the courts.

Investment is also broadly defined, encompassing not only direct investment by an enterprise, but also such things as a debt security or loan to an enterprise, or equity securities in an enterprise. A holder of a bond from a multinational enterprise is thus an investor, conferred with the extensive legal rights discussed below.

This broad definition has been extended by several rulings that have held that a company's *market share* is an investment asset that can be protected. When the US market share of Pope & Talbot – a US-owned forest products company operating in Canada – decreased as a result of Canadian government policy, the tribunal agreed that this market share itself was an 'investment' protected by the provisions of Chapter 11[1]. In effect, this approach has the potential to bring the full gamut of *trade* measures, such as bans and restrictions, under the purview of NAFTA's *investment* law, as most trade measures will affect market share. This would greatly extend the reach of the provisions, and would grant more access to the direct investor–state process (discussed below) than was arguably ever intended.

Expropriation

Article 1110 stipulates that any expropriation must fulfill four conditions. It must be:

- for a public purpose;
- non-discriminatory (that is, not targeted at a specific company or nationality);
- in accordance with the due process of law; and
- compensated by the expropriating government.

It also notes that its strictures cover both direct and indirect expropriation but, importantly, fails to define these terms. This is not so problematic with the former; direct expropriation – the physical taking or nationalization of an enterprise – is easy to identify, and there is a significant body of international law to guide arbitrators in addressing it.

But indirect expropriation is much more difficult. Indirect expropriation has three separate forms. One is commonly referred to as 'creeping expropriation'. This implies a series of measures that collectively have the effect of depriving an owner of their property, even where one individual measure would not do so. A firm, for example, might be subject to increasingly onerous reporting requirements, increased tax burden, mandated replacement of its foreign managers with locals, a permit system for importing key inputs, etc. By themselves none of these types of measures would constitute an expropriation, but combined they may be sufficient to drive a company out of business. Note that it is not necessary for a business to be 'taken' by the government in order for indirect expropriation to occur – depriving the owner of its investment, even if the investment does not then go to the state, is sufficient.

The second form is disguised expropriation, whereby a measure is really intended to deprive a person of their property or of all ability to use it, but does so through essentially indirect or disguised means. Rather than nationalizing an investment outright, for example, a country might levy an impossibly high tax on the firm involved, with the intent of putting it out of business. These two forms of indirect expropriation achieve more or less the same final effect as direct expropriation[2].

The third and most controversial concept of indirect expropriation falls under the notion of regulatory taking, a US concept that was, until NAFTA, largely foreign to international law. This doctrine holds that a regulation amounts to a form of indirect expropriation by virtue of having a significant negative impact on the economic value of an investment. For example, a government might enact land use regulations that preclude the kind of activity in which a firm is engaged. With the advent of NAFTA's Chapter 11, this expanded concept of expropriation moved to centre stage in the arbitrations initiated by foreign investors under its provisions. The comments that follow are focused on this third form of indirect expropriation – regulatory takings.

The key question in the NAFTA context is this: If a NAFTA government measure is undertaken for a clear public welfare purpose (such as health and safety, environment, public morals or order, etc.) and is non-discriminatory, but has the effect of harming a NAFTA foreign investor, are there any circumstances under which that measure can be held to be an indirect expropriation for which the government must pay compensation? If so, what are those circumstances?

The concern is obvious: most people would agree that taxpayers should not be paying investors to alter behaviour that is contrary to the public interest. A secondary concern is that regulators who are held liable for their impacts on investors will not regulate to the extent that they should (the *regulatory chill* argument).

What might allay these concerns? Most obvious would be a clear statement that regulations that apply to all firms (that is, non-discriminatory regulations of general application) cannot be held to constitute expropriation. However, such an approach would leave a very wide scope for governments to cloak expropriation in the guise of regulation. Even critics of Chapter 11 concede that such a broad statement is not workable (Mann and Soloway, 2002).

Failing that, we might look for some delineation that would exempt *bona fide* public welfare regulations from being considered expropriation. That is, non-discriminatory regulations that are obviously intended to serve the public good, such as environmental protection and human health and safety measures, while they might impact on the profitability of some companies, could not be held to be expropriation. This would necessarily involve defining the 'untouchable' regulations, or at least giving guidance as to their characteristics.

But drawing that bright line in the sand has proven too difficult a task for the NAFTA parties, despite years of debate and discussions. In the words of one of the tribunals, it is difficult to say 'when governmental action that interferes with broadly-defined property rights . . . crosses the line from valid regulation to a compensable taking, and it is fair to say that no one has come up with a fully satisfactory means of drawing this line' (Marvin Feldman *v* Mexico, 2002, para 100).

Finally, failing guidance from the lawmakers, we might hope to see some signs that the tribunals were at least considering the purpose of regulations, as opposed to simply looking at the extent to which they affected investors. Such a consideration would, in the end, come close to being a case-by-case determination of what regulations should be exempt, presumably on the basis of their *bona fides* and their public welfare objectives.

In one of the first cases to consider the expropriation argument, the Metalclad tribunal considered the case of a US hazardous waste company (Metalclad Corp.) that was eventually denied the ability to establish a hazardous waste processing facility in Mexico, first by bureaucratic means and finally by the decree that the land on which the plant was located would henceforth be a nature reserve for the preservation of rare cactus species. The tribunal in this case ruled that 'the tribunal need not decide or consider the motivation or intent of the adoption of the Ecological Decree' (Metalclad, 2002, para 111). The fact that there was substantial interference was enough to establish expropriation, and it was unnecessary to ask *why* that interference had occurred.

The tribunal in Pope & Talbot (2000), which considered whether that company's Canadian forest products export business had been expropriated by Canadian forest management regulations, took a similar tack: the test of whether there has been an expropriation has nothing to do with the measure's objectives but is judged only by the degree of interference (Pope and Talbot *v* Canada, 2000, para 102). If followed, this reasoning threatens to seriously erode the ability of governments to regulate in the public interest. Or, more precisely, it would have governments pay each time such regulations sufficiently impacted the private sector, even if the regulations were non-discriminatory and were legitimately designed to serve the public good.

Subsequent rulings have taken a different approach, holding that while a regulation can clearly constitute an expropriation, this will only rarely be the case. But there is still no guidance on how to distinguish between those that do and do not cross the line based on their purpose.

One positive development is a test introduced by the tribunal in the S.D. Meyers case, where a US-based processor of PCBs complained that its investment in Canada had been expropriated by a Canadian export ban on PCBs. While the tribunal still did not go to the purpose of the measure in denying a finding of expropriation, it did rule that 'expropriations tend to involve the deprivation of ownership rights; regulations a lesser interference' (S. D. Meyers Inc. *v* Canada, 2000, para 282). Specifically, the tribunal noted that an expropriation usually amounts to 'a lasting removal of the ability of an owner to make use of its economic rights'.

This same standard was followed in the subsequent Feldman case, where the Mexican tax authorities in effect shut down a 'grey market' cigarette exporting business through regulations that the business could not possibly meet (Marvin Feldman *v* Mexico, 2002, paras 152–153). This is a higher standard than one that simply looks at the degree of interference, and one that if followed would save most regulatory measures from being found to be expropriation.

Also hopeful in the Feldman ruling is the fact that the tribunal was guided in its considerations by the American Law Institute's 'Restatement of the Law Third, the Foreign Relations of the US', which says on the subject of regulatory expropriation:

> *A state is not responsible for loss of property or for other economic disadvantage resulting from* bona fide *general taxation, regulation, forfeiture for crime, or other action of the kind that is commonly accepted as within the police power of states, if it is not discriminatory. . . .*
>
> (American Law Institute, 1987)

In other words, if the measure in question is propounded in good faith and is non-discriminatory, then it cannot constitute an expropriation no matter what the extent of the damage. The Feldman tribunal did not go so far as to use this reasoning in its findings and did not actually consider whether the measure met these criteria. But the fact that it referenced this passage and used it as guidance shows at least that there is a viable alternative to the approach used in Metalclad and Pope & Talbot.

National treatment

Article 1102 obliges parties to 'accord to investments of investors of another party treatment that is no less favourable than that it accords, in like circumstances, to those of its own investors'. The main cause for concern here is the difficulty in determining whether circumstances are 'like'. Clearly the text does not mean 'identical', but neither does it give any guidance on how to determine whether circumstances are sufficiently similar as to trigger this obligation.

For example, if several existing firms are already polluting to the maximum allowed in a certain ecosystem, would a refusal to permit a foreign investor to open another plant at the same site amount to a breach of national treatment? Certainly the foreign investor is not being treated as well as the existing domestic firms. If there is existing legislation that applies to all firms this may not be an issue – any reasonable panel would give deference to regulatory authority in such a case. But if there is no existing legislation covering the situation, and the new entrant faces a licensing process that turns it down, or faces new legislation designed to deal with the new problem of potentially excess pollution at the site, then the jury is out as to how a panel would interpret such a situation.

The rulings to date have been mixed, and have left us not much closer to an agreed understanding of how to determine like circumstances. In a particularly convoluted piece of reasoning, the S. D. Meyers panel ruled that a Canadian processor of hazardous waste was in 'like circumstances' with a Canadian office established by the US investor for the purpose of brokering the export of hazardous waste. That being established, it was a simple matter to show that an export ban on hazardous waste accorded very different treatment to the two, although both were equally bound by it.

The ruling in the ADF case also gives pause for thought. ADF was a contractor bidding to supply structural steel components in a Virginia highway construction project, but as its offices are located in Canada it ran afoul of the Federal 'Buy USA' regulations that cover any project with Federal support. The tribunal ruled that both ADF and the US competitors were in like circumstances – both had to comply with the same local content regulations. But it also seemed to suggest that if ADF had more strongly made a case for economic damage as a result of the regulation, it would have successfully demonstrated a breach of the national treatment obligations (ADF *v* United States of America, 2003, para 157)[3].

The tribunal in Pope & Talbot (2000), on the other hand, used reasoning that gives more hope for the rational application of national treatment obligations. Pope & Talbot, a US-owned forest products company operating in the Canadian province of British Columbia, had argued that it was in like circumstances with producers in those provinces that were not restricted by the quotas of the Canada–US softwood lumber agreement. The tribunal rejected these arguments, noting that the differential treatment bore a 'reasonable relationship to rational policies not motivated by preference of domestic over foreign owned investments'. This is a welcome sign of deference to governmental authority in balancing the many competing priorities of public policy.

A second feature of NAFTA's national treatment provisions is that they are part of the rights of investors both before and after they have made an investment. In other words, foreign investors are due national treatment not only 'post-establishment' but also 'pre-establishment'. While NAFTA permitted exceptions to be made, and each party availed itself of this opportunity, the general principle of the right of foreign NAFTA investors to make investments into the territory of another party is established here[4]. While it appears in a limited number of pre-NAFTA investment treaties, the concept of a foreign investor's 'right to invest' reached a new breadth in the NAFTA context. This approach to pre-establishment rights is intimately linked with the ability of governments to establish and implement domestic development strategies.

Most-favoured nation treatment

Article 1103 states that parties shall accord to investors and investments of other parties: 'treatment no less favourable than it accords, in like circumstances, to investors of any other Party or of a non-Party . . .' In other words, all NAFTA parties shall be 'most-favoured'.

There is, of course, the same problem here as in the national treatment provisions: what constitutes like circumstances? But another concern haunts the most-favoured nation (MFN) obligations.

The MFN obligations may provide a way to import into NAFTA the most favourable treatment found in any of the bilateral treaties signed by the defendant in a dispute. That is, if a party is obliged under NAFTA to provide a certain standard of protection, but a higher standard exists in a treaty signed by that party with a non-NAFTA country, does the most-favoured nation obligation mean that the higher standard prevails? An example illustrates the power of this possibility. The US and Zaire have a bilateral investment treaty that sets a very low threshold for finding regulatory expropriation, protecting against any measures that cause, 'the impairment of [the investment's] management, control or economic value'. Such a standard would arguably be unacceptable to the NAFTA parties, and was arguably not part of the accord they thought they were signing[5].

Should this US–Zaire standard be accorded to Mexican and Canadian investors in the US by means of Chapter 11 MFN obligations? This possibility is more than speculative. At least one bilateral investment treaty dispute (Maffezini *v* the Kingdom of Spain) found in favour of such a use of the treaty's MFN provisions[6]. Closer to home, several Chapter 11 claimants have argued that the NAFTA Free Trade Commission's 2001 interpretive statement (discussed below) – on minimum international standard of treatment – is worthless, since a stronger standard of treatment exists in various BITs, and since Article 1103 obliges the parties to accord the higher standard. This argument was favourably considered in Pope & Talbot (2000), although the tribunal did not find it necessary to rule on it: 'The tribunal's view is well known – the Commission's interpretation would, because of Article 1103 . . . produce the absurd result of relief denied under 1105 but restored under 1103.'[7] The tribunal is arguing, in other words, that it is absurd that the MFN provisions in BITs can 'restore' the protections the FTC's interpretation has allegedly removed.

The ADF tribunal considered this argument as well, but did not have to rule on its validity since it held that the obligations the claimant was trying to import (from US BITs with Albania and Estonia) were equivalent to those in Chapter 11 (ADF *v* United States of America, 2003, paras 194–195).

The above description points to the need to carefully consider the relationship between different treaties when they are drafted. If the inclusion of an MFN provision along the lines used in NAFTA results in the risk of a reading in of investor rights and remedies negotiated in another context, and the potential expansion of any rights, obligations and remedies negotiated in the WTO context, this would raise very significant concerns from both a legal and policy perspective. Note, however, that even in the Maffezini context the tribunal was careful to stress that MFN could not, in their view, reach across different issues (e.g. import a transparency standard into a minimum international standards obligation that does not already deal with transparency), or act so as to thwart the clear wishes of the parties.

Performance requirements

Article 1106 of NAFTA prohibits host countries from imposing certain types of requirements on investors as a condition of entry and establishment. Among the requirements proscribed are demands to export a certain percentage of sales, demands to purchase locally for certain inputs and demands to transfer certain technologies to the host country.

The concerns that arise from this type of prohibition are twofold. First, many developing countries have expressed the view that this approach prohibits them from adopting the very types of tools that developed countries have used to promote their own development. Thus, a direct relationship with setting and implementing domestic development goals and strategies is implicated by performance requirement prohibitions. This is not an environmental problem per se, but falls clearly within the wider remit of sustainable development.

Second, there is a connection to certain types of regulatory measures. It has been argued in several cases now (although no ruling has yet been issued) that an import ban constitutes a performance requirement by forcing an investor to use only domestically sourced materials in its production processes or services. This was part of the claim in the Ethyl case[8]. Canada had banned the import of a gasoline additive – MMT, a suspected neurotoxin – and Ethyl argued that this meant its Canadian subsidiary would have to substitute local alternatives for imports from its US parent plant. Because the case was settled out of court, there was no ruling on this argument.

The same argument is now part of the claim against Canada in the Crompton case, where Canada banned the import of lindane-based seed treatments for canola on environment and health grounds. Crompton US, the manufacturer, plans to argue that the ban forces its Canadian subsidiary to buy local substitutes, and thus is in effect a local purchasing requirement (Crompton Corp *v* Government of Canada, 2001).

It is clear that the obligations on performance requirements were not intended to provide a remedy for measures that limit imports or exports for the sake of public protection from environmental and health hazards. However, this issue continues to arise in various cases. It is equally clear that prohibitions on performance requirements are intended to curtail the same types of development policies used by western countries over the entire 20th century. Thus, both the environmental and developmental pillars of sustainable development face challenges from this type of article.

Minimum standard of treatment

Article 1105 requires that investors shall receive treatment 'in accordance with international law, including fair and equitable treatment . . .'. The text leaves this requirement undefined, and before it was specifically ruled out by a Free Trade Commission (FTC) interpretive note dated July 2001, several cases interpreted it to mean that investors were due treatment spelled out in *any* international law, including the WTO, and even non-Chapter 11 parts of NAFTA[9]. The interpretive statement narrows the scope considerably, asserting that the parties meant to commit to treatment in accordance with customary international law.

Still, this does not leave matters completely resolved, as there is no clear-cut consensus on what constitutes customary international law in this area. But it has at least narrowed the scope for bringing into Chapter 11 a wide variety of law that is not specified anywhere in its text.

Possible Solutions

It has been argued above that the provisions of Chapter 11 are being interpreted, or risk being interpreted, in ways that are overly broad. This problem, of course, is compounded by the expansive definitions of investments and measures, giving a wide scope to extremely effective investor protections.

It needs to be asked: What is wrong with giving broad, effective protection to investors? Investment, after all, can be an engine of sustainable development. And the growth it brings can, if managed appropriately, bring real welfare benefits (although note the critical caveats offered in Chapter 1).

Whether the NAFTA parties are currently equipped to manage growth appropriately is beyond the scope of this chapter. The issue of more direct relevance to the present enquiry is one of balance. Expanding the rights of private investors typically comes at the expense of the rights of the public at large. This is perhaps most clearly demonstrated in the granting of patents, which allow a limited monopoly (monopolies always being against the public interest, other things being equal) as a reward to investment and innovation. To use an example from the context of investment law, Metalclad Corp.'s right to run a hazardous waste processing facility outside San Luis Potosi, Mexico, must be balanced against the public's right to an ecological preserve on that same land. Neither right is absolute, and it is normally the task of governments to find the appropriate balance.

The concern expressed by many with NAFTA's Chapter 11 is that there seems to be real potential to shift the balance unduly in favour of investor protection and away from the public good. It is not at all clear that the parties anticipated the broad readings of Chapter 11's provisions now being accepted or contemplated. Or, if they did, it is not at all clear that the balance they strike, or threaten to strike, would be acceptable to the public at large.

The issues discussed above have at their core a concern that NAFTA's Chapter 11 may restrict the parties' ability to exercise their legitimate authority to regulate in the public interest. That is, in seeking to protect investors from egregious government behaviour, Chapter 11 may tip the balance too far in their favour, to the detriment of non-commercial, public policy objectives such as environmental integrity and public health and safety.

Given those concerns, and the public policy implications of many of the cases to date, there is also concern at the closed nature of the dispute resolution proceedings, although there are welcome signs that this situation is changing. Still unaddressed is the problem that experts in international law are being asked to preside over proceedings that must balance between the private rights of investors and the public good – a position for which they are arguably not qualified.

There have therefore been a number of calls for reform both of the substance of NAFTA's Chapter 11 provisions and the process of dispute resolution. In examining them, it is useful to keep in mind that the two types of reform are very different propositions. As discussed below, some of the proposed solutions work better for one type than for the other. The proposals fall into three main categories, the pros and cons of which are discussed below:

- Interpretive statements issued by the FTC.
- Exceptions in Chapter 11 for environment, health and safety.
- Amendment of the Chapter 11 text to narrow its scope, add precision to provisions, and to improve the dispute resolution process.

Interpretive statements

NAFTA states: 'An interpretation by the [Free Trade] Commission of a provision of this Agreement shall be binding on a tribunal established under this Section' (NAFTA, Article 1131 (2)). In other words the FTC – the three NAFTA ministers of trade – may issue binding interpretations of the Chapter 11 provisions, presumably in circumstances of uncertainty. Given the concerns that have been voiced about the overly-broad interpretation of Chapter 11's provisions, an obvious solution would seem to be interpretive statements issued by the FTC clarifying exactly what the drafters meant by, for example, indirect expropriation.

In fact the FTC did issue such a statement (hereafter, the FTC statement) in July 2001 (NAFTA Free Trade Commission, 2001). It had two parts: first, an interpretation of Article 1105 (minimum international standards of treatment); and second, a clarification and commitment on the issue of transparency. (A more recent statement, discussed above, dealt only with process issues.) An analysis of this statement illustrates the limited function such a mechanism can play in reforming some of the problems identified in this chapter (Cosbey, 2001).

The FTC statement had asserted that NAFTA's drafters, when promising treatment in accordance with international law, in fact meant *customary* international law – a much weaker standard of protection. The FTC interpretation of the obligations on minimum standards of treatment has been criticized on two grounds. First, it has been argued that Chapter 11's MFN provisions can end-run any attempts to limit the scope of those obligations by reference to bilateral investment agreements where the parties have already committed to a stronger standard of protection. This is arguably not much of a stumbling block, since the FTC could simply issue a subsequent interpretation limiting this sort of reading of the MFN provisions.

Another fault is that in several cases the investor has argued that the 'interpretation' was in fact an amendment, since it actually changed the meaning intended by the drafters. While the FTC has authority to render binding interpretations, actual amendment is a much more difficult process, and is outside the FTC's jurisdiction. The Pope & Talbot tribunal was inclined to agree with this argument, but did not in the end rule on it. Several panels since then have ruled against this argument and the growing consensus is that the FTC interpretation will not be successfully challenged as an amendment (Mondev, 2002; ADF *v* United States of America, 2003).

This brings us back to the proposition that the interpretive statement is a solution to the problems identified in this chapter. While the early attacks on the FTC's first interpretive statement as an 'amendment' dimmed hopes that this mechanism would be useful, the recent cases have given more cause for optimism. Probably any interpretation worth its salt will repeatedly be the target of the same type of legal attack, but at this point such attacks look likely to fail. This leaves the interpretive statement as a good potential tool for reinterpreting the troubling provisions surveyed above.

However, the potential is much lower that interpretive statements can address Chapter 11's problems with the process of dispute resolution[10]. The discussion above of the October 2003 FTC statements indicated that this route might be problematic. Using the 2001 statement is also instructive. The statement commits the parties to 'make available to the public in a timely manner all documents submitted to, or issued by, a Chapter 11 tribunal'. This pledge is subject to three possible exceptions, one of which is vitally important: except for 'information which the party must withhold pursuant to the relevant arbitral rules, as applied'.

Early Chapter 11 tribunals established high levels of secrecy which would have been fundamentally altered by the parties' commitments, were they fulfilled[11]. But then again, in none of these cases *could* they have been fulfilled, since the information in question was being withheld pursuant to the relevant arbitral rules. The problem here is one of jurisdiction. By ICSID and UNCITRAL rules, each tribunal at the outset agrees with the parties on rules of procedure, including confidentiality orders. While the parties may have authority to issue interpretations of the NAFTA provisions, they have no authority to interpret or change the procedural rules of ICSID or UNCITRAL. The only way this agreement will have any impact is as a morally binding commitment on the part of the governments to promote more transparent proceedings when such issues arise for decision-making by a tribunal (Cosbey, 2001). This may assist in setting a better direction.

On other process issues, such as changing the selection process for arbitrators, and opening up the process to public input and observation, the FTC has even less sway, although the 2003 FTC statements contained commitments by the US and Canada to consent to, and ask for, Chapter 11 hearings that are open to the public. These are not part of the rules of procedure on which parties agree in each case, and are either the prerogative of the tribunal, or are laid down in the rules of ICSID and UNCITRAL.

Thus, while in some cases interpretive statements may help curtail some expansive readings of the provisions, they may be subject to attack as *de facto* amendments. And because the process of arbitration is governed outside the NAFTA's legal framework, there is only so much that FTC statements can do to address Chapter 11's process faults.

An environment, health and safety exception in Chapter 11

An exception would be an addition to the text of NAFTA that exempted parties from their Chapter 11 obligations when applying specified types of measures. The most commonly called for types are those aimed at protection of human health and safety, and protection of the environment, but it is not difficult to think of other important public policy goals that might also merit inclusion on the list.

The proposal for such a mechanism derives in large part from the existence of similar exceptions in trade law. Perhaps the best known example is Article XX of the General Agreement on Tariffs and Trade (GATT): General Exceptions. This article lists ten types of measures that can be exempted from GATT law, including measures:

- necessary to protect public morals;
- necessary to protect human, animal or plant life or health;
- relating to the products of prison labour;
- imposed for the protection of national treasures of artistic, historic or archaeological value;
- relating to the conservation of exhaustible natural resources;
- essential to the acquisition or distribution of products in general or local short supply.

Before a measure can be considered as benefiting from these exceptions, it must qualify as per the opening paragraph to Article XX (the *chapeau*), which demands that the measures in question not be 'applied in a manner which would constitute a means of arbitrary or unjustifiable discrimination between countries where the same conditions prevail, or a disguised restriction on international trade'. In other words, GATT will allow exceptions, but the drafters wanted to make sure that the exceptions were not abused to protect domestic producers under the guise of loftier principles.

Three considerations make this option questionable. First, to request an exception for a given behaviour is to concede that such behaviour is not normal and acceptable in the first place. Some argue that in the investment arena there should be a presumption of the right to regulate in the public interest, especially given the life span and potentially broad societal impacts of a productive investment (Mann, 2002). This right may be circumscribed by international agreement, but to *start* by assuming that regulating in the public interest is illegal (save for certain exceptions) seems a weak position. It has been suggested throughout the above analysis that some of the expanded interpretations have gone beyond what was intended by the drafters of NAFTA – an argument that would be severely compromised by seeking exceptions to cover the newly prohibited behaviour.

But if the effect is the same, should we care how the objective is achieved? The second cause for worry is that the effect is not the same. The experience of the GATT shows that the Article XX exceptions are an extremely tough hurdle to clear. Any wording intended to prevent protectionism will undoubtedly cause a great deal of error on the side of caution. For example, the term 'necessary' in the environmental exception above has been read by the panels to mean 'least trade-restrictive' – a characteristic possessed by relatively few measures.

A third cause for concern is that an EH&S exception would not by itself address the process problems identified above. This is not a serious fault, since addressing those problems and creating exceptions are not mutually exclusive endeavours. Since the NAFTA would have to be amended to accomplish the former, the latter could be revised at the same time.

A final cause for concern is precisely that adding exceptions would involve amending the NAFTA. This would be an extremely difficult proposition. The problem is that most trade agreements (or, more accurately, trade, investment and other related policy agreements) are something like an over-packed storage trunk that one has had to greatly compress to finally get it closed and locked. They are usually nailed down at the last minute, under great pressure, by way of compromises that none of the parties is particularly happy with, but with which they all can live. It will not be a simple matter to go into the storage trunk to retrieve just one pair of socks – once it is sprung open all manner of things are coming out again. As of this writing, for example, the Mexican government is under extreme pressure to reopen NAFTA's Chapter 7 to obtain more protection for its agricultural sector. Further, Mexico is being pressured by partners in other trade agreements to re-open those agreements in *their* favour, and the precedent set by renegotiating NAFTA would be impossible to downplay. It is no wonder the trade ministries are loathe to bring the trunk out of the closet.

Given the first two weaknesses cited above, if we are to embark on amendment, it would seem wiser to undertake a comprehensive repacking while we have the trunk open. The next section considers such a course of action.

Amending Chapter 11

The previous section made it clear that there is little political appetite for re-opening the NAFTA to fix Chapter 11. The paradox is that amendment would be the most direct route for implementing the types of fixes discussed above. In terms of substantive concerns, it would be theoretically simple to open the NAFTA to insert language specifying in greater detail the intent of the original drafting on provisions such as expropriation and minimum standards of treatment. Such an approach would not suffer the fate of interpretive statements that have been challenged as amendments in disguise.

The difficulty, particularly with respect to expropriation, would be in finding language that gave appropriate space to legitimate government regulations, exempting them from being found compensable expropriations, without creating a gaping loophole for government misbehaviour. As noted above, the challenge of how to draw this fine line was deemed too tough by the original negotiators, and has been a stumbling block for the FTC in saying anything on the subject by way of interpretation.

In terms of changes to the process of dispute resolution, the amendment route would be more effective than either an interpretive statement (which has only persuasive force) or an exception (which has no force). It could not involve the FTC dictating changes to the rules of UNCITRAL or ICSID, the frameworks in which the arbitrations actually take place; these are multilaterally agreed conventions. But within those frameworks it could do either of two things.

It could commit the parties to certain types of transparency that depend on the will of the parties under the current rules. For example, it could commit the parties to agreeing to release case documents (as do the FTC statements of October 2003, discussed above), but could also make such agreement on the part of the investor a prerequisite to launching a case.

It could set up a dispute settlement system that was entirely ad hoc and separate from either the UNCITRAL or ICSID rules. Of course any such system would be modelled in large part on such rules, but as an ad hoc system could, for example, specify the procedures to be followed in accepting *amicus* briefs, an area under which the FTC has no legal jurisdiction within the UNCITRAL and ICSID frameworks.

The difficulty of amending the NAFTA boils down to the fact that if it is opened for one purpose (such as amending Chapter 11), it is effectively open for all purposes – a prospect that would put the political leaders of the time under intense pressure to renegotiate key areas, and which might doom the talks to years of difficult wrangling. It might be possible for the parties to draft an agreement in advance of re-opening the agreement, specifying exactly which elements were touchable. The key question is whether such an agreement would be respected once the negotiations were underway.

In concluding, it is worth noting that the NAFTA itself was actually completed in 1992, although it entered into force in 1994. Thus, the text is already over 11 years old. In the lifespan of any major trade treaty, it is inevitable that after a decade or so the parties seek to expand, alter and fine tune an agreement. In the case of NAFTA, there is a risk that amendments might be made through additions, without revisiting some of the more controversial elements such as Chapter 11. This potential should be carefully monitored.

Amending ICSID and UNCITRAL

If amending NAFTA is the most direct route to giving greater clarity to its substantive provisions, amending the ICSID and UNCITRAL rules is similarly the most direct route to fixing NAFTA's problems of process. But just as opening the NAFTA to agreement among three parties would be extremely difficult, opening the ICSID Convention and negotiating changes to the UNCITRAL rules (both would need to be altered) would be a Herculean task.

The ICSID Convention has some 140 parties, and UNCITRAL rules would have to be changed from within the UN system by consensus. The types of change proposed here (transparency of proceedings, openness to *amicus* briefs, a roster of arbitrators) are certain to be a hard sell to some governments, particularly those with a tradition of closed dealings with their citizens, and those worried about the embarrassment of having their possible misbehaviour aired in full public view.

This option should not be ignored, as it represents a powerful way to change the way disputes are handled not only in the NAFTA, but in the myriad of bilateral investment treaties and investment contracts that resort to ICSID and UNCITRAL as frameworks of arbitration. The challenges involved, however, are daunting.

Conclusions

NAFTA's Chapter 11 aims to protect investors from unfair treatment at the hands of host governments, with the desired result of greater investment flows. Whether, and in what circumstances, such investment is beneficial to the host country, has been studied elsewhere (see Chapter 1 and Chapter 2). This chapter has focused on the unintended effects of the rules themselves.

The substantive provisions of Chapter 11 are being tested in the early years of the agreement by imaginative claimants who seek to stretch its intended interpretations to afford ever greater protections for investors[12]. Those protections may come at the expense of other public policy objectives; as this chapter has shown, there are a number of troubling ways in which the provisions might be interpreted that would restrict the parties' ability to regulate in the public interest. Moreover, as such claims notch up victories, the mere *threat* of a Chapter 11 suit may constitute an attractive weapon in the arsenal of firms looking to forestall or weaken regulations that affect them.

These problems are compounded by the procedural weaknesses of Chapter 11's dispute settlement system. While it looks as though the issues of public access and transparency are being addressed, if slowly, there remain a number of worrying institutional problems, such as the lack of an effective appeal mechanism, and the questionable selection process for arbitrators.

Further, it is inappropriate that the balancing of public policy priorities such as health and safety, the environment and economic growth be conducted outside of government and with few of the procedural safeguards that help ensure legitimacy, transparency and accountability.

Interpretive statements seem to be the repair tool of choice for the NAFTA trade ministers, and there is some reason to hope that these will have a positive influence, at least in terms of interpreting the obligations. As to reforming dispute settlement, that particular tool is not well suited since the process relies on rules over which the parties have little control – ICSID and UNCITRAL. Reforming those rules, or opening up the NAFTA to reform the process by amendment, present seemingly intractable difficulties.

It is, however, important to get it right in the NAFTA context, if only because the NAFTA parties and others are busy drafting investment rules in other contexts including the Free Trade Area of the Americas, various bilateral agreements and possibly the World Trade Organization. Just as NAFTA has served as an instructive laboratory for the weaknesses of the typical investment agreement, it should strive to serve as an example of how the shortcomings of such agreements can be addressed, such that investment agreements actually help to achieve sustainable development.

When it is expressed in those terms, such an objective seems eminently reasonable, even uncontroversial. And so it should be. It is a pity that the propriety of the objective is not matched by the simplicity of the solutions.

ENDNOTES

1 The tribunal in the end ruled, however, that this 'investment' had not suffered enough of an impact that the measure in question could be held to be expropriation. See Pope & Talbot paras 97–98.
2 Article 1110 also refers to measures 'tantamount to' expropriation. The consensus to date is that this is equivalent to indirect expropriation.
3 Note that this breach itself would have been saved by the fact that the tribunal found the Virginia contract to be 'government procurement' as defined in the NAFTA, and therefore not subject to Chapter 11's non-discrimination obligations (as per Article 1108(7)).
4 See Annex I of NAFTA for these exceptions.
5 This assertion is based on the language of the recent US Trade Promotion Authority Act, which mandates that in future trade and investment agreements 'foreign investors in the United States are not accorded greater rights than United States investors in the United States' – a condition that would be violated if foreign investors were accorded the US–Zaire-level of protection. And it is based on the public comments by Canada's Minister of Trade questioning the value of a broad interpretation of Article 1110. The author has no evidence of a Mexican position on expropriation but strongly suspects that the US–Zaire language would be unacceptable. Also see Been and Beauvais (2003).
6 ICSID Case No. ARB/97/7, 25 January, 2000; 40 ILM 1129 (2001).
7 Letter to the investor and defendant from The Hon. Lord Dervaird, Chair, Pope & Talbot tribunal, dated September 17 2001.
8 The case of Ethyl Corp *v* Government of Canada never proceeded to final ruling, but rather was settled in 1998 by the Government of Canada, which, among other things, paid Ethyl CAD$13 million. For details, see www.dfait-maeci.gc.ca/tna-nac/ethyl-en.asp
9 See www.dfait-maeci.gc.ca/tna-nac/NAFTA-Interpr-en.asp
10 In fact such statements are not 'interpretive' in the sense of clarifying the intent of NAFTA's drafters – rather, they seek to give FTC guidance to the conduct of the panels.
11 More recent tribunals have been less secretive; to date, two have opened their proceedings to the public, and most case documents are now available on government websites.
12 While the NAFTA itself is now ten years old, the cases actually settled under Chapter 11 arbitration number less than a dozen.

References

ADF *v* United States of America (2003) 'Final Award,' InternationalCentre for the Settlement of Investment Disputes, Case No. ARB/AF/00/1. January 9, www.state.gov/documents/organization/14442.pdf.

American Law Institute (1987) 'Restatement of the Law Third: the Foreign Relations of the United States', Philadelphia, American Law Institute

Been, V. and J. C. Beauvais (2003) 'The Global Fifth Amendment? NAFTA's Investment Protections and the Misguided Quest for an International "Regulatory Takings" Doctrine', *New York University Law Review*, no 78, pp30–143

Cosbey, A. (2001) 'Note on NAFTA Commission's July 31 2001, Initiative to Clarify Chapter 11 Investment Provisions', Winnipeg, International Institute for Sustainable Development, www.iisd.org/publiations/publication.asp?pno=375

Crompton Corp *v* Government of Canada (2001) 'Notice of Intent to Submit a Claim to Arbitration', November 6, www.dfait-maeci.gc.ca/tna-nac/documents/CROMPTON-CORP.pdf

Greider, W. (2001) 'The Right and US Trade Law: Invalidating the 20th century', *The Nation*, October 15, pp21–29.

Maffezini *v* Kingdom of Spain (2001) ICSID Case No ARB/97/7, 25 January; 40 ILM 1129

Mann, H. (2001) *Private Rights, Public Problems*, Winnipeg, International Institute for Sustainable Development, www.iisd.org/trade/private_rights.htm

Mann, H. (2002) 'The Right of States to Regulate and International Investment Law: Comment'. Paper prepared for the UNCTAD conference: 'Expert Meeting on the Development Dimension of FDI: Policies to Enhance the Role of FDI in Support of the Competitiveness of the Enterprise Sector and the Economic Performance of Host Economies, Taking into Account the Trade/Investment Interface, in the National and International Context', Geneva, 6–8 November, www.iisd.org/pdf/2003/investment_right_to_regulate.pdf

Mann, H. (2003) 'The Free Trade Commission Statements of October 7, 2003, on NAFTA's Chapter 11: Never-Never Land or Real Progress?', Winnipeg, International Institute for Sustainable Development, www.iisd.org/publications/publication.asp?pno=578

Mann, H. and J. Soloway (2002) 'Untangling the Expropriation and Regulation Relationship: Is there a way forward?', A Report to the *Ad Hoc* Expert Group on Investment Rules and the Department of Foreign Affairs and International Trade (Canada), www.dfait-maeci.gc.ca/tna-nac/regulation-en.asp

Mann, H. and K. von Moltke (2002) 'Protecting Investor Rights and the Public Good: Assessing NAFTA's Chapter 11', Winnipeg, International Institute for Sustainable Development, www.iisd.org/trade/ilsdworkshop/pdf/background_en.pdf

Marvin Feldman *v* Mexico (2002) 'Final Award', International Centre for the Settlement of Investment Disputes (Additional Facility), Case No. ARB/AF/99/1, December 16,www.economia-nci.gob.mx/sphp_pages/importa/sol_contro/consultoria/Casos_Mexico/Marvin/laudo/laudo_ingles.pdf

Metalclad Corporation *v* United Mexican States (2002) 'Final Award', International Centre for the Settlement of Investment Disputes (Additional Facility) Case No. ARB/AF/97/1. December 16.

Methanex Corp. *v* United States of America (2001) 'Decision of the Tribunal on Petitions from Third Persons to Intervene as "Amici Curiae"', January 15, www.state.gov/documents/organizations/6039.pdf

Mondev International Ltd. *v* United States of America (2002) 'Final Award', International Centre for the Settlement of Investment Disputes (Additional Facility) Case No. ARB/AF/99/2. October 11, www.state.gov/documents/organization/14442.pdf

NAFTA Free Trade Commission (2001) 'Notes of Interpretation of Certain Chapter 11 Provisions', July 31, www.dfait-maeci.gc.ca/tna-nac/NAFTA-Interpr-en.asp

NAFTA Free Trade Commission (2003) 'Statement of the Free Trade Commission on Non-disputing Party Participation', October 7, www.dfait-maeci.gc.ca/nafta-alena/Nondisputing-en.pdf

Pope & Talbot *v* Canada (2000) 'Interim Award', June 6, www.dfait-maeci.gc.ca/tna-nac/documents/pubdoc7.pdf

S. D. Meyers Inc. *v* Canada (2000) 'Partial Award', November 13, www.dfait-maeci.gc.ca/tna-nac/documents/myersvcanadapartialaward_final_13-11-00.pdf

Tollefson, C. (2002) 'Games Without Frontiers: Investor Claims and Citizen Submission Under the NAFTA Regime', *Yale Journal of International Law*, vol 27, no 1, pp141–192

US Trade Representative (2003) 'Statement on Open Hearings in NAFTA Chapter 11 Arbitrations', October 7, www.ustr.gov/regions/whemisphere/nafta2003/statement-openhearings.pdf

Vandevelde, K. (1992) *United States Investment Treaties: Policy and Practice*, Boston, Law and Taxation Publishers

Chapter 7

The Environment and the Principle of Non-discrimination in Investment Regimes: International and Domestic Institutions

Konrad von Moltke

Abstract

Non-discrimination is a universal principle that applies in a wide range of international regimes, including trade, investment and environment. It also applies at national and sub-national levels of governance. The institutions required to secure non-discrimination will vary, however, according to the problem that is being addressed.

This chapter identifies concerns that need to be taken into account when seeking non-discrimination in international investment by considering how environmental regimes approach this issue. Investment is central to the prospects for achieving more sustainable forms of development. The chapter concludes that investment rules at all levels must be capable of balancing private rights and public goods in a manner that is legitimate, transparent and accountable. Since most existing international regimes are incapable of meeting this standard, it suggests a pragmatic approach based on a framework agreement outlining principles and their implementation in a range of individual international agreements that seek to protect public goods.

Introduction

The central principle embodied in international investment agreements is that of 'non-discrimination', the principle that under like circumstances, all investors should be treated in a non-discriminatory manner. The desirability of treating all investors in a non-discriminatory manner under like circumstances seems self-evident. Yet there has not been much discussion about the principle and how best to achieve it, and virtually none about the likely impact of international agreements on domestic institutions that seek to ensure 'non-discrimination' between investors within a country, whether they are foreign or not.

It is widely assumed that the trade regime offers a template for achieving 'non-discrimination' in investment since 'non-discrimination' is also the fundamental goal of the trade regime. Most-favoured-nation treatment, national treatment, a measure of transparency, and a dispute settlement mechanism are the institutions that are used to achieve non-discrimination in trade[1]. The assumption that these institutions will also secure 'non-discrimination' for investors has been embodied in most investment agreements over the past decades.

There are many such agreements: several multilateral agreements and more than 2000 bilateral agreements, as well as investment provisions in some regional trade agreements such as the North American Free Trade Agreement (NAFTA) and in the General Agreement on Trade in Services and the Energy Charter Treaty. One indicator of the differences between trade in goods and investment is that the EU treaties, the basis of the most highly developed international regime, deal quite differently with the two issues.

Upon closer scrutiny it becomes evident that even though a goal of both trade and investment regimes is non-discrimination, the institutions required to achieve this goal are actually quite distinct. This counter-intuitive result reflects the fact that institutions must reflect the structure of the problem that is being addressed[2].Thus, issues that exhibit different problem structures require different institutions even when pursuing an identical goal. The central challenge of legislation or international negotiation is to ensure a proper fit between institutions and the goals that are being pursued.

Over the past 50 years, the trade regime has evolved from an agreement for mutual tariff reductions and non-discrimination to a complex structure involving numerous 'behind-the-border' issues such as non-tariff barriers to trade, technical barriers to trade, sanitary and phyto-sanitary measures and hidden forms of protectionism – i.e. discrimination. The reality of increasingly integrated markets forced governments to dig deeper and deeper into a range of domestic practices to ensure that gains made in the area of tariff reductions were not dissipated by further layers of protection.

The central dilemma has been the need to distinguish between legitimate measures with unavoidable protectionist effect and protectionist measures masquerading as legitimate. The original framers of the General Agreement on Tariffs and Trade (GATT) were well aware of the problem but it is doubtful that they anticipated the complexities involved in addressing it. Fortunately, there was time to develop multilateral disciplines as trade expanded.

Investment agreements are likely to exhibit a similar dynamic, with a need to delve deeply into domestic investment practices to ensure that hard won gains at the international level are not lost to continued discrimination. Indeed, because of the nature of investment, the scope for such practices is much larger. Investment is at the centre of economic development and touches virtually every aspect of economy, society and environment.

Moreover, because globalization is now in full swing, there is much less scope for trial and error. It is inexcusable to negotiate international investment agreements that are not fully aware of the domestic implications, that is, their possible impact on existing institutions designed to ensure non-discrimination with respect to investments within countries. Yet, there has been only limited consideration of these institutions in the international debate about investment agreements.

The lack of attention to the interplay between international agreements and domestic institutions may be due, in part, to the fact that the earliest investment agreements were bilateral treaties between OECD countries and newly sovereign states that had emerged from colonization. The purpose of these agreements was to ensure the rights of colonial investors in the newly independent states. There was not much concern about the existence of domestic institutions to promote non-discrimination because most of these countries did not have such capabilities.

The situation is dramatically different when similar investment agreements involve countries with highly developed regulatory structures designed to ensure a proper balance between private investor rights and the protection of public goods[3]. If drafting is not sufficiently prudent, the resulting dynamic between international rules and domestic institutions is bound to be full of surprises.

Environmental regimes illustrate the issue of institutions and 'fit'. The ultimate goal of any environmental regime is to preserve the environment so that it supports human activities and other living organisms. Many of the institutions that are used to achieve these goals recur in most environmental regimes: scientific research, assessment, monitoring, transparency and public participation. Yet different environmental issues require different institutional mixes. The hazardous waste regime uses highly developed documentation systems and bans. The toxics regime uses packaging, labelling, classification, testing, and hazard assessment and risk assessment. The stratospheric ozone regime is based on the control of production and use. Wildlife regimes typically require habitat protection. The common institutions are modified in each regime to fit the changed circumstances that are defined by the nature of the problem that is being addressed.

Thus the two central questions that must be addressed in any investment agreement are first, the interplay between international and domestic institutions, and second, the fit between the problem and the institutions employed to address it. This chapter will seek initial responses to these questions by focusing on the relationship between investment and sustainable development.

Non-discrimination and sustainable development

It is hard to overstate the importance of investment to the attainment of sustainable development. To the extent that current economic activity is unsustainable, it will take investment to replace it with more sustainable activities. Indeed, investment is the tool of choice to shift from less sustainable to more sustainable activities. Consequently, all investment agreements are of vital concern from the perspective of sustainable development, even as policy-makers face the hard question of how to channel investment – a private activity – towards the goal of achieving greater sustainability – a public good.

Foreign investment represents a particular case where the investor is a foreign national, whether a person or a corporation, and consequently is not integrated into the legal order in the same way that a domestic investor would be. Given the growth of foreign direct investment, the development of an international legal framework that permits a proper balancing of investor rights and public goods is a priority for promoting sustainable development.

The first question that needs to be answered is whether non-discrimination in an investment structure is always desirable from the perspective of sustainable development. The response to this question is much like the response to the idea that *economic growth* is environmentally beneficial: it depends. Clearly, a highly discriminatory investment system will be inefficient, subject to distortion, and exhibit large rents that are liable to be defended with no regard to any broader societal values, including sustainable development. Consequently, discriminatory investment regimes are more likely to be unsustainable than non-discriminatory ones.

This does not, however, imply that the converse holds – that all non-discriminatory investment systems will necessarily promote sustainability. Inappropriately rigid investment rules that do not provide for the use of essential market disciplines, or lax rules that provide tools for irresponsible investors to escape legitimate regulation, will both be detrimental to sustainable development, whether they are non-discriminatory or not.

Similarly, there may be *discriminatory* investment regimes that actively promote sustainable development, such that their replacement by non-discriminatory principles without taking account of the need to protect public goods could result in a net loss of environmental values. In other words, investment frameworks need to explicitly address sustainable development. That is more easily said than done.

Promoting sustainable development through investment agreements requires further analysis and discussion in order to ensure that the issues are properly framed, that the institutions needed to achieve desired results are properly identified, and that an appropriate organizational framework is created to ensure that results correspond to the identified needs. It is unlikely, however, that this goal can be achieved by making marginal adjustments to the trade regime so as to incorporate investment disciplines.

The central dilemma of any investment regime is the need to balance private rights of investors with the promotion of public goods. This is also central to the achievement of non-discriminatory environmental management in domestic society.

Non-discrimination in domestic environmental policy

Non-discrimination is a fundamental principle of democratic societies. It is generally articulated as equal treatment before the law. This is achieved through a complex institutional structure, designed to balance the rights of individuals against the needs of the community. In terms of investment and environment, investor rights are typically individual rights, while environmental measures are typically of community interest.

In an increasingly globalized world, there is a need to extend the principle of non-discrimination in an appropriate manner to foreigners. In doing so, however, it is vital to respect the rules that have grown up around the principle of non-discrimination within many jurisdictions – in other words, to ensure that foreigners have the same rights *and the same obligations* as citizens.

Non-discrimination is also an issue at all levels of environmental policy, within countries as well as at the international level. It reflects the need to craft policies that meet essential criteria of fairness and equality before the law, while still reflecting the diversity of environmental conditions. Since this is a new area of environmental policy, only a few suggestive comments can be made at this point.

Environmental problem structure

The environment poses some unusual challenges to the institutional capabilities of even the most highly developed societies. Knowledge of the environment is limited and is largely derived from scientific research that was never intended to lead to practical policy measures. Environmental management itself represents an attempt to change the behaviour of people so as to change the natural environment. It is difficult enough to change behaviour through regulations or economic incentives but the ultimate goal of environmental management is not changed behaviour but improved environmental conditions. The result is something like shooting around corners, fraught with uncertainties and consequently subject to contestation. A number of phenomena are characteristic for the resulting problem structure of environmental management.

Exhaustible resources

It is by now well-established that every natural system has a limited capacity to tolerate human interference, although technology can be used to reduce such impacts. Indeed, the traditional distinction between 'renewable' and 'non-renewable' resources turns out to be increasingly dubious, at least insofar as it suggests that exhaustion of renewable resources is less serious than exhaustion of non-renewable ones. 'Non-renewable' resources are by definition inert; it also turns out that they are often substitutable and their useful life can be extended by technological means. 'Renewable' resources are living resources or flow resources. They depend on the ecosystems within which they exist and are consequently sensitive to ecosystem changes. Moreover, renewable resources are often substitutable by other renewable resources, perpetuating the problem. The paradox is therefore that 'renewable' resources may ultimately prove to be more exhaustible than 'non-renewable' ones.

Ecosystems that once appeared inexhaustible turn out not to be. The allocation of these scarce resources is at the heart of the economic dimension of environmental management. Claims on them are frequently cumulative in nature. The classic example is a river that can accommodate some discharges without recognizable environmental damage. Certain limits are eventually reached, as the number of dischargers grows, and environmental policy-makers must balance the rights of established dischargers against the right of new dischargers to establish their activities.

In environmental policy, it is widely accepted that a new facility may need to be subject to significantly more stringent requirements than existing facilities – or may have to pay to reduce discharges from existing facilities. Existing facilities will need to converge towards the new standards as they are modified and updated. Nevertheless, much discretion remains for those responsible for issuing permits. The overall result is that there is an important time factor governing the stringency of environmental controls. Later entrants are unlikely to be treated in the same manner as earlier ones.

Irreversible effects

Some environmental changes are irreversible, or at least within a period that is economically or socially meaningful. Atmospheric emissions, for example, are effectively irreversible, making necessary a more precautionary approach. Moreover, atmospheric emissions tend to be widely dispersed, so that effects can occur some time after the emissions have occurred or at some distance. As time and distance increase, it becomes progressively difficult to establish causality, rendering the balancing between private rights and public goods more uncertain and more difficult.

In other areas of environmental management, not the action but the effects of human intervention can prove to be irreversible. The most extreme case is that of species extinction, a natural phenomenon that has been vastly accelerated by human intervention. But numerous other environmental effects can prove irreversible, at least within a time frame that is relevant to policy-making. Thus a natural forest that is cut down will take many generations to regenerate, with temperate forests recovering faster than boreal ones, which in turn are more likely to regenerate in their original state than tropical forests. Similarly, mutation, caused by the introduction of toxic substances or by the release of genetically modified organisms, is effectively irreversible.

Cumulative effects

A variety of factors can cause emissions to have a cumulative effect. Certain toxic substances may be emitted in very small amounts yet have a disproportionate effect because of the presence of other substances, either naturally occurring or anthropogenic. Persistence can lead to similar outcomes because recent emissions must take into account the presence of a pool of previous emissions. Finally, existing facilities can exhaust the absorptive ability of ecosystems, making any additional emission unacceptable.

A vivid example is the accumulation of lead in the soil in London, attributable to the presence of trace amounts of lead in coal burned over more than a century. On account of the properties of lead, the result is high background values that make the addition of further emissions an unacceptable risk. This led the British government to adopt measures to phase out leaded petrol at a time when most other European countries did not consider the health effects associated with lead use sufficient to warrant action (as opposed to the need to introduce catalytic converters). Again, the outcome is formally different treatment of individuals under otherwise like circumstances.

Threshold phenomena

Ecosystems are complex and not entirely understood. In some instances, they exhibit threshold phenomena. An environmental resource that appears to be holding up fairly well under human pressure will suddenly deteriorate dramatically. Threshold phenomena are particularly problematic when harvesting exhaustible natural resources from stocks. Thus fisheries are prone to collapse. As stocks are depleted, harvest effort increases so as to maintain yield. What is actually happening is an acceleration of decline, often manifested in deteriorating quality such as smaller and immature fish.

Similarly, lakes and waterways may exhibit threshold phenomena when it comes to pollution exposure. As acidity or nutrient concentrations increase, not much response is observed until a certain threshold is reached, after which a sudden change may occur. Acidity for example, may reach critical levels for certain species or overwhelm the buffering capacity of adjacent soils. Elevated concentrations of nutrients, or eutrophication, may lead to a change in the aquatic plant community to fast-growing, prolific species such as filamentous algae, which overgrow competitors. Organisms that feed on the decaying plant matter proliferate, eventually depleting dissolved oxygen.

Threshold phenomena pose particular challenges, as the limited resource must be allocated to competing uses in such a manner that natural functions are maintained. This creates particularly difficult problems where a resource faces competing claims for human uses – such as irrigation, navigation and power generation on a river – and for ecosystem functions – such as maintenance of healthy fish populations. The resulting conflicts require highly sophisticated institutions to ensure that decisions achieve the acceptance necessary for their respect and implementation.

Changing knowledge

Knowledge about the environment has increased over time. Nonetheless, it remains fragmentary in many areas. This poses two dilemmas: the uncertainty associated with fragmentary knowledge, and the need to adjust to changing knowledge. Scientific research is an institution to generate reliable information about natural phenomena. Yet it is always also associated with uncertainty. Coping with this uncertainty has given rise to some of the most intractable international conflicts.

As scientific information accumulated, and as public perceptions of environmental hazards changed, it became necessary to engage in a continual process of adjusting environmental standards. Countries dealt with this process differently, largely depending on their legal traditions. In some countries, permits were initially viewed as akin to 'property rights', so that changing them was comparable to a 'taking' and possibly subject to compensation.

In other countries, public authorities issued only temporary permits, anticipating a continuous need to adjust over time. As a consequence, new investments were treated differently in different countries: authorities who anticipate opportunities for later improvements can be more lenient initially than those who must attempt to maximize the initial impact. In the latter case, there is also likely to be a much greater difference between requirements for new and existing facilities (von Moltke, 1985, 1983).

Under these circumstances, non-discrimination requires an elaborate structure of standards and extensive procedural safeguards. These institutions differ from one country to another, reflecting political and social traditions and historical experience. Nowhere are these differences more pronounced than when dealing with the problem of scientific uncertainty, largely encapsulated in the debate about risk assessment and the precautionary principle (von Moltke, 2000).

As knowledge evolved, so have the available technologies. Again, this leads to significantly different treatment for new and existing facilities. Moreover, complex industrial facilities are each unique in terms of their technology and environmental impact. Even the permits for facilities as comparable as large combustion plants turn out to be difficult to compare with one another (von Moltke, 1983).

'Cross-media' effects and integration

'Environmental policy' is actually a complex of related policies designed to map the natural environment and its problems onto political, social and economic institutions. Issues as diverse as air pollution and landscape protection, biodiversity and water pollution, climate change and waste management, or toxic substances and ozone depletion all form part of environmental policy. Each of these issues has its own problem structure, requiring a range of institutional responses and frequently involving a number of organizations (von Moltke, 1995).

The result is a very large and complex mix of policy interests. In some countries, environmental law by now represents the largest single body of law. At the international level, similar developments can be observed. While no reliable measure of comparison exists, it is a plausible assumption that international environmental law is, or soon will be, the largest single body of international law.

At a relatively early stage in addressing environmental issues, it became clear that there were certain trade-offs between areas of policy. Vigorous control of air and water pollution led to a dramatic increase in waste streams – pollutants were removed from one medium only to be deposited in another, resulting in a crisis of hazardous waste management. In some processes, the choice is between waste disposal to water or to the atmosphere, so that reducing atmospheric emissions resulted in a much increased need for wastewater treatment, and *vice versa*. The control of persistent pesticides led to the introduction of pesticides that were more toxic but less persistent. Increased wastewater treatment caused additional air pollution as pollutants were volatized from the treatment facility.

Each of these trade-offs represented regulatory choices, with consequences for economic actors. To ensure that these choices are made in a non-discriminatory manner requires extraordinarily elaborate regulatory activities, and involves not only the specification of *standards* but also (increasingly) the definition of *procedures*, from environmental assessment, to public information, to public participation. In most OECD (Organization for Economic Cooperation and Development) countries, these procedures have become an integral part of the work of environmental agencies at all levels.

Maintaining non-discrimination under these circumstances has become a continuing preoccupation of environmental authorities, requiring substantial institutional resources. This is particularly true for federal systems, which can exhibit quite significant variations in actual practice, despite the best efforts of federal authorities to achieve a measure of uniformity in the interests of non-discrimination (Liroff et al, undated; von Moltke, 1985).

Institutional consequences

The issues raised in the previous sections lead to a number of characteristic institutional responses in environmental management. One is the prevalence of procedural rather than substantive non-discrimination, that is, investors will be subject to the same procedures even though the outcomes may be significantly different. Another is the use of transparency and public participation as key policy tools.

Since non-discrimination in domestic environmental management is hard to achieve in substantive terms, the almost universal response has been the creation of an elaborate structure of procedural rules. The goal is to achieve non-discrimination by submitting investors to the same procedures, even though the outcome of these procedures may differ widely. Consequently, domestic environmental law is characterized by a large number of procedural requirements, involving testing, environmental assessment, permitting, public information, participation, monitoring, review, labelling or packaging. High procedural standards will require a strong, continuing presence of foreign investors in the relevant jurisdictions, and the first and most fundamental right of these investors is equal access to all domestic procedural safeguards against discrimination.

Environmental management is not just a matter of public authorities applying certain rules in the process of issuing licenses to applicants. Because a facility's environmental performance can have unanticipated effects on people and property in its neighbourhood and beyond, and because public authorities cannot monitor all facilities continuously, public participation has become a major feature of environmental management in democratic societies. In practice, public participation helps identify environmental impacts that may otherwise be overlooked. Public participation also helps authorities in monitoring and setting priorities for enforcement action. Consequently, environmental law in many countries is characterized by extensive procedural safeguards to ensure timely and adequate information and to create opportunities for public participation. This has profound implications for non-discrimination.

The problem structure of investment

Investment is the heartbeat of an economy and a crucial arena for decision-making for any corporation because it largely determines future operations. In market economies, investment is largely a private activity. Public budgets do not include a balance sheet of assets and liabilities, nor is there any requirement to achieve a return on public 'investments' to amortize them. Thus a road or a school may generate economic benefits akin to investment, but there is never any accounting for those benefits nor an economic penalty – other than higher taxes – when they fail to materialize. The central dynamic of investment is the relationship of risk to return. In practice, however, investment decisions are influenced by a large number of factors, including most importantly the existence of markets for output and the ability to access those markets.

Other than access to markets, factors which influence investment decisions and returns include the availability of labour and of skilled labour in particular, access to inputs, energy costs, taxes and charges, transportation and other infrastructure concerns, waste disposal and other environmental issues, and the regulatory environment, especially whether decisions are reasonably predictable and reliable. All of these factors involve public resources or public goods in some fashion.

Attempts to identify causality of specific investment decisions to these numerous secondary factors generally founder on the reality that none of them is determining by itself. Moreover, existing investment agreements affect only a few of these secondary factors. It is consequently hardly surprising that there is no clear empirical evidence that investment agreements actually contribute to changing investment flows.

Like most economic processes, investment benefits from an unambiguous metric. Ultimately all factors are measured in financial terms, and the overall outcome of an investment can be calculated in a convincing manner in terms of its return on capital. This clarity of metric stands in stark contrast to the agenda of environment and sustainable development where no such measurements exist.

Non-Discrimination in International Environmental Management

Environmental management has an inescapable (and growing) international component. This has resulted in the development of a substantial body of international environmental law, which has implications for non-discrimination in both trade and investment. International environmental law promotes equivalency in environmental safeguards across national frontiers, because environmental protection efforts in one country can be defeated by lack of similar efforts in another, and also to ensure that these measures do not distort economic competition. They also seek to allocate effort between countries when confronting international environmental issues such as global warming, or the allocation of resources in a shared river basin.

The international dimension of environmental management creates a unique interface with the trade regime – and with an incipient international investment framework – taking it beyond the realm of national jurisdictions alone. As noted earlier, this part of international environmental law is characterized by a high degree of reliance on procedural and institutional, rather than substantive, responses.

Trans-boundary environmental management

A web of legal provisions, developed bilaterally and regionally, rather than at the global level, extends domestic rules for non-discrimination across borders, especially in border regions (OECD, 2001). These rules date back more than 70 years to the Trail Smelter case between Canada and the US, which established the responsibility of polluters in one country for damage in the neighbouring country (Sands, 1995).

Cross-border responsibility was further elaborated in Principle 21 of the Stockholm Declaration, which reaffirmed the sovereign right of states to exploit their own natural resources, but imposed a 'responsibility to ensure that activities within their jurisdiction or control do not cause damage to the environment of other states or of areas beyond the limits of national jurisdiction' (Sands, 1995).

In many instances, this has led to the recognition of rights of residents to participate in administrative proceedings when they may be affected by actions on the other side of the border. In the NAFTA countries, these rights have been codified in the so-called 'environmental side agreement', establishing the Commission on Environmental Co-operation, which has rights of investigation and reporting, especially when inadequate or discriminatory applications of environmental measures are alleged (Johnson and Beaulieu, 1996).

These broad rights and responsibilities become much more problematic when the principle of non-discrimination is extended to cover the activities of citizens of one country in another. In some industries, it has become common practice for enterprises to establish universal standards that are applied to all facilities wherever they may be established, and in some instances even to suppliers. This approach is desirable where no relevant local regulations exist, or where these are less stringent. Nevertheless, it does not pre-empt the right of public authorities to impose other standards on operations within their jurisdiction, provided this is done in a non-discriminatory manner.

Non-discrimination in the EU

The EU has developed a large and detailed body of environmental law, including more than 300 legal instruments covering virtually every aspect of environmental management. Arguably, this entire effort can be viewed as a structure to ensure non-discrimination in environmental affairs within the EU. European environmental law utilizes a number of instruments to achieve this goal, and specifies a number of procedures (see Table 7.1).

The EU process is increasingly complemented by agreements at the broader European level, sometimes including countries that are candidates for EU membership, sometimes a broader range of European countries such as the Council of Europe, and sometimes all the members of the United Nations Economic Commission for Europe – that is, also the US and Canada. The result is a network of international environmental agreements that range from the Treaty on Long Range Transboundary Air Pollution (LRTAP) to the Århus Convention on Access to Information, Public Participation in Decision-Making and Access to Justice in Environmental Matters.

International environmental regimes

International environmental regimes are designed to frame environmental issues that require international action in an equitable fashion. In dealing with countries, they impose equal obligations in some areas; in others, these obligations are 'equal but differentiated', reflecting a range of additional considerations, such as level of development, technological capability, and 'historical responsibility' for the environmental problem being addressed. This is analogous to 'special and differential treatment' for developing countries in trade agreements.

The task of allocating the attendant obligations within their country is the exclusive responsibility of the respective governments, subject to the procedures and safeguards that exist in each country to ensure non-discrimination. Consequently, the extent to which differential treatment carries over to individuals within a country remains a matter of subsequent negotiation. In several regimes, a number of issues have arisen that may cause complications in ensuring that the consequences of international environmental regimes are non-discriminatory.

The Convention on Biodiversity (CBD) is concerned both with the preservation of biodiversity and with its utilization. Concerns have arisen over the exploitation of traditional knowledge and the registration of patents based on biological materials found in developing countries. These concerns have clear

Table 7.1 *Selected EU Legal Instruments and Institutions for the Environment*

Source	Title	Institutions
76/464/EEC	Directive on pollution caused by certain dangerous substances discharged into the aquatic environment of the Community	Black list substances; grey list substances; pollution reduction programmes; discharge permits; designation of competent authority; emission standards; quality objectives; limit values; best technical means; monitoring; reporting; publication; priority list of substances; new facilities; comparative assessment; daughter directives.
75/442/EEC 91/156/EEC	Directive on waste	Waste prevention, reduction and recovery; technology development; best available technology not entailing excessive cost; network of disposal installations; competent authorities; waste management plans; permits; record-keeping; polluter pays principle; list of wastes; implementation reports.
96/62/EC	Directive on ambient air quality assessment and management	Air quality standards; daughter directives; limit values; alert thresholds; target values; guidelines; monitoring; modeling; zoning; reporting; improvement plans; scientific and technical progress; committee; competent authorities.
67/548/EEC 92/32/EEC	Directive on the approximation of the laws, regulations and administrative provisions relating to the classification, packaging and labelling of dangerous substances	Classification, packaging, labelling, notification; testing; assessment; inventories; safety data sheets; competent authority; committee for adaptation; confidentiality; reporting.

Source: European Commission, DG Environment

implications for the principle of non-discrimination in an investment regime and need to be addressed explicitly, particularly in light of a growing perception that the Agreement on Trade-Related Intellectual Property Rights (TRIPs) has led to the creation of significant rents for holders of patents from developed countries without equivalent benefits for developing countries.

Many multilateral environmental agreements (MEAs) also articulate the notion of preferential access to the technologies needed to address a particular environmental problem, but none has yet been able to operationalize this notion very effectively[4]. The implications for investments incorporating such technologies are clear, and once again, need to be addressed explicitly. At the very least, technological preferences parallel the idea of 'performance requirements' – and are therefore closely related to the principle of non-discrimination.

The Basel Convention on the Transboundary Transport of Hazardous Wastes and Their Disposal is based on dividing countries into several groups – primarily OECD and non-OECD countries (although not all OECD countries have ratified the convention and the key provisions concerning export bans have not yet entered into force). It involves a ban on the transport of hazardous wastes from OECD to non-OECD countries but does not develop any rules for enterprises operating in non-OECD countries but controlled by enterprises based in OECD countries. Certainly, any investment to relocate production with a view to escaping controls on the disposal of hazardous wastes would be viewed as a highly controversial and problematic development, and could give rise to calls for more far reaching controls than are currently in place.

Finally, the Framework Convention on Climate Change (UNFCCC) is in many respects an international investment agreement. Its purpose is to shift investment (in particular, in energy, transport and infrastructure) towards projects that involve fewer greenhouse gas emissions. The UNFCCC distinguishes between Annex I countries and other countries, and its Kyoto Protocol has established several 'flexibility mechanisms' that build on this distinction. Investments and investors are treated differently in this structure, depending on both the country of origin and the host country. While the resultant treatment may be 'fair and equitable', it may not be viewed as strictly 'non-discriminatory'.

SUBSIDIARITY

The principle of subsidiarity – the idea that action should be taken at the lowest level of governance consistent with effectiveness – is in many ways a basic principle of good governance. This principle has given rise to extensive discussions within the EU, where it is enshrined in Article 3b of the Treaty of Maastricht[5].

Subsidiarity applies differently to economic and environmental regimes. While economic regimes deal largely in 'universals' and generally seek to develop global rules of equal application wherever they apply, environmental regimes more closely follow the subsidiarity principle. This difference is likely to render the balancing of economic and environmental priorities within an international investment framework increasingly difficult as economic decisions become more globalized.

All countries struggle to a greater or lesser degree with the problem of subsidiarity in environmental affairs. Specific decisions on environmental quality (and on permitting) must be locally based. In a few countries (e.g. the UK), permits for the largest installations involving the greatest environmental hazards are undertaken by a national inspectorate. This inspectorate operates on the basis of 'guidance' – indicative standards that recognize the need to vary decisions to take local conditions into account.

Even a country as relatively small as Denmark must address the problems associated with subsidiarity, especially when confronting EU and other international requirements:

> *Under the Danish Environmental Protection Act and other environmental legislation, the competence to set standards is decentralised to local councils (municipalities and counties) – supported by guidelines from the Danish Environmental Protection Agency, together with access by way of administrative appeal to national agencies and boards. With few exceptions, local councils are also granted the discretion to decide when and how to enforce environmental legislation.*
>
> (Pagh, 1999)

It is clear that such a system requires an elaborate institutional structure to ensure non-discrimination.

Federal countries have much the most elaborate institutional structures for achieving a measure of balance between the need for nationally consistent, non-discriminatory rules and local authority in those areas where differentiation is viewed as essential. The US, with its unique system of independent branches and levels of government that exercise often competing jurisdiction over the same issue, resorts to extensive judicial interpretation to maintain an appropriate balance. Germany achieves a high degree of subsidiarity by reserving the implementation of many federal laws (e.g. income tax collection) to the Länder. All federal environmental laws are implemented exclusively by the Länder, with nominal federal supervision (although strong federal supervision has traditionally been limited to the rather special domain of nuclear power).

Apart from posing significant challenges to the national implementation of certain international mandates, the principle of subsidiarity poses major difficulties for the balancing of conflicting international priorities. This problem has not even been resolved within the highly developed institutional framework of the EU.

During the Third WTO Ministerial in Seattle in 1999, a conflict arose when the European Commission made certain concessions concerning biotechnology, based on authority derived from the 'Article 133 Committee'. This committee, established by Article 133 of the EU Treaties, was designed to remove trade policy from the purview of the foreign ministries, which control the EU Council. While nominally subject to the council, the Article 133 Committee enjoys much autonomy in the day-to-day conduct of trade negotiations. It is composed of high level officials of the economics ministries of the EU member states.

The concessions made in Seattle were immediately opposed unanimously by EU environment ministers, acting through the council. With the inconclusive outcome of the Seattle meeting, this conflict did not need to be resolved in a definitive manner, but it did demonstrate a continuing problem in determining who has the authority to make decisions when an issue subject to the exclusive jurisdiction of the EU (such as trade) must be balanced against one subject to shared jurisdiction and operating within a framework of subsidiarity (such as environmental management). For the time being, significant aspects of the EU investment agenda are handled separately from the trade agenda, and are therefore not dealt with within the Article 133 committee structure[6].

The problems created by an incoherent international policy-making structure are magnified at the wider international level where no institutions exist to balance conflicting priorities. In many ways, they are at the heart of the relationship between environment and trade, and contributed significantly to public perceptions of both the Seattle Ministerial and the Multilateral Agreement on Investment (MAI). Such problems can be 'dodged' for some time in relation to relatively simple issues like trade liberalization. However, they are central to any broadly based investment framework, and must therefore be resolved before any such framework can be implemented, especially if public acceptance is to be obtained.

Enforcement and Voluntary Measures

The complexities of environmental management imply that public authorities must be selective in which enforcement measures they undertake. Obviously, most public authorities seek to exert effort where there is an expectation of results, so that any significant enforcement measure also implies an assessment of an enterprise's record, the quality of its management and the likelihood of encountering problems. This in turn creates a range of discretionary authority and involves an inescapable degree of discrimination. Achieving an appropriate level of protection against unjustifiable discrimination against foreign investors is a delicate task.

In this context, public awareness and public perception can play important roles. On the one hand, neighbours of an enterprise observe its activities on a continuing basis, in a manner not possible for public authorities. They are an important source of information. On the other hand, unrelated conflicts between an enterprise and affected citizens can lead to a range of unwarranted responses. Again, protection against discrimination solely on account of the nationality of an investor is not easy.

Faced with insurmountable difficulties in establishing systematic controls, public authorities are increasingly turning to voluntary action on the part of enterprises to secure environmental quality. Such voluntary programmes are liable to be monitored by industry associations (generally dominated by domestic enterprises, and with possible biases against foreign investors) or by a process of self-reporting that requires a high degree of trust between public authorities and the enterprise. Such trust can generally only be built up over time.

In some instances, perceptions about the quality and stringency of environmental management in the country of origin of a particular investor could play a role in deciding how much trust is warranted. It is certainly conceivable, and may in fact be appropriate for industries likely to have a long-term impact on environmental values, that foreign enterprises may be denied the opportunity to invest on account of information available concerning their past practices, the practices of their associates, or the stringency of environmental controls in their home jurisdiction. It is hard to imagine, for example, that the Malaysian forest product company, Kumpulan Emas, would not face vigorous scrutiny as a foreign investor after its operations were suspended by the government of the Solomon Islands. Similar constraints may face Jaya Tiasa, which has 'been heavily criticised for its operations in Papua New Guinea' (Grieg-Gran et al, 1998).

Some environmental effects can be long-lasting, creating significant problems with regard to the assignment of liability. This has been a major obstacle to implementing the US Superfund legislation, which provides for clean-up of sites containing hazardous wastes. A foreign investor with limited interests in a given country may decide to withdraw from that country, rather than face its environmental liability. This has occurred in the US and Australian mining industries and leaves public authorities in the host country with no effective recourse against the foreign investor. Insurance schemes or performance bonds can be used to internalize known future liabilities but are generally not effective with respect to unanticipated effects.

Attention also needs to be paid to the potential for a 'flag of convenience' problem in an international investment framework. Numerous enterprises, including most large multinational corporations, utilize off-shore jurisdictions as 'havens' to shield their investments from taxation. In some instances, the controlling interests are clearly identified and can be held accountable for actions relating to their foreign investments. In others, however, they cannot be identified, and no controls over environmental performance exist in the off-shore jurisdiction. It appears reasonable for a host country to submit such investors to much closer scrutiny than those who are openly identified, especially when sensitive environmental resources are at stake.

Problem Structure, Institutions, Organizations

The preceding analysis is suggestive rather than exhaustive. The issues surrounding the integration of environmental (and other) policy considerations into an international investment framework require significant additional research. Nevertheless, some preliminary conclusions concerning the most appropriate approach are already possible.

In developing international environmental regimes, the standard practice has been to first identify the structure of the problem being addressed, and then to consider the institutions that may be appropriate for its management. Only as a last step are the legal and organizational forms considered. The result has been a remarkable degree of institutional innovation in international environmental regimes, presumably necessitated by the demanding problem structure of most environmental issues, as well as by the limited range of options available in traditional international regimes.

The process of developing international *economic* regimes, on the other hand, has seen a very different dynamic. Although institutional innovation has occurred at a sometimes breathtaking pace in the private sector, international economic governance has been characterized by great reluctance to innovate.

This may be because of the risks involved in false starts, such as the various attempts to maintain exchange rate stability once fixed exchange rates were abandoned.

Even the creation of the WTO, the last major organizational innovation in this field, was marked by a lack of institutional innovation, with the notable exception of the Dispute Settlement Understanding. Nor has there been much general discussion in the literature of the need for institutional innovation. Consequently, crises such as the breakdown of the MAI negotiations or the failure of the Seattle Ministerial leave the economic policy community with few options and limited experience of the processes required to innovate.

An issue such as the interface between environment and investment is very likely to require some measure of institutional innovation if it is to be successfully addressed. The precise details will emerge as the structure and functions of an international investment regime come more clearly into focus. What is evident thus far is that none of the available templates – BITs, NAFTA, MAI – meet the requirements set out in this chapter.

Non-discrimination in environmental affairs is achieved at the domestic level through a complex institutional structure. Any international agreement that impacts upon that structure – as an effective agreement on investment must – will therefore be measured by the standard of these institutions. To promote non-discrimination at the international level, an investment agreement must meet the fundamental standards of legitimacy, transparency and accountability that have been achieved through many years of institutional innovation in environmental policy at the national and international level.

In light of the complexity of the underlying issues, and the need to balance private investor rights against the protection of public goods such as the environment, it is reasonable to assume that an international investment regime will have to be characterized by institutional sophistication and a significant level of review and accountability to avoid mistakes that could undermine its acceptance. On the other hand, one of the great strengths of the trade regime is its institutional simplicity, or elegance, in that it achieves the goal of promoting non-discrimination in trade with relatively modest institutional means. It is inconceivable that these institutional structures, largely replicated in the draft MAI, will be sufficient to meet the needs of integrating environment and investment objectives.

The central dilemma faced by a multilateral investment agreement is how to balance trade and investment priorities with other legitimate goals of public policy – represented at the international level by regimes that have traditionally been entirely separate from each other – while still ensuring the necessary degree of predictability that is one of the most important fruits of international cooperation.

An initial approach to this dilemma in the trade context sought to avoid the issue by pointing out that all states can choose the level of social and environmental protection they desire. This is presumably adequate to deal with most social issues, including labour rights. This approach does not work in the case of environmental issues because a large number of environmental issues have an international dimension, a dimension that is not adequately represented by the preferences of individual states.

Most likely, addressing the investment/environment interface will entail a set of agreed rules setting out certain procedural safeguards. These must be designed to ensure an adequate degree of non-discrimination while recognizing that actual levels of protection – and the institutional means to achieve them – will first need to be determined by environmental regimes at the appropriate levels, and only later become incorporated within the investment framework.

Clearly, institutional innovation will be needed in the environmental arena as well. Most importantly, the highly fragmented structure of environmental regimes – actually one of the strengths of the international environmental management structure – makes it all but impossible to articulate the international environmental interest in a manner that is readily comprehensible to economic policy-makers (von Moltke, 1995).

To resolve this problem, some analysts have suggested the creation of a 'World Environment Organization' modelled after the WTO (Esty, 1994). A more appropriate response, one which respects the problem structure of environmental management, has emerged through the UNEP (United Nations Environment Programme) process on International Environmental Governance (UNEP). The UNEP proposal recognizes the need to strengthen the overall system of international environmental governance as well as its essential elements. To do so, UNEP must obtain the necessary legal and financial means to provide focus and structure to international environmental governance. Steps must be undertaken to ensure greater coherence among the multilateral environmental agreements (MEAs), probably through a process of clustering (von Moltke, 2001). The work of UN organs in environmental matters must be better integrated.

THE 'ARCHITECTURE' OF A SUSTAINABLE INVESTMENT REGIME

Non-discrimination is a universal principle but it requires specific institutional realization. To achieve non-discrimination between goods in international trade, it has sufficed to apply the disciplines of MFN and national treatment, to provide for a measure of transparency, and then to deal with problems that may arise through a dispute settlement process. These disciplines hinge on the interpretation of the notion of 'like product'. Difficulties have arisen as the trade regime has expanded to TRIPs and has had to confront environmental issues that require that distinctions be made between otherwise 'like' products on the basis of process and production methods (PPMs). These difficulties are surmountable, yet they provide some indication of the increasing institutional sophistication that will be required as increasingly complex issues, involving the rights of an ever larger number of individuals, are addressed.

It is unlikely that a single universal regime will be able to address the investment dimension of sustainable development. The distance is too great between actual environmental decision-making and the broad principles underlying a global investment system. Moreover, the balancing of individual rights and the needs of communities, which is implied in most productive or long-term investments, should be undertaken as close as possible to the actual investment, perhaps with provisions for subsequent review at a more global level (but limited to issues of universal significance).

Such a balancing act requires a credible structure of accountability if it is to be acceptable to a wide range of people. At least for democratic societies, it must also be seen to be legitimate and transparent. No existing international economic regime other than the EU meets these criteria. The World Bank has struggled to move in that direction, despite a governance structure that tends to favour the interests of developed countries. In general, this suggests that an international investment structure will need to be multi-tiered and well-integrated with relevant international environmental regimes. It will probably need organizational realization at regional and global levels, as well as within key environmental regimes (such as the climate regime, the regime for biodiversity, commodity regimes, or regimes governing certain commons such as the oceans and, possibly, Antarctica).

Most international investment agreements have utilized two existing institutions for dispute settlement: the International Center for the Settlement of Investment Disputes (ICSID), attached to the World Bank, and the United Nations Commission for International Trade Law (UNCITRAL). Both institutions are clearly inadequate for the needs of balancing private rights against public goods because they lack legitimacy, transparency, and accountability (see Chapter 5). UNCITRAL dispute settlement procedures are somewhat more problematic than those of ICSID because a complete lack of transparency leads to a corresponding lack of accountability, which undermines whatever legitimacy the process may have. In fact, however, the processes of ICSID are also deeply problematic (von Moltke and Mann, 2001).

An international investment framework must first of all respect the elaborate institutional arrangements in many countries (and within groups of countries, such as the EU), to achieve non-discrimination. It should act only when the opportunities for redress offered by these institutions have been exhausted – or when they have been denied.

When a country has strong safeguards guaranteeing equality before the law and extends these to foreigners in a non-discriminatory manner, an international investment structure should 'second-guess' the results of these institutions only under the most exceptional of circumstances. When a country has weak safeguards, a way needs to be found to strengthen these without immediate reliance on an international dispute settlement procedure. It does not seem sensible to attempt to fill a domestic institutional void through an international institution, which will almost always be lacking in essential attributes to ensure legitimacy, and which will be dangerously remote from the actual level of decision-making.

In general, the institutions required to determine whether unjustifiable discrimination between otherwise 'like' investments has occurred are unlikely to be effective at the global level. They involve a degree of understanding of domestic processes, a respect for differences in environmental and social conditions, and an ability to weigh conflicting policy priorities that is unlikely to be achievable at the global level. This suggests that it may be appropriate to develop a general framework at the global level, but to undertake its implementation primarily in other contexts, where a better balancing of rights and obligations may be achieved, and where similarities and differences between jurisdictions can be properly weighed. Regional agreements and certain specialized global agreements offer obvious advantages in this respect.

A global framework agreement on investment should set out the underlying principles but should leave implementation to subsequent agreements – protocols in effect – and to regional efforts. In addition to articulating the principle of non-discrimination and the goal of sustainable development, such a framework agreement must reaffirm the rights of public authorities to set priorities, and to ensure that all market participants contribute to the achievement of these priorities.

The EU is, among other things, a 'regional economic integration organization'. It has the institutional capacity to make difficult distinctions appropriate to balancing conflicting policy requirements. It is certainly an appropriate location for investment provisions, and for balancing these with the overarching requirements of sustainable development. After a lengthy process, the EU Treaties now properly reflect these factors and the process of implementing these requirements is now under-way.

The original EU Treaties were modified versions of trade agreements from the immediate post-war era, including the GATT. During the 1970s, the EU attempted to address emerging environmental (and a range of social) issues within this original legal framework. This approach proved untenable, ultimately leading to several treaty amendments, beginning with the Single European Act, followed later by the Maastricht Treaty and the Treaty of Amsterdam[7]. This process continues today. The result has been comprehensive institutional reform, including the development of treaty norms and institutions related to the environment. The complexity of this process is illustrated by the fact that each of the treaty amendments thus far has included further adjustments to the existing environmental provisions (von Moltke, 1994).

While the EU experience may be viewed in some respects as a 'benchmark,' it remains a unique phenomenon in international society. Lessons should be drawn with some caution. The EU experience does, however, suggest that the environmental issues are complex and that the necessary responses may take several steps and a significant amount of time to develop. Any attempt to compress the entire process into a single step is likely to be fraught with great risks, as illustrated by the MAI experience.

Other regional economic agreements – notably NAFTA and MERCOSUR – are not designed to achieve a comparable level of integration or institutional development. Nevertheless, they may provide an appropriate forum for addressing some of the issues that link investment and sustainable development. The NAFTA provisions on investment are problematic, but they are susceptible to being improved (von Moltke and Mann, 2001). MERCOSUR is modelled on the original EU Treaties and consequently has a potentially significant institutional structure. At present, MERCOSUR provisions on investment are cautious, keeping national governments in control of the process. They have not yet been tested (Fundacion Ambiente). NAFTA represents a development of the principles and institutions of the GATT/WTO system. It involves few innovations, and one of the most important – the investor–state dispute settlement provisions of Chapter 11 – was poorly designed (von Moltke and Mann, 2001; Chapter 6).

In the case of both NAFTA and MERCOSUR, even the limited institutional provisions of the treaties have not (yet) been fully implemented. For example, NAFTA's trade secretariat is not a single institution but has been formed from three national secretariats. This leaves individual governments in charge and that may be the intention. The lack of implementation creates problems, however, when specific provisions of the treaties need clarification, when common regional interests need to be articulated, and when problems arise with implementation. It also creates a significant deficit in terms of accountability, since the actions of the individual governments concerned are not reported together, and relevant information frequently cannot be accessed. An appropriate goal would therefore be an institutional structure that is less highly developed than the EU but stronger than either NAFTA or MERCOSUR.

Investment is a significant issue for a number of MEAs, both in terms of creating economic incentives to allocate investment in the desired fashion, and to ensure that investors who follow the 'rules of the game' defined by the MEA investment framework are appropriately secure in their rights. In some instances, notably in the climate regime and in those frameworks concerned with the sustainable use of renewable resources, it may be appropriate to introduce the necessary investment provisions directly into the environmental agreement. Dispute settlement could then reflect the dual concerns of the framework (investment and sustainable development).

This approach has already been used in the General Agreement on Trade in Services (GATS) and the Energy Charter Treaty. The GATS contains modest provisions concerning investments necessary for certain 'modes' of delivery of services – which are, of course, bolstered by the state-to-state dispute settlement system of the WTO. The Energy Charter Treaty seeks to create a legal framework for OECD energy investments in the former Soviet Union. It incorporates a full range of provisions providing protection to investors, as well as an investor–state dispute settlement procedure[8]. Neither approach is directly transferable to the agenda of sustainable development but both create clear precedents for sectoral approaches to investment agreements.

The multi-tiered approach outlined above responds constructively to the investment needs of sustainable development. The main objection is presumably the risk entailed in fragmenting the investment framework. The need for 'universal rules' is, however, not as great for an investment regime as it is for the trade regime. Investments (at least the major productive investments) represent single, complex decisions with highly individual characteristics. While international investment flows are very large, this is the result of many case-by-case decisions, rather than the outcome of increasing or decreasing the volume of production in a process that is widely replicable. Consequently, an international investment framework must reflect the structure of the issue that it addresses, and retain the ability to make case-by-case determinations on a routine basis.

Forty years ago, the OECD adopted the Code of Liberalisation of Capital Movements and the Code of Liberalisation of Current Invisible Operations. Twenty-six years ago, it adopted the Declaration and Decisions on International Investment and Multinational Enterprises. All these instruments have been updated.

Over the past 20 years, however, the international economy has changed beyond all recognition. At the same time, environmental issues have emerged as a major issue on the international policy agenda. By some measures, MEAs now constitute one of the largest 'enterprises' in international society[9]. It may be time to rethink not only the details, but also the basic structure of the approach to investment agreements, and to consider whether it still meets the needs of a globalizing economy with interdependent states confronting global environmental challenges.

ENDNOTES

1 The term 'institution' is used in this chapter to mean the 'agreed rules of the game'. In this sense, marriage is an institution, as are property rights or scientific research. 'Institutions' are distinguished from 'organizations', which are entities with budgets, staff and buildings. See Young, 1999a and 1999b.

2 For a discussion of the underlying theory, see Young, 2002.

3 Public goods have three characteristics. They yield to *non-rivalrous* consumption – that is, one person's use of them does not deprive others from using them. They are non-excludable – that is, if one person consumes them it is impossible to restrict others from consuming them. They are *non-rejectable* – that is, individuals cannot abstain from their consumption even if they want to. Many environmental goods – for example, clean air, clear views, wildlife, and ecosystems – are public goods.

4 For example, the Framework Convention on Climate Change, Article 4: 'All Parties, taking into account their common but differentiated responsibilities and their specific national and regional development priorities, objectives and circumstances, shall . . . promote and co-operate in the development, application and diffusion, including transfer, of technologies, practices and processes that control, reduce or prevent anthropogenic emissions of greenhouse gases not controlled by the Montreal Protocol. . .' Article 16 of the Convention on Biodiversity deals entirely with Access to and Transfer of Technology. See, in general, on differential treatment, Halvorsen, 1999.

5 'In areas which do not fall within its exclusive competence, the Community shall take action, in accordance with the principle of subsidiarity, only if and in so far as the objectives of the proposed action cannot be sufficiently

achieved by the Member States and can therefore, by reason of the scale or effects of the proposed action, be better achieved by the Community.' See also Commission of the European Communities, 1990.

6 During the most recent revision of the EU Treaties in Nice in December 2000 the European Commission sought to have investment included in Article 133 but this was not accepted.

7 For one of the earliest critiques, see von Moltke, 1977.

8 For more information about the Energy Charter see www.encharter.org.

9 *The Earth Negotiations Bulletin*, a reporting service of IISD, provides one measure. It covers more than 30 formal sessions every year, involving over 150 days of negotiation. See www.iisd.ca.

REFERENCES

Commission of the European Communities, (1990) 'The Principle of Subsidiarity', *Communication of the Commission to the Council and the European Parliament*, SEC(92) final 27.10.92

Esty, D.C. (1994) *Greening the GATT*, Washington, D.C., Institute for International Economics

Grieg-Gran, M., W. Westbrook, M. Mansley, S. Bass and N. Robins (1998) *Foreign Portfolio Investment and Sustainable Development: A Study of the Forest Products Sector in Emerging Markets*, London, International Institute for Environment and Development,' pvi. 23

Halvorsen, A. M. (1999) *Equality Among Unequals in International Environmental Law: Differential Treatment for Developing Countries*, Boulder, Colorado, Westview Press

Johnson, P. M.' and A. Beaulieu (1996) *The Environment and NAFTA*, Washington, D.C., Island Press

Liroff, Rich et al, *Environmental Policy in a Federal System: The United States and the European Community*, report prepared for the Netherlands Ministry of Housing, Physical Planning and Environment (Contract DGM/ABJ no. 1439053)

Organisation for Economic Co-operation and Development (OECD) Groupe de travail conjoint sur les échanges et l'environnement, le principe pollueur-payeur et le commerce international, COM/ENV/TD(2001)44/FINAL

Pagh, P. (1999) 'Denmark and EC Environmental Law,' *Journal of Environmental Law*, vol 11, no 2, pp303–304

Sands, P. (1995) *Principles of International Environmental Law, vol I: Frameworks, Standards and Implementation*, Manchester, Manchester University Press

United Nations Conference on Trade and Development (UNCTAD), *World Investment Report*, New York and Geneva, United Nations (annual)

von Moltke, K. (1977) 'The Legal Basis for Environmental Policy of the European Communities', *Environmental Policy and Law*, vol 3–4 (December)

von Moltke, K. (1985) 'Rechtsvergleich deutsch-niederländischer Emissionsnormen zur Vermeidun von Luftverunreinigungen Teil 1: Bundesrepublik Deutschland; Teil 2: Niederlande; Teil 3: Tabellen. (Teil 1 also in Dutch: Rechtsvergelijking van duits-nederlandse emissienormen ter bestrijding van luchtverontreiniging), Bonn, Institute for European Environmental Policy (with Boerwinkel F. and H. Meiners)

von Moltke, K. (1993) *Comparison of Regulatory Trends in the West and Central and Eastern Europe*, Report for the European Bank for Reconstruction and Development, London von Moltke, K. (1994) *The Maastricht Treaty and the Winnipeg Principles on Trade and Sustainable Development*, Winnipeg, International Institute for Sustainable Development; also at www.iisd.org/trade/pubs.htm

von Moltke, K. (1995) *International Environmental Management, Trade Regimes and Sustainability*, Winnipeg, International institute for Sustainable Development, www.iisd1.iisd.ca/trade/pubs

von Moltke, K. (2000) *The Precautionary Principle, Risk Assessment and the World Trade Organistation*, Winnipeg, International Institute for Sustainable Development, 2000, www.iisd1.iisd.ca/trade/pubs

von Moltke, K. (2001) 'On Clustering International Environmental Agreements', Paper for the French Ministry of Environment, July, www.iiss1.iisd.ca//trade

von Moltke, K. and H. Mann (2001) 'Misappropriation of Institutions: Some Lessons from the Environmental Dimension of the NAFTA Investor–State Dispute Settlement Process', *International Environmental Agreements*, vol 1, no 1 (January), pp103–123

Young, O. (2002) *The Institutional Dimensions of Environmental Change: Fit, Interplay, and Scale*, Cambridge, MIT Press

Young, O. (1999a) 'Towards a Theory of Institutional Change', in Young, O., *Governance in World Affairs*, Ithaca, NY, Cornell University Press, pp133–162

Young, O. (1999b) 'Science Plan for the Project on the Institutional Dimensions of *IHDP Report No. 9*. Bonn, International Human Dimensions Programme on Global Environmental Change

Chapter 8

Corporate Governance and Global Disclosure: Let the Sun Shine In

Sandy Buffett

ABSTRACT

Rules, relationships, and expected standards for accountability and disclosure are at the heart of corporate governance. Traditional shareholder-led models of corporate governance have not clearly defined accountability for environmental and social impacts or a company's responsibility to its stakeholders. Yet, recent corporate accounting and governance scandals and growing calls by civil society for minimum corporate environmental and social standards provide traction for elevating an enhanced corporate governance and disclosure framework into the international policy arena.

This chapter examines the potential scope and substance of a 'multi-stakeholder corporate governance framework' to increase the transparency and accountability of large global companies. As a starting point, such a framework could be modelled on the Organization for Economic Cooperation and Development's (OECD) Corporate Governance Principles and Guidelines for Multinational Enterprises section on disclosure. However, further work is needed to reconcile and strengthen these voluntary principles. Convergence between corporate governance and corporate social responsibility in Europe and elsewhere provides useful policy precedents for the creation of a binding and international multi-stakeholder corporate governance framework.

INTRODUCTION

> *The governance of the corporation is now as important in the world economy as the government of countries.*
>
> (Wolfensohn, 1999)

In recent years, the governance and ethical failures of high-profile developed country companies, including Enron and Worldcom, have generated a crisis of accountability of markets and corporations. As a result, regulators have scrambled to put corporate governance rules and guidelines into place to restore the public's trust. These new rules and guidelines, which seek to strengthen accountability of corporate executives and boards of directors, are meant to be the expression of society's expectations for corporate behaviour and to serve as a foundation for corporate regulation.

Yet, many activists involved in the international corporate accountability movement remain bystanders to these current policy debates. While they call for global environmental and social regulation of corporations, international policy-makers and activists remain remarkably disconnected from the corporate governance reform movement emanating from Wall Street, London and other financial centres.

The definition of rules, relationships, and expected standards for accountability and disclosure are at the heart of these debates. Corporate governance reform is reshaping the rules and information flows among a company's management, board of directors, shareholders and stakeholders. Should environmental and social justice advocates join and broaden this debate on corporate governance, it would provide a potentially powerful 'point of entry' to redefine corporate rules and relationships. Elevating environmental and social issues into the corporate governance debate and disclosure reforms could have profound implications for whether or not foreign direct investment (FDI) by corporations will contribute to sustainable and responsible development in the developing world.

In the face of numerous examples of poor environmental performance and human rights abuses by transnational corporations (TNCs) operating in developing countries, international activists are increasingly calling for global rules for corporations. Leading up to the 2002 World Summit for Sustainable Development (WSSD), several NGOs and citizen's groups called for a binding framework to hold corporations accountable. One proposal put forward, the Corporate Accountability Convention, called for corporations to adhere to binding environmental, human rights, and labour performance standards and reporting requirements[1]. Although this and similar proposals gained some momentum prior to the WSSD, a binding international framework regulating multinational performance has yet to be realized.

As the main drivers of international trade and investment, TNCs have become powerful drivers of development within many developing and transition economies. TNCs can bring much needed jobs and potential technology transfer to these regions. However, many of the countries that are destinations for FDI frequently lack the resources, regulatory capacity, or political will to hold TNCs to high environmental, labour, and human rights standards. Some companies claim that they are operating according to international best practice. However, the absence of a global regulator for corporate activity and the lack of capacity for developing countries to unilaterally impose rules on foreign investors have resulted in a vacuum of corporate oversight.

To date, investment and trade policy-makers pushing the FDI liberalization agenda have failed to heed the implications of recent corporate crises and the ensuing calls for greater oversight, transparency, and protection of stakeholders. The World Bank, for example, cautions that 'agreements on investment policy are likely to have strong development effects only if they deal with the big issues facing developing countries' (World Bank, 2003). To deal with the 'big issues', it suggests that pro-development investment policies should include protection of investors' rights, liberalization of investment flows, and minimization of distortions. On a similar track, in international and regional trade negotiations, one of the most contentious issues is whether to extend rights such as national treatment, non-discrimination, and dispute settlement to international investors.

Sorely missing from these policy prescriptions are mechanisms to ensure that TNCs that benefit from liberal international investment and trade rules operate to a high standard of corporate governance and social responsibility. Global market players require global rules. Policy-makers, business, and civil society need to connect the dots between corporate governance reform, corporate social responsibility, and international investment policy to forge a coherent and binding framework defining the rules and responsibilities of TNCs in the 21st century.

This chapter seeks to illuminate the potential for a convergence and elevation of corporate governance principles, disclosure, and corporate social responsibility at the international level as a first step towards global rules. Following this introduction, Section 2 defines corporate governance and describes the current state of debate and reform in the US and at the multilateral level. Section 3 looks specifically at the role of disclosure and sustainability reporting as a governance mechanism. Section 4 illuminates promising trends in international corporate governance, disclosure and corporate social responsibility. Section 5 provides initial recommendations for a way forward.

THE CURRENT STATE OF CORPORATE GOVERNANCE REFORM

> *Corporate governance is concerned with holding the balance between economic and social goals and between individual and communal goals. . . . The aim is to align as nearly as possible the interests of individuals, corporations, and society.*
>
> (Cadbury, 1999)

What is meant by the term 'corporate governance' and how does it relate to governing global corporations? Corporate governance establishes the relationships and rules among a company's management, the board of directors, shareholders, and stakeholders, such as employees and local communities. More broadly, corporate governance defines both the legal obligations and societal expectations of companies (Gregory, 2000).

Corporate governance frameworks have evolved from the realm of technical and arcane shareholder concerns to move to the forefront for national regulators and emerging public policy networks. Corporate governance frameworks are shaped by stock exchange commissions, disclosure regulations, shareholder actions, and decisions by the board of directors. Ultimately, a company's board of directors is responsible for corporate governance.

Models of corporate governance vary between different countries and cultures and there is an unresolved debate over which model is superior. The dominant Anglo-American model, the so-called shareholder model, emphasizes the protection of shareholders, whereas the European or Asian model provides more rights to stakeholders, such as labour, and to an intermediary such as a bank. The pillars of the Anglo-American model – as it is currently exercised – relate to a company's financial audits, executive compensation, shareholder rights, and board organization and independence.

The US-led model of corporate governance and its related accounting, reporting, and audit standards, for the most part, overlook material risk factors such as the environment, reputation, and worker health and safety (Keefe, 2002). From the spate of recent scandals where shareholders, employees, the environment, and communities all suffered from corporate greed, it is clear that the traditional frameworks of corporate governance have failed both shareholders and stakeholders.

Companies criticized for having some of the most environmentally or socially egregious activities are likely to have inadequate corporate governance mechanisms in place. Indeed, 'socially responsible investors' consider that a company's commitment to and management of environmental and social issues often serves as an indicative proxy to gauge the quality of its overall management and governance.

While investors were buying Enron at high stock valuations in the late 1990s, for example, activists were decrying the company's environmental and social record and raising concerns about the company's governance. NGOs pointed to Enron's alleged complicity in human rights abuses and charges of corruption at the Dabhol power project in India, and its environmental destruction at the Bolivia-Brazil pipeline (Friends of the Earth, 1999). From these allegations, poor environmental and social performance and charges of corruption should have served as a red flag to investors that larger management failures existed. Redefining corporate governance to include the management and disclosure of worldwide environmental and social risks would better protect both shareholders and stakeholders.

In reaction to recent US corporate scandals, the US Congress hastily signed into law the Sarbanes-Oxley Act (SOX) of 2002 'to protect investors by improving the accuracy and reliability of corporate disclosures made pursuant to the securities laws, and for other purposes'[2]. Its primary intent is to hold corporate executives and the accounting bodies that audit corporations more accountable to shareholders. SOX addresses issues such as auditor independence, strengthens criminal penalties for corporate fraud and corruption, and creates an accounting oversight board. Interestingly, it requires a company's chief executive officer and chief finance officer to personally certify that its financial disclosures are true and that all relevant material information has been presented.

While some commentators on Wall Street and overseas markets believe that SOX goes too far, many investors in the US who have long been involved in the promotion of good corporate governance believe it does not go far enough. The US Social Investment Forum, a 500-member socially responsible investment organization, released a series of 26 additional suggestions to initiate 'the next wave of reform'. The statement calls for the replacement of a business model of shareholder governance to one that democratizes corporate governance and prioritizes all stakeholders. The suggested categories for further reform include proxy voting disclosure, expensing of stock options, reigning in executive compensation, audit reforms, and social and environmental disclosure (Baue, 2002).

The OECD corporate governance principles

The non-binding OECD Principles of Corporate Governance, ratified in 1999, reflect the consensus of the 30 OECD member countries, as well as additional country observers.

The four pillars of the OECD Corporate Governance Principles – equitable treatment, responsibility, accountability, and transparency – are increasingly seen as universal values for corporate governance (Witherell, 2003). The principles recognize the rights of stakeholders and call for the development of mechanisms to increase access to information. Some have referred to the OECD Principles as the emerging 'gold standard' for corporate governance (Shinn and Gourevitch, 2002).

Box 8.1 *OECD Principles of Corporate Governance*

Fairness: Protect shareholder rights and ensure the equitable treatment of shareholders.
Transparency: Make timely and accurate disclosure on all material matters.
Accountability: Ensure the strategic guidance of the company, monitoring of management by the board, and the board's accountability to the company and shareholders.
Responsibility: Recognize the rights of stakeholders as established by law (i.e. compliance) and encourage active cooperation between corporations and stakeholders in creating wealth, jobs and the sustainability of financially sound enterprises.

Source: www.oecd.org

These overarching principles allow for a wide degree of interpretation. It is likely that the attempt to synthesize key principles between the Anglo-American governance model and the European or Asian models of governance required such vagueness. One key uncertainty for policy-makers, corporations, investors, and civil society is how to measure and benchmark these concepts of fairness, transparency, accountability and responsibility. How can regulators judge if companies 'encourage active cooperation between corporations and stakeholders'? How does a company recognize the rights of stakeholders in countries with oppressive regimes? Does the word 'sustainability' mean sustainability of the planet or of a company's profits? It is clear that more work remains to be done to broaden and deepen the debate on universal principles of corporate governance.

Section IV of the OECD Corporate Governance Principles specifically addresses disclosure and transparency and advises that disclosure should include, but not be limited to, material information on:

- the financial and operating results of the company;
- company objectives;
- major share ownership and voting rights;
- members of the board and key executives and their remuneration;
- material foreseeable risk factors;
- material issues regarding employees and other stakeholders; and
- governance structures and policies.

The 'materiality' of risk factors and stakeholder issues is generally defined as information 'whose omission or mis-statement could influence the economic decisions taken by users of information'. However, the delineation of whether specific information is material is left to the country or market actor to define (OECD, 1999).

The points above relating to the disclosure of foreseeable risk, employees and other stakeholders, and governance policies are of particular interest for considering how corporate governance has the potential to hold corporations accountable on global environmental and social issues. Further definition of these sections could serve as a minimum baseline for mandatory environmental and social disclosures required of OECD-based corporations. For example, if a company is paying a military dictatorship in a developing country to provide security for its pipeline, or a project loses its insurance coverage because it is poisoning a community's drinking water with mine tailings, this could be 'material' information that the company would be forced to disclose to its investors and the international community.

International corporate governance

International policy-makers began taking note of corporate governance following the 1997 Asian financial crisis. Many analysts blamed the Asian crisis on the banks and corporations in the Asian countries that lacked transparency and 'good governance'. Since then, the World Bank and the International Monetary Fund have used the OECD Corporate Governance Principles as a benchmark for measuring the uptake of corporate governance by domestic companies and developing country regulators, in a sense providing a seal of approval for TNCs looking for safe and sound business climates.

The World Bank has launched the Global Corporate Governance Forum (GCGF) as a way to disseminate best practice, foster research, and provide technical assistance among the private sector in developing countries. So far, this initiative aims at improving the governance of local industries in the developing world, but does not address improving the governance of TNCs operating in those developing countries.

The pre-eminent policy network addressing corporate governance is the International Corporate Governance Network (ICGN). The ICGN, founded in 1995, is a global, non-governmental organization that represents over 250 institutional and private investors, corporations and advisers. It is dedicated to the promotion of sound corporate governance and promotes international dialogue on this issue.

The ICGN considers the OECD Principles to be a baseline of minimum acceptable standards for companies and investors and has put forth an expanded set of standards for best practice. Notably, the ICGN declares that 'boards that strive for active cooperation between corporations and stakeholders will be most likely to create wealth, employment and sustainable economies. They should disclose their policies on issues involving stakeholders, for example, workplace and environmental matters' (ICGN, 2000).

Corporate governance has only been touched upon as a peripheral and aspirational issue within trade and investment fora. Any discussion linking corporate governance to development has related to spreading the 'gospel' of the Anglo-American style of corporate governance to developing country corporations. For example, China committed to improve corporate governance and transparency of Chinese banks and companies ahead of its accession into the WTO. There has been, to date, no official reference to corporate governance benchmarks, such as the OECD Principles of Corporate Governance, as a standard to be followed by TNCs as a condition of access to new markets and dispute resolution mechanisms. The bar needs to be raised, not only on developing country companies, but on the governance of TNCs that seek legal protections and rights through investment regimes.

To date, the most comprehensive set of corporate social responsibility guidelines that reference corporate governance and disclosure are the OECD Guidelines for Multinational Enterprises (MNE). First compiled in 1976 and most recently revised in 2000, the MNE Guidelines establish voluntary principles to promote responsible business practices and to enhance corporations' contribution to sustainable development.

The scope of the guidelines includes labour, corruption, environment, human rights, technology transfer and corporate governance principles derived from international law and other standards adopted from the Universal Declaration on Human Rights and the ILO. The 30 member countries of the OECD, including the US, have ratified the OECD guidelines and several non-OECD countries, such as Brazil and Singapore, have agreed to adhere to the guidelines. However, corporations are not legally bound to adhere to the voluntary MNE guidelines (OECD, 2003).

Box 8.2 *Disclosure Principles of the OECD Guidelines for Multinational Enterprises*

1. Enterprises should ensure that timely, regular, reliable and relevant information is disclosed regarding their activities, structure, financial situation and performance.
2. Enterprises should apply high quality standards for disclosure, accounting, and audit. Enterprises are also encouraged to apply high-quality standards for non-financial information, including environmental and social reporting, where they exist. The standards or policies under which both financial and non-financial information are compiled and published should be reported.
3. Enterprises should disclose basic information showing their name, location, and structure.
4. Enterprises should also disclose material information on corporate governance.
5. Enterprises are encouraged to communicate additional information that could include:
   a. Value statements or statements of business conduct intended for public disclosure including information on the social, ethical and environmental policies of the enterprise and the other codes of conduct to which the company subscribes.
   b. Information on systems for managing risks and complying with laws, and on statements or codes of business conduct.
   c. Information on relationships with employees and other stakeholders.

Source: www.oecd.org/

Section III of the OECD MNE Guidelines addresses disclosure. Much of the MNE disclosure recommendations mirror the OECD Corporate Governance Principles' wording on disclosure. But the MNE Guidelines go further by explicitly encouraging disclosure on social, environmental and risk reporting, as well as a company's use of codes of conduct and stakeholder relationships. Moreover, while the OECD principles state unequivocally that companies 'should' disclose financial issues, the MNE Guidelines merely 'encourage' disclosure of non-financial environmental and social information.

Each of the countries that ratified the MNE Guidelines agreed to establish a 'National Contact Point' (NCP) to implement the guidelines and to provide a national context for handling enquiries about them. The NCPs are tasked with promoting the guidelines and serve as the central contact for any person or organization to bring cases where companies have allegedly failed to uphold the voluntary guidelines. The US NCP is the director of investment affairs in the Department of State; in the UK, the NCP is located in the Department of Trade and Industry.

A new coalition of NGOs, called OECD Watch, monitors the role and the effectiveness of the NCPs. OECD Watch observes that there is wide variance among countries in NCP procedures and handling of enquiries brought by NGOs and labour unions. At this time, signatory countries do not appear to be integrating the NCPs into broader current debates and national policies on corporate responsibility and governance (OECD Watch, 2003). It is likely that corporate securities regulators (such as the SEC) and lawmakers are not even aware of the existence or the role of the NCP, nor of the MNE Guidelines. NCPs could play a central role in the current review of corporate governance and disclosure regimes in each of their respective countries to include a debate on disclosure of multinational corporate activities overseas as laid out in the guidelines.

The Central Role of Disclosure and Sustainability Reporting

Sunlight is said to be the best of disinfectants.

(US Supreme Court Justice Louis Brandeis, 1934)

Disclosure of a company's financial assets and liabilities is mandated and regulated by national governments. However, the lack of statutory disclosure on environmental and social issues provides little incentive for companies to voluntarily disclose this type of information to the public. Even mandatory environmental disclosures in the US and some European countries are narrowly defined, broadly subjective, and full of loopholes. For example, if left undefined, who determines if an environmental liability is 'material' (that is, a threshold where information is deemed important enough for investors to want to know)? Since securities regulators have failed to clearly define 'material' in relation to non-financial risks, companies and the investment community continue to deem environmental and social issues as immaterial.

Companies claim that disclosure is unnecessary, cumbersome, and potentially damaging to competitive advantage. Consumer pressure and NGO campaigns have put a flame under some companies to provide more information, but without a standardized reporting and disclosure framework, companies can selectively disclose and 'tell a story' favourable to the company. Notably, several large European companies have voluntarily adopted sustainability reporting as part of a 'triple bottom line' approach. But some companies simply engage in blatant 'greenwashing' as a public relations strategy (Komisar, 2002). Clearly, there is a need for 'systematic, comprehensive and reliable data' to inform shareholders and stakeholders (Lydenburg, 2002).

The investment community needs credible information about a company's operations in order to get a true picture of the company's performance, non-financial risks, and liabilities. Measurable data must be provided not only for domestic activities, but also for a company's global operations. Currently, there is no regulation anywhere in the world that mandates TNCs to disclose to their home country regulator the same level of information about overseas operations as are required for domestic operations. While some progressive companies have made strides towards transparency and increased information on their worldwide operations, TNCs still operate within a regulatory vacuum at the international level, enabling them to evade scrutiny and evaluation of their true impacts on the environment, employees, public health, and communities.

Among the OECD countries, the incoherence between disclosure requirements for domestic versus global corporate operations has created a substantial information gap. It should be noted that even the existing disclosure regulations in the 'home' or headquarter countries of TNCs (if they are enforced) fall short of providing robust, meaningful data. This schism raises two potential policy options to increase social, environmental, and ethical corporate disclosure:

- 'Closing the gap' – The first baseline approach would be to require all TNCs to disclose the same level of information (to their headquarter-based regulator) for overseas activities as required for home-based domestic operations. This would be a substantial first step for obtaining information on MNC activities in developing countries.
- 'Raising the bar' – The more ambitious approach calls for an upward harmonization of all domestic and global disclosure standards, improving access to environmental, social, and ethical information for corporate activities worldwide. Raising the bar requires both a 'catch up' on international operations disclosure and a strengthening of existing domestic disclosures.

Environmental disclosure rules in the US

In the US, the most important environmental disclosure law is the Emergency Planning and Community Right-to-Know Act of 1986 (EPCRA). Within this law is a section called TRI, the Toxic Release Inventory, which requires facilities to disclose to the US EPA data on toxic emissions to air, water and land. TRI was the first attempt to make an inventory on a facility-by-facility basis of toxic releases from corporate activity. Ironically, the EPCRA was prompted by the Union Carbide Bhopal Tragedy, yet TRI does not extend to a US corporation's overseas activities. TRI extends only to US-based facilities. TRI data has enabled many affected US communities to organize, inform the media, and pressure companies to reduce pollution (World Resources Institute, 2003).

In the US, a coalition of over 200 groups is advocating for international right-to-know legislation. Based on successful community right-to-know legislation in the US, the IRTK (International Right to Know) Campaign would require US companies to match their mandatory domestic reports on issues such as worker injury and releases of toxic chemicals with reports on their overseas activities. It encompasses disclosure labour reporting requirements, such as workplace injuries and fatalities and hazardous materials in the workplace as required by the US Occupational Safety and Health Act (IRTK Campaign, 2003).

IRTK also would require human rights disclosures, such as the existence of security arrangements (for example, paramilitary or state police arrangements), violations of international human rights standards, and information regarding the displacement of indigenous peoples. The IRTK Campaign has proposed legislation in the US Congress. If passed, it would be implemented and enforced by relevant US agencies (EPA, Department of Labor, State Department) in the same manner that the US departments of Justice and Commerce have authority to enforce the Foreign Corrupt Practices Act[3].

The US mandates certain types of environmental accounting within financial reports for investors. US securities disclosure laws are defined by the Securities Act of 1933 and the Securities Exchange Act of 1934, and are overseen by the Securities Exchange Commission (SEC). Within financial statements, material environmental expenses must be disclosed quarterly and in the annual 10-K statement, the annual financial reporting mechanism for publicly traded companies.

Regulation S-K in the US requires disclosure by publicly traded companies of material effects that environmental regulation, trends, or uncertainty may have upon the company. It also requires a company to disclose environmental legal proceedings or claims of US$100,000 or more. However, a 1998 Environment Protection Agency study found that 74 per cent of publicly traded companies had failed to disclose legal proceedings on the environment in their 10-K disclosures, as required by the SEC[4].

A US alliance comprising NGOs, unions, public interest groups, and socially responsible investors, known as the Corporate Sunshine Working Group (CSWG), is lobbying the US Securities and Exchange Commission to enforce and expand mandatory disclosure of environmental and social information within a company's financial annual report. The CSWG has a proposal with 20 comprehensive points for expanded SEC disclosure. These include such things as changing the threshold on cumulative environmental liabilities, disclosing major suppliers and countries of operations, levels of unionization of a company's worldwide work force, corporate contributions for political lobbying, disclosure on compliance with the Foreign Corrupt Practices Act, and political risk disclosure related to security arrangements with military or paramilitary forces (Corporate Sunshine Working Group, 2003).

Corporate social responsibility and voluntary sustainability reporting

Despite a lack of political will at the international level for binding corporate performance standards, some companies have adopted the 'triple bottom line', that is, a management belief that economic, environmental, and social issues are bottom-line issues. As a key element of corporate social responsibility (CSR), several large corporations have voluntarily disclosed through 'sustainability reports' a broader set of environmental and social indicators. These disclosures can provide useful and empowering information to communities and stakeholders, which 'can speed the transition to a greener business model' (World Resources Institute, 2003). However, there is as yet little evidence that voluntary CSR and disclosure, by itself, has compelled the majority of TNCs operating in developing countries to raise their environmental and social performance.

While stakeholders have demanded greater disclosure and transparency of corporations, the lack of a standardized framework for social, environmental, and ethical reporting allows companies to craft their own stories. To resolve this, the Global Reporting Initiative (GRI), is trying to create a common framework for voluntary reporting of economic, environmental, and social impacts of corporate activity. GRI's proponents want to elevate 'sustainability reporting' to the same accepted level as financial reporting (White, 1999). GRI reports require disclosure on a company's economic, environmental and social performance. Firms must report on company-wide materials, energy and water use, emissions and effluents. GRI also requires, *inter alia*, company information on labour practices and human rights, product stewardship and supply chain issues, bribery and corruption, and broader economic impacts.

In 2002, GRI became a permanent, independent international body with a multi-stakeholder governance structure. Draft guidelines have been test piloted by over 60 companies and GRI is seeking input from various stakeholders into its current revision. By September 2003, 322 companies and organizations had begun to use GRI in some capacity, including TNCs such as Ford, Deutsche Bank, Nike and Mitsubishi. GRI is also committed to developing 'sector supplements' to provide more detailed sector-specific information. GRI sector supplements have been released in pilot form for the financial services sector and for tour operators (tourism).

Perhaps the key challenge for GRI remains the creation of a uniform reporting format that is meaningful, yet still flexible enough to be useful across industry sectors and within different country and cultural variations. Moreover, it provides a framework for company-wide compiled data, rather than facility-specific data sorely needed by communities around the globe. However, in 2002, affiliated groups, CERES (the Coalition for Environmentally Responsible Economies) and the Tellus Institute, launched a compatible and complementary reporting initiative for facility-level and site-specific environmental and social sustainability reporting.

PROMISING TRENDS IN GOVERNANCE AND DISCLOSURE WORLDWIDE

> *. . .the topic of 'corporate governance, accountability, and transparency' is out of its shaded box, historically overseen by learned and powerful interests. . . .*
>
> (Zadek and McIntosh, 2002.)

The impetus for corporate disclosure on social, environmental and ethical issues is gaining steam around the world. Currently, in Europe, South Africa and Australia, the rethinking and reform of corporate governance criteria is gaining momentum. With the dual emerging phenomena of recent high-profile corporate scandals and the increasing influence of institutional investors, corporate governance frameworks are slowly evolving to embrace notions of stakeholder rights and disclosure of social, environmental and ethical issues. The movements of 'corporate social responsibility' and corporate governance appear to be slowly overlapping as non-financial issues and a company's relationship with its stakeholders become relevant to shareholders.

South Africa appears to be at the forefront of the convergence of corporate governance and corporate social responsibility. The South African King II report, released in 2002, is a set of principles for corporations listed on the Johannesburg Stock Exchange (JSE), banks and financial services regulated by South Africa. The Corporate Governance Code calls on companies to provide 'integrated sustainability reporting' annually on social, ethical, safety, health and environment practices, and to report regularly to stakeholders on the policies and procedures to monitor and verify compliance. Notably, it directly references the Global Reporting Initiative (GRI) as a standard for sustainability reporting. It also states that the board should take into account the business environment in South Africa, including an HIV/AIDs corporate strategy/policy (already a listing requirement of the JSE) and disclosure of procurement practices as they relate to black economic empowerment.

The code also recommends that not only its domestic companies, but also all multinational companies operating in South Africa, should give due consideration to the application of the code. While there is no enforcement mechanism for the principles, the JSE has indicated that it will 'compel' companies listed on the exchange to comply. Even though it is a set of guidelines rather than company law, the King II report is significant for its inclusion of CSR and disclosure within a corporate governance code, and it will allow shareholders in South Africa, as well as shareholders of companies operating there, to bring environmental and social corporate governance issues to the attention of the board.

South Africa has also enacted an innovative right-to-know law, the Promotion of Access to Information Act of 2000 that seeks to improve transparency and accountability. Most remarkably, the unprecedented legislation allows citizen access to information not only from the State regulators, but also directly from private corporate sector actors. An individual can pay an access fee and submit a request to a private sector corporation. The company has 30 days to accept or refuse the request. If it is refused, the company must provide written explanation. An individual can appeal this refusal in a South African court. Grounds for refusing to disclose include 'trade secrets', competitive disadvantage, or likely commercial or financial harm from the disclosure (Hofmeyr, 2002).

Regulators in the UK, France and South Africa, and international bodies such as UNCTAD and the EU, have explicitly defined material risk factors and issues to include impacts on the environment, communities and other stakeholders. These governance innovations set a useful precedent for interpreting the OECD Corporate Governance Principles to embrace environmental and social disclosure.

Disclosure for institutional investors

Institutional investors, such as Hermes in the UK and the California Public Employees Retirement System (CalPERS), have used their clout to force significant changes in corporate management to make the companies in which they

Table 8.1 *International Trends in Social and Environmental Disclosure*

Country/region	Name & Date	Coverage
France	**Nouvelle Regulations Economique NRE**, mandates 'sustainability reporting', came into effect in February 2002	Requires companies to report on the on their employee relations and environmental performance within their annual reports, including community impacts, human resources, labour standards, emissions, and resource consumption. The law does not clearly delineate whether a company must report on its global operations, or just its French-based operations and provides no sanctions for non-compliance. (*Source:* Ethical Performance, April 2002)
UK	**Company Law Review**, published in July 2001	Requires directors to report annually on 'material' social and environmental matters. Within a company's annual report, publicly traded and large private companies must provide an 'operating and financial review' (OFR), that must contain an assessment of past performance and future prospects, including impacts on the environment, communities and employees. *(www.dti.gov.uk/cld/review.htm)*
UK Institute of Chartered Accountants	**Turnbull Report, 1999** Internal Control: Guidance for Directors on the Combined Code. Often referred to as the Turnbull Report (after the chairman)	Provides guidance for board directors on how to implement and disclose board policies on risk management and internal control to comply with requirements of the London Stock Exchange. The report states that companies should regularly report on 'significant internal and external operational, financial, compliance and other risks'. These include market, liquidity, credit, technological, legal, health, safety and environmental, brand value, reputation and business probity issues. *(www.icaew.co.uk/cbp/index.cfm?aub=tb2I_6242)*
UK The Association of British Insurers	**ABI Guidelines 2001**	A set of disclosure guidelines to provide a 'basic benchmark' for companies to develop best practice for reporting on social responsibility. Notably, the disclosure guidelines relate specifically to the responsibilities of Board Directors. These recommendations include disclosure of how the board takes regular account of social, environmental and ethical (SEE) matters, the identification of risks arising

Table 8.1 *Continued*

Country/region	Name & Date	Coverage
		from SEE matters, and a description of the company's policies, procedures, risk management systems, and compliance with these policies. It recommends that a company obtain an independent external verification of its SEE disclosures. (*www.abi.org.uk/*) (Cowe, 2001)
UNCTAD	The Intergovernmental Working Group of Experts on International Standards of Accounting and Reporting **(ISAR) UNCTAD 1998 position paper**	The position paper, 'Accounting and Financial Reporting for Environmental Costs and Liabilities' provides guidance on best practice for reporting on environmental transactions within a company's financial statement. According to its website, it is the sole intergovernmental working group on accounting and auditing for multinational corporations. (*http://r0.unctad.org/isar/*)
European Community (EC)	**Voluntary guidelines for environmental costs and liabilities reporting by EU companies (C[2001] 453/EC), 2001**	Based on the 1998 ISAR position paper, the guidelines clarify existing rules as part of the European Union Financial Reporting Strategy, an effort to harmonize EU standards with International Accounting Standards. The scope of the guidelines pertains to a company's environmental costs and liabilities that should be disclosed in annual and consolidated financial reports. (*http://europa.eu.int/eur-lex/en/index.html*)

invest in more transparent and accountable. Thus, they have been key players in promoting good corporate governance.

Beyond this catalytic role, the recent application of disclosure regulations to this sector in some countries is also having a remarkable ripple effect on the convergence of corporate social responsibility and corporate governance. New disclosure regulations, elegantly simple in design, are being promulgated in several countries for institutional investors. According to the conference board, nearly US$24 trillion in corporate assets is held by institutional investors (76 per cent of which is held by US and UK institutional investors) (Conference Board, 2003).

The new trends in the convergence of corporate governance and corporate social responsibility offer promising tools for corporate accountability. However, the coverage and regulatory reach of these innovative policy mechanisms is still relatively insignificant to the overall operations of TNCs operating worldwide. These regulations apply to a small number of mostly European corporations.

Table 8.2 *Recent Disclosure Regulations for Institutional Investors*

Country	Name	Coverage
UK	UK pension law 1999	In 1999, the government amended the 1995 Pensions Act requiring all pension fund trustees to make an annual disclosure statement, which would comment on 'the extent, if at all, to which social, environmental, or ethical considerations are taken into account in the selection, retention, and realization of investments'.' France, Germany, and Belgium have passed similar legislation.
Australia	Corporation Law 2001	An amendment to Australia's Corporations Law requires, at the point of sale of the investment product, that the issuer or seller disclose to the consumer: 'the extent, if any, to which labour standards, environmental, social or ethical considerations are taken into account in the selection, retention and realization of the investment'. This amendment applies not only to pension funds, but to all institutional investors such as retail mutual funds, superannuation products and life insurance products. The Australian law also requires investors to disclose whether an investor considers labour standards.

Source: www.socialfunds.com

None of the above mechanisms explicitly requires companies to report on their overseas activities.

THE WAY FORWARD: RECOMMENDATIONS FOR SUSTAINABLE AND RESPONSIBLE CORPORATE GOVERNANCE

In a global market, corporate governance and disclosure must have a global reach. Corporate accounting and governance scandals and parallel calls by civil society for minimum corporate accountability standards have created a political climate ripe for elevating a corporate governance framework into the international policy arena.

Corporate governance has evolved from an enigmatic boardroom aspiration into official accounting and disclosure regulation. As the concept of corporate governance evolves to embrace corporate responsibility and the role of stakeholders, national and international regulators need to evolve accordingly (Chan-Fishel, 2002). A harmonized and binding international corporate governance regime may be an effective and politically strategic starting point for balancing the private rights of corporations with the social good of sustainable and responsible corporate activity.

A rules-based framework for sustainable, multistakeholder corporate governance should have the same internationally binding status as the rules which govern international trade and investment. Indeed, such a framework could be embedded in bilateral, regional, or multilateral trade and investment agreements. It could also be created and implemented through a stand-alone or joint agreement through the OECD, the UN, the International Organization of Securities Commissions (IOSCO), or other relevant international law bodies.

A politically feasible and effective starting point for holding multinational corporations accountable worldwide could be to require the 'home' countries of foreign investors to strengthen environmental, social, and ethical disclosure and reporting requirements for TNCs. The countries where TNCs are headquartered and domestically regulated (predominantly the richest of the OECD countries) have the capacity to regulate their companies' global operations through enhanced corporate governance and disclosure rules.

Regardless of which is the most desirable or politically feasible, an enhanced governance framework should reflect the best, state-of-the-art governance policies that promote accountability to stakeholders and robust disclosure of environmental and social performance. The framework would represent the convergence of corporate social responsibility with mainstream corporate governance principles. Ultimately, it must serve to move the corporate sector from a shareholder model to a more inclusive multistakeholder model. The development of a 'Multistakeholder Corporate Governance Framework', or MCGF, should incorporate the following principles:

- ***Build on emerging norms:*** The MCGF should start with the spirit of the OECD Corporate Governance Principles, together with the enhanced disclosure guidelines provided in the OECD MNE Guidelines. But the MCGF must go further and look to new emerging legislation and mechanisms such as the South African corporate governance code, the UK Company Law Review, UK pension law, and France's Nouvelle Regulations Economique. Additional standards, such as the recommendations of the US Social Investment Forum, the proposal by the Corporate Sunshine Working Group, and the IRTK Campaign should also be incorporated[5].
- ***Hold boards accountable:*** Just as new corporate governance reforms require accountability of a company's board of directors, ultimate accountability – and liability – for the tenets of a MCGF must rest with the board. The MCGF could require a board-level subcommittee responsible for dealing with social, environmental and ethical governance. The guidelines of the Association of British Insurers could serve as a template as they provide particular guidance for board responsibilities.
- ***Involve the GRI:*** The GRI is evolving quickly as the best practice for voluntary sustainability reporting and represents an important step towards mandatory reporting. As a first step, a MCGF could include mandatory reporting using the GRI format. A GRI global secretariat, with an accompanying level of enhanced authority and funding, would be responsible for monitoring the content and verity of GRI reports and for coordinating with

the UN or national governments to make the reports available in relevant local languages. The MCGF should create an international data clearing-house where any citizen of the world could have access to a company's relevant MCGF disclosures.

- ***Consider linkages with trade agreements:*** If linked to or embedded within trade and investment agreements, all signatory countries, developing and developed, would be party to an MSCG Framework. The framework would apply to both foreign multinational companies and to large domestic companies. The commitment would be mandatory only for large TNCs and would allow exemption of small and medium-sized enterprises (SMEs) in developing countries that may not be positioned to comply in the same manner as TNCs. The Free Trade Area of the Americas (FTAA) may be a viable point of entry for a MCGF since the US, Mexico and Canada (OECD members) and Brazil, Chile and Argentina (non-OECD members) have already declared adherence to the OECD Corporate Governance Principles and the Guidelines on MNEs (OECD, 2003).

Why should activists and policy-makers champion a framework of corporate governance and disclosure rather than push for a comprehensive set of binding environmental and social performance standards for TNCs? A corporate governance and disclosure approach to make corporations accountable is attractive for the following reasons:

- **The regulatory burden would be on the home country:** Rules for TNCs will not succeed politically if they rely on FDI-hungry developing countries to unilaterally implement and monitor MNC adherence to complex social and environmental standards[6]. In the absence of a global regulator, securities regulators are the only governmental bodies responsible for monitoring of multinational corporate activity[7].
- **Mandatory disclosure is effective**: Disclosure regulations have improved overall corporate performance on the environment in developed countries[8]. There is an often-mentioned saying, 'What gets measured gets managed'. Disclosure empowers communities, activists, and consumers with accurate information on worldwide, and potentially facility-specific, corporate activities. As demands for corporate accountability increase, companies – especially those companies that claim to be leaders in corporate responsibility – should welcome binding disclosure as a way to 'level the playing field'. The enforcement and verification of environmental and social disclosures would be held to the same regulatory standard as financial disclosures.
- **Many investors would support it**: The investment community, particularly socially responsible investors (SRI), would likely rally behind mandatory disclosure and reporting to provide more credible data and reduce its current dependency on unverifiable surveys and questionnaires. The most powerful institutional investors would also likely welcome binding disclosure. Indeed, in 2003 a group of influential US institutional investors created

the National Coalition for Corporate Reform (NCCR) to advocate for improved corporate governance (Baue, 2003).

- **It is politically attractive:** Currently, the mechanism with the most momentum and recognition for improving the accountability and transparency of corporations is corporate governance. It is the buzzword *de jour* among financial regulators and boardrooms around the world. Since strong corporate governance strengthens transparency and trust in international capital markets and is believed to facilitate flows of FDI, policy-makers concerned with global financial stability and liberalized markets may champion elevating a corporate governance framework to the international level (Shinn and Gourevitch, 2002).
- **It is a good first step**: A corporate governance framework would not set out to hold companies to single global standards, such as uniform pollution standards or a global minimum wage. A governance and disclosure approach would provide a powerful snapshot of corporate performance to shareholders and stakeholders and would likely help activists, policy-makers, and the corporate sector operationalize what further work needs to be done. A corporate governance and disclosure framework does not preclude the future promulgation of minimum global standards for the environment, labour and human rights. Such a framework would greatly increase the flow of sorely lacking corporate information, facilitating parallel and future efforts towards binding environmental and social standards.

Policy-makers, corporations and investors must respond to the crisis of corporate accountability. The OECD announced recently that it 'has embarked on a drive to strengthen corporate governance practices world wide in the wake of a series of business scandals that have undermined public trust in companies and stock markets' (OECD, 2002). This is a notable opportunity for this organization and its member countries to revisit the Corporate Governance Principles, to reconcile the principles with the farther-reaching disclosure recommendations included in the MNE Guidelines, and to provide further guidance and clarification on disclosure of a company's global operations.

At the same time, civil society must demand social, environmental and ethical issues to be integral to a corporate governance framework. To paraphrase the OECD Principles, stakeholders must be involved in creating wealth, jobs and sustainability. It is time to elevate multistakeholder corporate governance and disclosure to apply to all TNCs. That would be a big first step towards meaningful governance of corporations in a global economy.

ENDNOTES

1 The Friends of the Earth International proposal provided rights of redress for affected citizens and methods for sanctions against alleged corporate violators, such as fines, extension of liaibility to corporate directors, and withdrawal of a company's limited liability status. See www.foei.org/corporates/towards.html

2 Sarbanes-Oxley Act 2002, H.R. 3763, US Congress, 107th Congress, Washington, D.C.

3 The US FCPA prohibits corrupt payments to foreign officials for the purpose of obtaining or keeping business. The Department of Justice is the chief enforcement agency, with a coordinate role played by the Securities and Exchange Commission (SEC). See www.usdoj.gov/criminal/fraud/fcpa.html

4 Many companies considered each legal proceeding in piecemeal, rather than aggregated, fashion, leaving a sum of liabilities unreported (i.e. Company X has ten legal proceedings or claims at US$99,000 each – a potential liability of nearly a million dollars, but since each claim is under the US$100,000 threshold, none of them is reported). New voluntary guidelines, the Standard Guide for Estimating Environmental Liabilities and the Standard Practice for Disclosure of Environmental Liabilities (the 'ASTM standards'), developed by the American Society for Testing and Materials, require companies to aggregate environmental liabilities and report them in the company 10-K, the annual financial reporting mechanism for publicly traded companies in the US.

5 The MCGF would need to be designed to avoid the possibility of running afoul of trade rules such as 'non-discrimination' that requires equal treatment of foreign investors, and 'national treatment' that requires the same treatment of foreign and domestic investors.

6 A threshold test for applicability could be applied, exempting any company with less than, say, US$1 billion in annual revenue. Such a threshold commitment would automatically capture all the largest TNCs (all the companies in the Global 500 *Fortune Magazine* list exceed annual revenues of US$10 billion) and it would also apply to the large corporations headquartered in developing countries, such as Brazil's Petrobras, or Singapore's Asia Pulp and Paper.

7 The Convention on Combating Bribery of Foreign Public Officials in International Business Transactions, which was agreed upon in late 1997, commits each signatory party to enact domestic legislation criminalizing bribery of a foreign official. The convention was negotiated under the auspices of OECD; as of November 2002, 34 countries had ratified the convention.

8 According to the US Environmental Protection Agency (EPA), the US pollution register, the Toxics Release Inventory, has helped companies cut industrial pollutant releases by 48 per cent from 1988 to 2000, with some companies reducing pollution beyond government compliance (World Resources Institute, 2003).

References

Baue, W. (2002) 'Social Investment Forum Outlines "Next Wave" of Corporate Governance Reforms', December 20, www.socialfunds.com

Baue, W. (2003) 'Influential Institutional Investors to Form National Coalition for Corporate Reform', September 10, www.ishareowner.com/

Brandeis, L. (1932) *Other People's Money, and How the Bankers Use It*, Frederick A. Stokes Co., New York

Cadbury, A. (1999) 'Corporate Governance: A Framework for Implementation', in M Iskander and N Chamlou (eds.) *Private Sector Development*, Knowledge Management Unit, World Bank, Washington, D.C.

Chan-Fishel, M. (2002) 'After Enron: How Accounting and SEC Reform Can Promote Corporate Accountability While Restoring Public Confidence', www.corporate sunshine.org/afterenron.pdf

Corporate Board (2003) *Commission on Public Trust and Private Enterprise: Finding and Recommendations*, The Conference Board, New York

Corporate Sunshine Working Group (2003) 'Proposed Expanded SEC Disclosure Regulation', www.corporatesunshine.org/

Cowe, R. (2001) *Investing in Social Responsibility: Risks and Opportunities*, London, Association of British Insurers

Ethical Performance (2002) 'French Set the Pace on Reporting', vol. 3, issue 11, April, London

Friends of the Earth (1999) 'Corporate Accountability', www.foe.org/camps/intl/corpacct/bushcorp.html

Gregory, H. J. (2000) 'The Globalisation of Corporate Governance', Global Counsel, October, Weil, Gotshal, & Manges LLP (available at www.worldbank.org/Papers Links/)

Hofmeyr (2002) 'Final King II Report Released', www.hofmeyr.co.za/king.htm

ICGN (2000) 'Statement of Global Corporate Governance Principles', www.icgn.org/documents/globalcorpgov.htm

IRTK Campaign (2003) 'International Right to Know: Empowering Communities Through Corporate Transparency', www.irtk.org

Keefe, J. F. (2002) 'Statement on Corporate Scandals and Proposals for Reform: The Perspective of Socially Responsible Investors and Proposals for Reform', Social Investment Forum, www.socialinvest.org

Komisar, L. (2002) 'Transnational Corporations Push Voluntary Self-Regulation at Johannesburg Earth Summit', *Pacific News Service*, August 26

Lydenburg, S. D. (2002) 'Envisioning Socially Responsible Investing: A Model for 2006', *The Journal of Corporate Citizenship*, New York

OECD (1999) 'Corporate Governance Principles', www.oecd.org/document/62/

OECD (2002) 'OECD Launches Drive to Strengthen Corporate Governance', November 15, www.oecd.org

OECD (2003) 'Annual Report on the Guidelines for Multinational Enterprises: 2003 Edition', www.oecd.org

OECD Watch (2003) 'Review of National Contact Points', http://208.55.16.210/OECD Watch-June-2003.htm

Shinn, J. and P. Gourevitch (2002) 'How Shareholder Reforms Can Pay Foreign Policy Dividends', New York, Council on Foreign Relations

White, A. L. (1999) 'Sustainability and the Accountable Corporation: Society's Rising Expectations of Business', *Environment*, October, vol 41, no 8

Witherell, W. (2003) 'The OECD Guidelines for Multinational Enterprises: A Key Corporate Responsibility Tool', *OECD Observer Policy Brief*, June

Wolfensohn, J. D. (1999) 'A Battle for Corporate Honesty', *The Economist: The World in 1999*, p38

World Bank (2003) *Global Economic Prospects and the Developing Countries*, Washington, D.C., World Bank

World Resources Institute (2003) 'Driving Business Accountability' in *World Resources 2002–2004: Decisions for the Earth: Balance, Voice, and Power*, United Nations Development Programme, United Nations Environment Programme, World Bank, World Resources Institute

Zadek S. and M. McIntosh (2003) 'Corporate Transparency, Accountability and Governance', *The Journal of Corporate Citizenship*, Issue 8, Greenleaf Publishing, pp16–20

Index

Århus Convention on Access to Information, Public Participation in Decision-Making and Access to Justice in Environmental Matters 183
Aberfoyle Holdings 83
ADF 159
AES corporation 90–1
Africa *see* Sub-Saharan Africa
Aguas Del Tunari 133, 134, 141–2
aid *see* foreign aid
Aluminium Company of America (Alcoa) 55
American Society for Testing and Materials (ASTM) 216n4
Amnesty International 109
Andonova, L. 55, 56, 60, 61
Angola, FDI 83, 84
arbitrators
  bilateral investment treaties (BITs) 131–3
  NAFTA, Chapter 11 153
Argentina, water dispute 140–1
Ashanti Goldfields Corporation (AGC) 85
Asia *see* East Asia; Southeast Asia
Asian Brown Haze 103, 115n8
Asian Corporate Governance Association 108
Asian Rare Earth case 116n13
'Asian tigers' 100
Association of British Insurers 109
Association of Southeast Asian Nations (ASEAN), environmental policies 100–1
Association for Sustainable and Responsible Investment in Asia (ASrIA) 108
Australia, corporate disclosure 212
Azurix Corporation 141

banks, environmental policies 64–5
Basel Convention on the Transboundary Transport of Hazardous Wastes and Their Disposal 185
Bechtel Corporation 20, 40n2
bilateral investment treaties (BITs) 3, 6–7, 17, 88–9, 123–43
  accountability in arbitrations 134–9
  arbitrators 131–3
  award publication 130–1
  dispute registration 128–30
  dispute settlement 124–5
  formal disputes 140–2
  informal disputes 139
  legitimacy in arbitrations 131–4
  origins and features 126–8
  transparency 128–31, 138
Blackman, A. 54
Bolivia, investment disputes 133, 134, 141–2
Botswana, FDI 84–5
British Petroleum (BP), shareholder activism 64
Brundtland Report 97
Buddhism, economic model 107
business communities, self-governance 108

Business Council for Sustainable Development 117n17

California Public Employees Retirement System (CalPERS) 209
Cameroon, FDI 83
Camisea project 64–5, 69n14
Canada, arbitration tribunal 134, 145n18, 157
Caron, David 141–2
Center for Transnational Corporations 6
Chevron 52, 68n4, 92
Chile, environmental impacts 57
China
  corporate governance 203
  environmental impacts 52
  environmental technology 54, 55
China Council for International Cooperation for Environment and Development (CCICED) 104–5
Christmann, P. 54, 61
civil regulation 63
civil society, environmental concerns 106
CME 135, 145n22
Coalition of Environmentally Responsible Economies (CERES) 117n17, 208
codes of conduct, environmental 64, 110, 117n17
Commission on Environmental Co-operation 182
competitiveness, transnational corporations (TNCs) 98–9
conditioned finance 110
conflicts, Sub-Saharan Africa 78
Convention on Biodiversity (CBD) 183
Convention on Combating Bribery of Foreign Public Officials 216n7
Convention on the Settlement of Investment Disputes between States 89
Corporate Accountability Convention 198
corporate governance
  Asia 108
  definition 199–200
  disclosure 205–12
  future of 212–15
  international 202–5
  OECD Corporate Governance Principles 9, 201–2
  United States 200–1
corporate social responsibility (CSR) 108, 207–8
Corporate Sunshine Working Group (CSWG) 207
Corporate Watch 63
corruption, cronyism and nepotism, Asia 106
Crompton US 161
Czech Republic, dispute arbitrations 135, 136, 145n22

Danida 62
Das, Bhagirath Lal 113
Dasgupta, S. 54
debt finance, environmental impacts 50, 58
Del Monte 83
Denmark, environmental regulations 62–3, 185–6
developing countries, FDI 15–21
Dezalay, Yves 132
dispute settlement *see* bilateral investment treaties (BITs); North American Free Trade Agreement (NAFTA), Chapter 11
domestic investment
  and FDI 24–6
  Mexico 33–4
Dow Jones Sustainability Index 48, 117n18

East Asia, environmental quality 29, 30
economic development
  environmental impacts 29–30

and FDI 21–6
Sub-Saharan Africa 77–80
ecosystems, threshold phenomena 178
Ecuador, environmental damage 52, 68n4
efficiency spillovers
environmental impacts 57–8
of FDI 21–4
Mexico 34–5
emissions, atmospheric 177–8
Energy Charter Treaty (ECT) 129, 193
Enron 200
environmental impacts
FDI 4–5, 26–31, 35–7, 46–67, 89–92
research themes 47–8
Environmental Kuznets Curve (EKC) 29–30, 40n6, 51, 101, 115n6
environmental management
cross-border 47, 49, 59–65, 182–3
enforcement measures 187–8
institutional structure 188–90
international environmental regimes 183–5
non-discrimination 175–6, 182–5
subsidiarity 185–7
environmental problems
changing knowledge 178–9
cross-media effects 179–80
cumulative effects 177–8
institutional consequences 180–1
irreversible effects 177
non-renewable resources 176–7
threshold phenomena 178
environmental regulation 30–1, 61–3
informal 63–5
international cooperation 103–5
environmental technology, literature review 54–5
environmentalism, international 109–11
Equator Principles 50, 58
Eriksen, J. 54, 62
Eskeland, G. 54
Ethiopia, FDI 83
Ethyl Corp 161, 169n8
European Union (EU)
corporate disclosure 211
environmental agreements 183, 184, 192
Export Processing Zones (EPZs), Kenya 87, 90

Feldman, Marvin 157–8
financial services, environmental effects 58
foreign aid, Sub-Saharan Africa 78–9
foreign direct investment (FDI)
Asia 97–115
bilateral investment treaties 88–9
conditionalities 110
determinants 16–17
developing countries 15–21
and economic growth 21–6, 68n3
efficiency spillovers 21–4, 34–5, 57–8
environmental impacts 4–5, 26–31, 35–7, 46–67, 89–92
future of 39–40, 67, 92–4
impacts of 2, 14–15, 89–92
Mexico 31–9
and poverty reduction 92
and privatization 19–21, 83–4
scale effects 51–2
sectoral analysis 82–3
structural effects 58–9
Sub-Saharan Africa 5, 74–95
and sustainable development 3–5, 7–10, 92–4, 97–100
technology effects 52–4, 55–7
trends in 1990s 17–19
see also international investment
Framework Convention on Climate Change (UNFCCC) 185, 194n4
France
corporate disclosure 210
FDI to Africa 82
Free Trade Area of the Americas (FTAA) 214
Free Trade Commission (FTC) 153, 163
Friends of the Earth International 216n1

García-Johnson, R. 56, 60
Garth, Bryant 132
General Agreement on Tariffs and Trade (GATT)
  Article XX 165
  non-discrimination 173
General Agreement on Trade in Services (GATS) 193
Gentry, B. 61, 62
Ghana, FDI 82, 85
Global Corporate Governance Forum (GCGF) 203
global–local inequalities 8–9
Global Reporting Initiative (GRI) 208, 213–14
governments, environmental role 66–7, 105–6
grassroots movements, environmental issues 107–8
Greenpeace 109
'greenwashing' 205
Guinea, FDI 82
Guoming, Z. 54, 55

Hansen, M. 54, 60, 62
Harrison, A. 54
He, J. 52
Hermes 209
Home Depot 69n11

India, environmental impacts 52, 54, 61
Indonesia
  environmental issues 52, 65, 106, 116n12
  self-governance 108
inequalities, Mexico 37–9
International Centre for the Settlement of Investment Disputes (ICSID) 125, 127–8, 129, 133, 137, 144nn4,12, 191
  Additional Facility (AF) rules 127, 137
  amendments 167–8
  case studies 141–2
  costs 136
International Chamber of Commerce, International Court of Arbitration (ICC rules) 127–8, 129, 137
International Corporate Governance Network (ICGN) 203
international environmentalism, Southeast Asia 109–11
International Institute for Sustainable Development (IISD) 133
international investment
  future sustainability 7–10, 112–13, 190–4
  governance of 5–7, 99
  non-discrimination 172–94
  see also bilateral investment treaties (BITs); foreign direct investment (FDI)
International Organization of Securities Commissions (IOSCO) 213
International Right to Know Campaign 63, 206
International Rivers Network (IRN) 91
investment agreements
  and domestic environmental policy 175–6
  non-discrimination 172–4
  and sustainable development 174–5
  see also bilateral investment treaties (BITs)
investment rules, international 2–3

Jaya Tiasa 188
Jha, V. 52

Kemp, M. 52
Kenya
  FDI 87, 90
  labour rights 90
knowledge, diffusion of 21–4
Kumpulan Emas 188
Kyoto Protocol 100, 185

labour rights, Kenya 90
Lauder, Ronald 135, 144n9, 145n22

lead, cumulative effects 178
Lonrho 83

Maffezni 160
Makarim, Nabiel 102
Malaysia
  Bakun Dam 116n13
  environmental policies 101, 106, 116n13
Mann, Howard 132, 134
market forces, environmental management 61
MERCOSUR 192–3
mergers and acquisitions (M&As) 19–20
Metalclad Corporation 136, 138–9, 145n24, 157, 162
Methanex Corporation 133
Mexico
  chemical industry 56
  domestic investment 33–4
  efficiency spillovers 34–5
  environmental impacts 35–7
  environmental regulations 62
  FDI impacts 4, 31–9, 54
  inequalities 37–9
  privatizations 19–20
Mohammed, Mahathir 101
most-favoured-nation treatment (MFN), NAFTA Chapter 11 159–60
Multi-stakeholder Corporate Governance Framework (MCGF) 213–14, 216n5
Multilateral Agreement on Investment (MAI) 3, 113, 117n20, 126, 187, 189
multilateral environmental agreements (MEAs) 9, 184–5, 193–4
Multilateral Investment Guarantee Agency (MIGA) 89
multinational enterprises (MNEs), OECD Guidelines 8, 28, 64, 203–5

National Coalition for Corporate Reform (NCCR) 215
New York Convention on the Enforcement of Foreign Arbitral Awards 137
Newell, P. 63, 64
Nigeria, FDI 82, 85
Nike 109
non-discrimination
  principle of 172–4
  and sustainable development 174–5
non-governmental organizations (NGOs)
  environmental action 109, 116n14
  environmental regulation 63, 105, 116nn12–14
North American Free Trade Agreement (NAFTA), Chapter 11 3, 6–7, 124, 134, 150–69, 192–3
  amendments 166–7
  arbitration process 152–4
  exceptions 164–6
  expropriation 155–8
  interpretive statements 163–4
  minimum standard of treatment 161
  most-favoured-nation treatment 159–60
  national treatment 158–9
  performance requirements 160–1
  problems with 162–3
  provisions of 154
  transparency 153
Novo Nordisk 54–5

O'Connor, D. 59
off-shore jurisdictions 188
oil exploration, Sudan 92
Oil Watch 63
Organisation for Economic Co-operation and Development (OECD)
  Corporate Governance Principles 9, 201–2, 213, 215
  and FDI 21
  Guidelines for Multinational Enterprises (MNE) 8, 28, 64, 203–5, 213, 215

OECD Watch 204–5
overseas development assistance (ODA), and FDI 18

Parra, Antonio 134, 137, 140
Patton Boggs LLP 144n10
Philip Morris company 139
Philippines, self-governance 108
pollution
Southeast Asia 103
threshold phenomena 178
see also environmental impacts
Pope & Talbot Company 134, 145n18, 155, 157, 159, 160
portfolio equity investments 48
poverty
Mexico 37–9
Sub-Saharan Africa 77–80
poverty reduction, and FDI 92
privatization, and FDI 19–21, 83–4
Project Firefight Southeast Asia (PFFSEA) 111
protectionism 173
PSEG Energy Holdings Inc 144n11
public goods 194n3

Rainforest Action Network (RSN) 69n11
Rasiah, R. 54, 55
regulations, environmental 30–1, 61–5
religion, and economics 107–8
renewable resources 176–7
Responsible Care® 56, 60, 61, 68n8
Rio Declaration 97, 104
Rondinelli, D. 55
Rosenn, Keith 84
Ruud, A. 54, 5661

Salacuse, Jeswald 125, 131
scale effects, foreign direct investment (FDI) 51–2
S. D. Meyers 157, 158
shareholder activism 64
Shell, shareholder activism 64
social indicators, Sub-Saharan Africa 78
South Africa
corporate governance 209
FDI 80, 82, 87
Southeast Asia
cooperation 103–5
economic crisis (1997) 102
environmental policies 100–5
FDI 5, 97–115
governance 106
grassroots movements 107–8
international environmentalism 109–11
self-governance 108
sustainable development 111–15
Southern African Development Community (SADC) 81, 89
Stern, Nick 104
Stockholm Chamber of Commerce, Arbitration Institute (SCC rules) 128, 129, 134, 137
Stockholm Declaration 182
Sub-Saharan Africa (SSA)
bilateral investment treaties (BITs) 88–9
economic development 77–80
FDI 5, 74–95
national policies 83–8
sustainable development 92–4
subsidiarity 8, 185–7
Sudan
FDI 87–8, 92
oil exploration 92
sufficiency economics 107
sustainability
and non-discrimination 174–5
voluntary reporting 207–8
sustainable development
and FDI 3–5, 7–10, 92–4, 97–100
future paradigm 111–15
investment regime 190–4

Tanzania, FDI 81, 82, 83, 85–6
Taylor, G. 54, 61
technology transfer, and FDI 21–4, 52–4, 55–7
Tellus Institute 208
Texaco Petroleum Inc. 52, 68n4

Thailand
 self-governance 108
 sufficiency economics 107
threshold phenomena, ecosystems 178
tourism, environmental effects 58
Toxic Release Inventory (TRI) 206, 216n8
trade-related aspects of intellectual property rights (TRIPS) 184
trade related investment measures (TRIMs) 6
transnational corporations (TNCs)
 competitiveness 98–9
 corporate governance 198, 199
 disclosure 205–6
 efficiency spillovers 21–4
 environmental performance 27–9, 101–2
 FDI 15–16
 international investment rules 5–7
 sustainable development 112
transparency
 bilateral investment treaties (BITs) 128–31, 138
 corporate disclosure 205–8
Treaty for the Establishment of the East African Community 88–9
Treaty on Long Range Transboundary Air Pollution (LRTAP) 183

Uganda
 Bujagali dam 90–2, 94
 FDI 80, 82, 86–7, 90–2
United Kingdom
 corporate disclosure 210–11, 212
 FDI to Africa 82
United Nations Commission on International Trade Law (UNCITRAL) 128, 130, 131, 133–4, 191
 amendments 167–8
United Nations Conference on Trade and Development (UNCTAD), corporate disclosure 211
United Nations Environment Programme (UNEP) 190
United Nations Global Compact 64
United Nations Industrial Development Organization (UNIDO) 57
United States
 corporate governance 200–1
 Emergency Planning and Community Right-to-Know Act (EPCRA) 206
 environmental disclosure 206–7
 Environmental Protection Agency (EPA) 216n8
 Foreign Corrupt Practices Act 207, 216n3
 and Kyoto Protocol 100
 Sarbanes-Oxley Act (SOX) 200–1
 Social Investment Forum 201
 Superfund legislation 188
 Trade Promotion Authority Act 169n5
Unocal 117n16

Vastag, G. 55
von Moltke, Konrad 132

WALHI 116n12
Warhurst, A. 55
water services
 disputes 140–2
 privatization 20
Woicke, Peter 91
World Bank 199
World Business Council for Sustainable Development (WBCSD) 57
World Environment Organisation 190
World Summit on Sustainable Development (WSSD) 198
World Trade Organization (WTO)
 investment treaties 124–5
 Seattle meeting 3, 116n16, 186, 189
World Wide Fund for Nature (WWF) 109, 111
Wu, X. 54

Zaire, and United States 160, 169n5
Zambia, foreign aid 79
Zimbabwe, FDI 83